WORDSWORTH: PLAY AND POLITICS

Wordsworth: Play and Politics

A Study of Wordsworth's Poetry, 1787–1800

John Turner

St. Martin's Press   New York

ISBN 0–312–88940–2

Library of Congress Cataloging-in-Publication Data
Turner, John (John F.)
Wordsworth: play and politics.
Bibliography: p.
Includes index.
1. Wordsworth, William, 1770–1850—Criticism and
interpretation. 2. Play in literature. 3. Politics
in literature. I. Title.
PR5888.T87 1986   821'.8   85–14535
ISBN 0–312–88940–2

For Sue

Contents

Preface

When Wordsworth wrote in *The Prelude* of the radical philosophy that had formerly tempted him 'to abstract the hopes of man / Out of his feelings' (x:808–9), he was picturing human reason as an alchemist promising to transform the mixed elements of the present into the purer element of the future. The hope of his youth was to see 'the man to come parted as by a gulph, / From him who had been' (xi:59–60); and the anxiety involved in this magical thinking makes itself clearly felt in the isolated journeying consciousness of his early political poems. Longing for the future, he had no home in the present.

The history I have followed in this book is that of a man who came to find himself in time and place, and who eventually came home, to Grasmere, in the winter of 1799–1800. It is the history of a man's struggle to come to grips with the mixed elements of the present without surrendering his radical hope for the future. It is a struggle, too, in which Wordsworth found poetry. The early poems are descriptive in manner, the mind observing the world. But from 1793 onwards, as he measured first the evil and then the good that he found in the world, Wordsworth came increasingly to find in poetry an intermediate area between that which was perceived as objective and that which was perceived as subjective. It provided an area with real existence in time and space, in which the minds of author and reader alike could both relax and concentrate, finding themselves recomposed by composing the world. The poet, that is, discovered he had a contribution to make. Wordsworth later spoke of this contribution in terms of a faculty, the imagination; but in these years the emphasis seems rather to fall upon it as a kind of *doing* – and I have accordingly spoken of it as *play*, an activity deriving from the young child's re-creation of the real world in order to feel really at home in it.

The importance of Wordsworth, it seems to me, lies here in the attention he paid to the discipline of subjectivity in that intermediate area where self and other interplay; for he saw that it was upon this area that our common capacity to form relationships, values and ideals depended. He saw indeed that perception itself was relationship, the mind participating in its world; and his poetry became a conscious attempt to resite the radicalism of his youth, to ground it not in the seemingly objective abstractions of reason but in an imagery that would appeal to passion, feeling and reason alike, with power (in the words of his *Essay on Morals*) 'to incorporate itself with the blood & vital juices of our minds' and thus to amend the relationships they enjoy. His thinking led him in two directions: towards psychology, and the processes of development of that play-area where poetry worked, and towards politics, and the circumstances in which that development might most favourably occur. It is this balance between play and politics that I have tried to keep in my book, as I trace Wordsworth's attempts to structure his hope for the future upon feelings he had proved good in the past, both of his own life and the life of his country as he found it in Grasmere.

I have written the book in the form of a commentary partly in response to the exploratory nature of the poetry. It seems to me that Wordsworth is often misrepresented because passages are isolated from their place in the particular meditative adventure upon which he has embarked; for the poems, like all relationships, are experiments in faith. They invite us to trust ourselves to play; and that is also why I have written in commentary form. For that is what interests me about literature – the meanings it brings into play. In an age when radicalism in academic circles is predominantly mistrustful and sceptical of the literature of the past, Wordsworth's poetry may serve to remind us of the value that might be found in play, not just of the intellect but of the whole sensibility.

In what I have written I have drawn upon the language and work of the object-relations tradition in British psychology and in particular upon the work of D. W. Winnicott. I first came across his book *Playing and Reality* in my attempt to think about the playing of the little cottage girl in *We are seven* and the playing of Wordsworth himself in *The Prelude*; I then found a whole tradition which in its interest in the development of the mind, its concept of the good, its capacity (at best) to observe feelingly and write poetically with its eye on the object seemed to me engaged in a modern form of the same exploratory, tactful inquiry into mental health and creativity that had preoccupied Wordsworth. It is right that I should acknowledge that debt here.

I should like finally to acknowledge my more personal debts: first and foremost to my wife, Sue Gagg, whose understanding and liking of Wordsworth's poetry has long been a pleasure and a challenge; second, to Peter Shoenberg, whose wisdom in guiding my reading was matched by his hospitality during the composition of this book; third, to Wynn Thomas, for the scrupulous quality of his teaching in the days when we taught Romantic literature together; and fourth, to Nick Potter and Ken Watkins, with whom Wordsworth was always one of the interesting subjects of conversation on Friday nights. My thanks are also due to Liz Watkins for preparing the typescript.

JOHN TURNER

List of Abbreviations and Texts

ABBREVIATIONS

PW   *The Poetical Works of William Wordsworth*, ed. E. de Selincourt and H. Darbishire, 5 vols (Oxford University Press, 1940–9).

EL   *The Letters of William and Dorothy Wordsworth*, ed. E. de Selincourt, 2nd edition, *The Early Years, 1787–1805*, rev. Chester L. Shaver (Oxford University Press, 1967).

TEXTS

All quotations from *The Prelude*, except those in Part VI (Chapters 10 and 11), are from the 1805 edition, ed. E. de Selincourt, 2nd edition, revised by H. Darbishire (Oxford University Press, 1959).

All quotations from Wordsworth's prose works are from *The Prose Works of William Wordsworth*, ed. W. J. B. Owen and Jane Worthington Smyser, 3 vols (Oxford University Press, 1974).

All quotations from *Lyrical Ballads* are from the edition by R. L. Brett and A. R. Jones (Methuen, 1968). I have not given line references for the shorter poems to avoid encumbering my text.

Part I   *An Evening Walk*, 1793 version, in *PW* i.
Part II   *Descriptive Sketches*, 1793 version, and *Imitation of Juvenal – Satire VIII*, in *PW* i.
            A Letter to the Bishop of Llandaff, in *Prose Works*, vol. i.
            Salisbury Plain and *Adventures on Salisbury Plain*, in *The Salisbury Plain Poems of William Wordsworth*, ed. Stephen Gill, Cornell Wordsworth (Ithaca, New York: Cornell University Press, 1975).

Part III   *The Borderers*, The Early Version, in *The Borderers*, ed. Robert Osborn, Cornell Wordsworth (Ithaca, New York: Cornell University Press, 1982).

Part IV   *The Ruined Cottage*, Ms.B, in *PW* v:379ff. All manuscript references, and references to *Incipient Madness* and 'The Baker's Cart', are to *The Ruined Cottage and The Pedlar*, ed. James Butler, Cornell Wordsworth (Ithaca, New York: Cornell University Press, 1979).
Lines left upon a seat in a Yew-tree, in *Lyrical Ballads*.

Part V   All references here to *Lyrical Ballads*, as above.
Peter Bell, in *PW* ii.

Part VI   *Tintern Abbey*, *Nutting* and 'There was a Boy' in *Lyrical Ballads*.
The two-part *Prelude*, in *The Prelude, 1798–1799*, ed. Stephen Parrish, Cornell Wordsworth (Ithaca, New York: Cornell University Press, 1977).

Part VII   *Home at Grasmere*, Ms.B, in *Home at Grasmere*, ed. Beth Darlington, Cornell Wordsworth (Ithaca, New York: Cornell University Press, 1977).
The Old Cumberland Beggar, *The Brothers* and *Michael*, in *Lyrical Ballads*.

Part I
An Evening Walk:
The Poet in Hiding

1   An Evening Walk (1787?–92)

'The Scenes which he describes have been viewed with a Poet's eye and are pourtrayed with a Poet's pencil' (*EL* 89). Dorothy in 1793 had no doubt of her brother's achievement in *An Evening Walk* and *Descriptive Sketches*. 'I am sure you must think that there are some very glaring Faults but I hope too, that you will discover many Beauties, Beauties which could only have been created by the Imagination of a *Poet*' (*EL* 90). An author's youthful works lie in the shadow of his mature successes, banished there all too often by his own later impatience with them. By 1801 Wordsworth had come to see both poems as apprentice works: 'They are juvenile productions, inflated and obscure, but they contain many new images, and vigorous lines; and they would perhaps interest you, by shewing how very widely different my former opinions must have been from those which I hold at present' (*EL* 327–8). He did not, however, disown them in his impatience; characteristically he kept his youthful work in print, even working extensively at a revision whose chief aim seems to have been to free his original intentions from their extrinsic imperfections. It is not only poor biography and poor history but also, in view of their merits, poor criticism to consign these early works to the shadows. They show in parts, as Dorothy claimed, what she and her brother thought in 1793 that a poet should be; and in so doing they reveal an aspect of the past that we too should work to keep alive in the present.

'What is a Poet? To whom does he address himself? And what language is to be expected from him?' These questions from the 1802 *Preface* to *Lyrical Ballads* have thus a particular appropriateness to *An Evening Walk*, which consciously offers itself as 'the history of a poet's ev'ning' (52). It is a mistake to identify the poem too closely with the usual topographical poem of the day, for it is much more than one of those catalogues of natural description whose organisational difficulties Dr Johnson

3

summarised in commentary upon Thomson's *The Seasons*: 'Of
many appearances subsisting all at once, no rule can be given why
one should be mentioned before another; yet the memory wants
the help of order, and the curiosity is not excited by suspense or
expectation.'[1] *An Evening Walk* is often an unwieldy poem, but it is
never a radically formless one. Its mechanical principle of
organisation – day passing through twilight into night – is given
life because the different lights of different times of day directly or
indirectly evoke the full reach of the poet's sensibility; and this
sensibility is his true subject. As Geoffrey Hartman wrote, '*An
Evening Walk* is a poem issuing from the mind of someone
interested in the mind, and especially the mind of a poet.'[2]
Wordsworth understood from the first that what we see is a
function of what we are; and this first completed poem brings
before us constantly the mind that sees – the child's mind, the
adult's mind, the vagrant's mind, all of them subsumed in the
precious seeing of the poet's mind. Of course, what he saw in 1793
was conventional, consciously literary; but not therefore
inauthentic or unfeeling.[3] What is a Poet? ... To ask these
questions of *An Evening Walk* is to begin to explore Wordsworth's
youthful sense of the poet's mind in the light of the conventions
and cultures of his time.

   The mind in which *An Evening Walk* finds its subject, however,
does not declare itself directly to us in chosen statement or willed
belief. It reveals itself gradually, through primarily unwilled
meditative activity; and if we are to understand it, we must attend
carefully to the character, range and balance of the moods and
affections that claim it. Clearly the organisational principles and
transitional points of such poetry are integral to its meaning, not
fortuitous as Johnson rightly found them in *The Seasons*; for they
are crucial to the poem's unity, as it harmonises the changing
relationships between the mind and the world through which it
moves. The attention which Wordsworth later gave to 'the
transitions, and the impassioned music of the versification' (*PW*
II:517) of *Tintern Abbey* should teach us how to read this early
poem, for it too demands an ear alert to the music of mood, in all
the variety of its forms and delicacy of its sequences. We may for
convenience divide the poem into the following movements: the
introduction (1–52); the poet's sheltering at noon (53–84); his
emergence and evening walk (85–240); his fancy of the widowed
vagrant and her children (241–300); the darkening of twilight into

night (301–88); and finally the rising of the moon and the poet's return (389–446). I want now to compose my picture of the poet's mind, and the culture in which he was writing, by carefully retracing these various stages of his walk.

The poet is a *melancholy* man; and the first two sections of the poem (1–84) describe the elements of personal and cultural alienation that blend to build up that melancholy. For we must remember that, like that of Jaques, the poet's melancholy is 'compounded of many simples, extracted from many objects'.[4] It is no single mood but a colour with many tones, a note with many harmonies; it belongs to that species of complacent grief in which, as Burke remarked, 'the *pleasure* is still uppermost'.[5]

First, the personal alienation. One approach to an anatomy of eighteenth-century melancholy is suggested by the inner emotional necessity of the poem's opening paragraph. Starting with the poet's separation from his beloved friend, it moves across a panoramic composition of Lake District scenery until it focuses upon Esthwaite, the landscape of his childhood pleasures; and here his initial loneliness is revealed as part of a far deeper sense of desolation. Some words of D. W. Winnicott's are relevant here:

> The subject of nostalgia comes into the picture: it belongs to the precarious hold that a person may have on the inner representation of a lost object.[6]

What is it that Wordsworth has lost? It is not the moral innocence of childhood; nor is it quite, as Paul Sheats argues, the capacity to fancy a nature 'adequate to the desires of his spirit'.[7] It is rather the wildness and the cheerfulness of those desires themselves – what Blake thought of as exuberance, the uninhibited energy that welcomes all times and all seasons and does not flinch in the face of experience. The child's cheerfulness, his mirth, his ecstasies and hopes all flow spontaneously into action; and it is upon this authenticity, the co-presence of the child within him, that Wordsworth has now so precarious a hold.

The poem is drawing upon a conventional understanding of the mind's capacity to sublimate its primary passions as the necessary precondition of civilised maturity. Such sublimation brings with it the adult capacity for those subtle and refined pleasures of thought, taste and sensibility in which a sympathetic consciousness of our shared humanity can grow (the adult's hopes, we read, are more social and reflective); and yet it is a refinement at the expense of a crucial sense of vitality. Burke paints the conventional picture composedly enough:

> In the morning of our days, when the senses are unworn and tender, when the whole man is awake in every part, and the gloss of novelty fresh upon all the objects that surround us, how lively at that time are our sensations, but how false and inaccurate the judgments we form of things? I despair of ever receiving the same degree of pleasure from the most excellent performances of genius which I felt at that age, from pieces which my present judgment regards as trifling and contemptible.[8]

Burke's despair (it seems a complacent expression of a real enough feeling) is counterbalanced in his prose by the gains of adult reason and taste; but in *An Evening Walk* there is no such sufficient compensation. Certainly the melancholy of its introduction is an adult pleasure, but its cost is high, dependent as it is upon the poet's inability to integrate the powers and the wildness of his childhood. Sublimation is incomplete, we might say: his melancholy seems – as it usually is – a directing against the self of energies otherwise disavowed. It was to take Wordsworth (as it took Blake) some time to realise those energies, both creative and destructive, in his verse; and the achievement was to take him far away from the culture that demanded their sublimation.

Within the frame of the poem, however, the mood of nostalgia passes. After the emergence of that extraordinary image of the sundial, it exhausts itself in the melancholy impotence of self-directed irony. Alas! man's tale is idle, he is the sport of some malignant power. . . . This sense that all is vanity, of course, is not the reason's judicial conclusion to its trial of life; it is no more than an imperfect cadence, summarising the powerful mood of the moment – for reason, like perception itself, is only a function of what at the moment we are. Now the tide of emotion turns. 'But why, ungrateful, dwell on idle pain?' (49) . . . and suddenly the painful pleasures of nostalgia seem no more than idle self-indulgence. But as Wordsworth turns to recount his joys, he first paints a picture of his noontide self in hiding; and here we glimpse the poet in a cultural alienation which also claims our attention.

The melancholy man had been in hiding from the sun for at least two hundred years. Monsieur Melancholy in *As You Like It* chose to lie 'under an oak, whose antique root peeps out / Upon the brook that brawls along this wood' (II:1:31–2); and now, with equal self-consciousness, Wordsworth invokes the more important model of *Il Penseroso*.

> There in close covert by some brook,
> Where no profaner eye may look,
> Hide me from day's garish eye,
>
> (139–41)

It is not simply the heat that Wordsworth shelters from: *An Evening Walk* re-creates by allusion that long pastoral tradition that found in the shade of tree and forest relief from what Marvell called 'our passion's heat'. The poet is not simply alienated from his own passionate life, irrecoverably fixed as it is in the distances of childhood; he is alienated too from the ongoing passionate life of his own civilisation. The energies of its unsublimated lusts and its unrefined labours assault his soul, as much as its garish colours assault his eye. The melancholy man, of course, was originally a satirist, and Jaques had once delighted to rail 'most invectively' by his brook against 'the body of the country, city, court' (II:1:58–9); but now in *An Evening Walk* this passion for satire has become characteristically muted. Denunciation has given way to self-defence, and the civilised sensibility calls upon all the resources of pastoral to hide itself from the contamination of its society.

This desire for a world within a world took many different forms in the eighteenth century. Hume expressed it quite matter-of-factly when writing 'Of the delicacy of taste and passion':

> One that has well digested his knowledge of both books and men, has little enjoyment but in the company of a few select companions. He feels too sensibly, how much all the rest of mankind fall short of the notions which he has entertained.[9]

He feels too sensibly. . . . Hume's essay uses centrally some of the keywords that valorise this typically eighteenth-century picture of

minority culture: taste, delicacy, refinement, elegance. At the end
of the century, Mrs Radcliffe in *The Mysteries of Udolpho* expressed
a similar desire in the idiom of romance:

> Virtue and taste are nearly the same, for virtue is little more
> than active taste, and the most delicate affections of each
> combine in real love. How then are we to look for love in great
> cities, where selfishness, dissipation, and insincerity supply the
> place of tenderness, simplicity and truth? (1:5)

The coarseness of so-called civilisation brutalises the truly
civilised sensibility. Marilyn Butler has remarked that 'the most
obvious feature common to all the arts of Western nations after
1750 was the refusal to validate the contemporary social world',[10]
shown in the popularity of pastoral, primitivism and 'historicism'.
There was, in other words, not only a refusal to validate but also a
common failure to engage the contemporary world – a failure
whose human cost is witnessed, as in *An Evening Walk*, by that
self-congratulatory melancholy which could find its tastes and
social impulses confirmed only in retreat. Hence such literary
oddities as Henry Mackenzie's *The Man of Feeling*, whose hero dies
a pleasurably melancholy death (unqualified by the satire and
irony of the earlier part of the book) simply because his finer
feelings unsuited him for the business of living. It is a melancholy,
too, capable of such tragic intensification as Rousseau's great cry
out of solitude that he had a heart perfectly formed for love. The
world within a world could scarcely shrink to a smaller compass or
be the cause of a more acute pain.

What we are dealing with is a question that will continue to
preoccupy us in our discussion of Wordsworth: the nature of
idealism, and the character of its psychological and social basis.
Clearly there is a wide range of possibility between Hume's
preference for the company of his friends and Harley's slow drift
into death in *The Man of Feeling*; and yet in each case the pleasures
of society are defined self-protectively, by prior appeal to a
language of dissociation. The assurance of writers like Hume and
Burke in handling their melancholy stems from the fact that,
despite their occasional luxurious distaste for the world, their
beliefs and their interests are geared to its good management. But
in the melancholy of writers like the young Mackenzie and the
young Wordsworth there is an effeteness that expresses a deep

cultural alienation from the centres of power in their society. It is an effeteness typical of much late eighteenth-century primitivism in pastoral or romance; and we may characterise it by recalling Walter Benjamin's words on historicism:

> It is a process of empathy whose origin is the indolence of the heart, *acedia*, which despairs of grasping and holding the genuine historical image as it flares up briefly. Among medieval theologians it was regarded as the root cause of sadness.[11]

Historicism is a failure in hope, a failure of the historical imagination to integrate present and past; and Marx in the *Grundrisse* passed the definitive judgement upon the historical failure that characterised much Romantic thought:

> It is as ridiculous to yearn for a return to that original fullness as it is to believe that with this complete emptiness history has come to a standstill. The bourgeois viewpoint has never advanced beyond this antithesis between itself and this romantic viewpoint, and therefore the latter will accompany it as legitimate antithesis up to its blessed end.[12]

The poet in hiding in *An Evening Walk* lacks substantial hope – it is a main theme of his poem. Nostalgia and melancholy are ways of trying to keep an ideal of sensibility alive; but their success is precarious and powerless when matched against the ongoing processes of time and history. The poet finds himself isolated from his society; and this opposition between culture and society debilitates both. The supposedly coarse ways of the larger world will go on, whilst poetry becomes specialised and marginalised to minister to the sensibilities of the smaller private world. It was against this impoverishment of society and marginalisation of poetry, this dissociation within bourgeois culture, that Wordsworth was to set himself to work in the period of his best poetry.

There is more to *An Evening Walk* than melancholy dejection, of course. Wordsworth's joys begin with his walk (85–240), and are the source of all that is best in the poem: its observation and organisation of pictures of human labour and 'the infinite variety of natural appearances' (*PW* I:319). Here we see 'the Imagination of a *Poet*' in the usual eighteenth-century understanding of that faculty – as a creative power which, to quote Burke's words again, is active 'in representing at pleasure the images of things in the order and manner in which they were received by the senses, or in combining those images in a new manner, and according to a different order'.[13] It is the power which, as Mary Warnock put it, 'enables us to go beyond the bare data of sensation, and to bridge the gap between mere sensation and intelligible thought'.[14] It is a constitutive power in perception, that is, but commonly considered subservient to the judgement and therefore unable to bring about what *The Prelude* would later call 'an ennobling interchange' (XII:376) between inner and outer reality. What is more, the pleasures appropriate to the imagination fit into the mind precisely as poetry fits into society: they minister compensation as a valued diversion from the main business of life.

We may take two examples of these compensatory adult pleasures, for which the child would have been too busy, too cheerful and too ignorant: and we shall see how much acquired skill Wordsworth had to sacrifice in the course of his future development. First, the poem's opening:

> Far from my dearest friend, 'tis mine to rove
> Thro' bare grey dell, high wood, and pastoral cove;
> His wizard course where hoary Derwent takes
> Thro' craggs, and forest glooms, and opening lakes,
> Staying his silent waves, to hear the roar
> That stuns the tremulous cliffs of high Lodore:
>
> (1–6)

This is poetry, composition, that makes the reader work: the eye follows, as under the harmonious discipline of a painting, the meandering sparkle of the River Derwent through dark crags and gloomy forests until it comes to rest upon the distant lake. There the ear becomes intent and still as the water itself to hear the thunder of the Lodore falls, created for us in a line as musically precise as Wordsworth ever wrote. It is a line much harder at work than comparable lines from the second book of Samuel Rogers' *The Pleasures of Memory*, where Florio, 'recoiling from the roar / Gazed on the tumbling tide of dread Lodoar' (II:228–9). Wordsworth seems to have been aware of the psychology of perception that underlay picturesque theory, for he is trying to re-create the pleasure that the restless, tyrannical senses of men experience when brought under the discipline of the quietening power of harmony. So the second, fourth and sixth lines of that opening passage slow down the running eye: its movement is checked by balancing contrasts of light and shade, height and depth, expansiveness and enclosure, roughness and smoothness, speed and slowness, until it comes to enjoy composition. Wordsworth's couplets are as distinctive as those of Pope or Johnson; and if they make us work more often and more rewardingly than those of his immediate predecessors like Rogers, it seems to be because of the force of the tension between his visual and aural appetite on the one hand and his ordering imagination on the other. I believe that the 'harsh and obscure construction'[15] noted by Coleridge in Wordsworth's early verses springs from the same source.

In our second example, the poetic imagination appears at first to reach out in sympathy to bridge those gulfs that define the adult in his alienated self-consciousness.

> Waving his hat, the shepherd in the vale
> Directs his winding dog the cliffs to scale,
> That, barking busy 'mid the glittering rocks,
> Hunts, where he points, the intercepted flocks.
>
> (165–8)

Through the skilful placing of verbs, we are drawn sympathetically into the goings-on of life, into the relationship of dog to master and the urging authority that controls the distance between them – the break of rhythm in the fourth line suggests perfectly the dog's pause to look back at his distant master for instruction, whilst the final prolepsis makes us visualise the dog's shepherding in action. It is subtle couplet-making; we work with time and space, with vision and sound, from two different standpoints, to compose the picture, and such work is part of the pleasure that there is in life itself. Interestingly, so early in Wordsworth's life, it is nature and rural walks that sustain him in the precariousness of his hold upon the feelings he values. But that hold remains precarious: even in such vigorous writing, we can still hear the note of melancholy at its heart. Indeed, the very clarity of its seeing is a function of the poet's distanced observation and isolated concern. He has already told us of his 'sad tides of joy' (22): the passivity of his melancholy and the activity of his joy are opposite moods, each implicit and co-present in its contrary, and always liable to give way to it – and it is this range of poetic sensibility which is, as we have said, the true subject of the poem.

Now, once more, Wordsworth's mood changes: as he enjoys the anthropomorphic contemplation of the domestic bliss of a pair of swans, the image itself – by what Hume called 'the relation of contrariety'[16] – stimulates the dialectically opposed imagination of the houseless vagrant and her children (241–300). Roger Sharrock found this long episode 'outside the frame of the poem' and therefore straining 'the ordinary character of the local poem to breaking point'.[17] But Wordsworth's sense of structure was, like Shakespeare's, from the first remarkable; and once we have seen that the poem's unity does not lie in its character as a topographical poem but in its exploration of poetic sensibility, we shall understand the real purpose of this passage. It is the moment when the poet displays his humane sympathy in an attempt at last to engage politically with the civilisation from which hitherto he has been in hiding.

The lines, although probably unattractive to modern taste, were deliberately written in a language and syntax which were new to the poem and yet familiar to the contemporary reader – that of the sublime, which enjoyed a conventional relation of contrariety with the language and syntax of the beautiful used elsewhere in the poem. Couplets now accumulate terror on terror, rather than weave a complicated tapestry of loveliness. In *A Philosophical Enquiry into the Origins of our Ideas of the Sublime and Beautiful* Burke had set out to discover the biological basis for these two categories of aesthetic pleasure; and he had traced the sublime to 'the passions which regard self-preservation' and the beautiful to 'those which are directed to the multiplication of the species' and to '*society in general*'.[18] The passions of self-preservation were pain and fear, passions so strong that they could easily overthrow the social passions in all their delicate pleasures of sympathy, beauty and love; and therefore true civilisation depended upon their sublimation. The imagined fact of the vagrant's pain and fear in *An Evening Walk* is thus Wordsworth's indictment of a society that denied any one of its inhabitants the opportunity of such sublimation, and his use of the mode of the sublime embodies his respect for her suffering. Of necessity, the poet's political responsibility demands imaginative responsiveness to the full range of human language and experience.

Wordsworth's political faith at this early period of his life lay deep in those paternalist traditions of the eighteenth century that aimed to pacify the revolutionary struggles of the seventeenth. It was a faith that mankind might be bound into a family by sympathy and the reciprocities of charity and gratitude, and that such sympathy would also harmonise man's relationship with nature. Hence the entire appropriateness of the consideration of political injustice in the course of a verse-epistle to a young lady upon the picturesque beauties of the Lake District. 'All is right, tho' man be wrong', wrote Henry Brooke in his *Universal Beauty*,[19] a poem whose title speaks for itself; and thus literature came to find for itself an almost scientifically precise function in the cultivation of those social passions that might reconstitute the family of man. It played its part in that 'important access of humanitarian concern among the upper classes'[20] by which E. P. Thompson characterised the two decades preceding the French Revolution. Marilyn Butler too agrees that 'it was reformist sentiment that was common and even fashionable among the gentry', and adds that such sentiment 'informs the work of creative writers of all shades of political opinion'.[21] But we need to remember the variety of those shades of political opinion and also to make that distinction which is always necessary in the assessment of liberal thought: the distinction between paternalism and a genuine radicalism in which the poor may speak and act for themselves. E. P. Thompson argues elsewhere that it is a feature of paternalism that 'the interior life of the poor cannot be handled, unless with condescension or as picturesque';[22] and certainly in *An Evening Walk* Wordsworth cannot handle the interior life of his vagrant – hence, in part, the melodrama and deadness of the verse. On the other hand, the poetry does have a radical drive in its indignation at the imperialism of king and aristocracy during the American War of Independence – a war commonly seen by radicals as a war of the ruling oligarchy against the peoples of both Britain and America. Thus we may recognise in the poet of *An Evening Walk* a young radical whose radicalism is still inseparable from the paternalist

attitudes typical of mainstream eighteenth-century culture. It was
to be the history of the 1790s that finally drew out the
contradictory tendencies of paternalism and radicalism, both of
which had been originally latent in the ideal conception of the
family of mankind and which from this period onwards would
diverge lastingly in our culture, sometimes mediated by liberalism
and sometimes not.

During this radical passage of the poem, Wordsworth's
melancholy has become activated into a disturbed and disturbing
indignation, a kind of mobilised pity. But it is a mood which he is
unable to sustain in a substantial way: the vagrant's fate proves to
be a tragic and prophetic intensification of Wordsworth's own
melancholy alienation. As she walks her own particular way to
dusty death, she and her children (like the poet) reach out to the
world around them for joy. They are moved by a glow-worm, by
the moon or a shooting star; but wherever they turn, the glimmer
of hope is rapidly extinguished. This search for a world
substantial with hope will be the great theme of Wordsworth's
poetry; but in *An Evening Walk* hope always proves to be an *ignis
fatuus* dying into the darkness of disillusion.

> For hope's deserted well why wistful look?
> Chok'd is the pathway, and the pitcher broke.
>
> (255–6)

Vanity of vanities, all is vanity . . ..[23] The old note in a new key:
once again we hear the betrayal of hope and the inhibition of love.
Wordsworth serves both hope and love, but as powers which he
cannot incarnate amidst the melancholy joys and griefs of his own
life: and so his indignation and engagement subside into an
impotent political quietism which, whilst not relinquishing its
radical faith, finds in the despair of the vagrant's death an image
of its own ultimate hopelessness.

What in fact happens is that the poet's imagination of the vagrant
runs its course, until his disturbing excitement subsides and
leaves him free once more to perceive the natural world around
him. Far from being 'the most violent transition in the poem',[24] it
is a moment of exhaustion when Wordsworth's breast is 'by the
scene compos'd' (309). Evening now slowly turns to night

(301–88); and in his astonishing sensitivity to the play of light and sound over landscape, Wordsworth once again reveals his melancholy consciousness of mutability, both endearing and threatening each human moment of beauty and significance. Nightfall thus brings the possibility of crisis: it causes 'baffl'd vision' (364) and a 'wilder'd mind' (376), and threatens to extinguish finally all those illusions of consciousness by which Wordsworth had maintained his precarious hold upon the feelings and things he valued in the real world. It is a type of death, threatening to turn all value into vanity.

Geoffrey Hartman has written well of this moment when the mind falters before 'apocalyptic intimations of the world's loss'.[25] His choice of the word *apocalyptic*, however, needs challenge, for a word that might be at home within American transcendentalism or Blake studies has an air of the bombastic about it when applied to Wordsworth, especially in these early verses. It seems to me that Hartman, in his account of the imagination coming to recognise itself within nature by the extinction of nature, neglects the subtleties of the eighteenth-century empirical psychology in which Wordsworth was grounded. *An Evening Walk* was written, as Dorothy said, to show the 'Imagination of a *Poet*'; and whether that imagination is at work upon the past, upon the fancied history of the vagrant or simply upon the recombination of beautiful images, it supersedes the nature before it as surely as it does under the sublime passion of fear. In other words, the impulses which prompt the imagination towards self-expression and self-recognition are manifold and everyday; *apocalyptic* is too grand, too rigid and (here) too religious a word to describe them. It is also, we may note, a word that works towards the depoliticisation of Wordsworth's poetry that has been characteristic of much recent American criticism. We distort and puritanise *An Evening Walk* if we make it enact 'the real, if submerged, drama' of a poetic imagination facing its own apocalyptic powers.[26] It is, as it says, the *history* of a poet's evening; and it unfolds a sequence of impressions, moods, feelings and thoughts which delicately check and balance one another within the constitution of Wordsworth's mind, none of them needing to be denied, and tending overall to a deepening love of the world, a greater concern for man and an enriched sense of the self which truly display the poet.

Of course, at nightfall there is, as Hartman says, a fear of loss –

of loss of relationship with man and nature, and of faith in the self, for Wordsworth's hold upon these things remains precarious. But the impulse of panic is small and quickly passes.

> Stay! pensive, sadly-pleasing visions, stay!
> Ah no! as fades the vale, they fade away.
> Yet still the tender, vacant gloom remains,
> Still the cold cheek its shuddering tear retains.
>
> (385–8)

Although the insubstantial pageant of the evening fades and leaves not a rack behind, the mind's relationships survive: the poet recovers his creative melancholy in the tender, vacant gloom that night induces and his human concern in the shuddering tear that belongs to the vagrant's history. Finally, in the night-piece that concludes the poem (389–446), he moves with gathering confidence from anticipation to observation of the moonlit world around him, and at last to expression of the hope that is the illusion of his inner world – the hope against hope, that he may one day enjoy shared cottage life with his friend. This fantasy achieves its immediate restorative effect; and as he turns for home, in lines as beautiful to eye and ear as he ever wrote, Wordsworth invokes a harmonious progression of images upon which the creative mind may close in the contented expectation of sleep.

To-morrow, and to-morrow, and to-morrow . . . Throughout *An Evening Walk* the imagination of the poet is trapped by the alienated melancholy which is the very condition of his being. In his hiding from the sun his capacity for joy is etiolated, confined to the search for self-protective consolation amidst the beauties of nature. But although the various lights of his declining day may interest his mind, they cannot enlighten it. Although the perception of needless human suffering may arouse his sympathy, it cannot bridge those paternalist distances which also serve to protect him. It seems that nothing radically new can ever happen to this poet, islanded as he is in the perpetual absences of time and place: his tomorrows hold out no substantial hope for him. He will walk again the round of his pleasures but only – it seems – as an exercise in the prison of that late eighteenth-century culture which is the marginalisation of poetry, the sentimentalisation of politics and the suburbanisation of nature. All of Wordsworth's future concerns are here already in *An Evening Walk* – the sustaining power of nature, the importance of illusion in perception, the growth of the poetic mind, the need for fraternal sympathy – but we see them only through a glass darkly. His way forward was to be through a deeper experience and understanding of alienation, in which the energies, angers and aggressions of the self were gradually released and disciplined to a richer relationship with the otherness of man and nature.

Part II
The Political Writings of 1791–5: The Poet and Politics

2 *Descriptive Sketches* (1791–2)

Descriptive Sketches is a very different poem from *An Evening Walk*; it is no local walk but a European tour, composed according to Wordsworth mostly 'upon the banks of the Loire in the years 1791, 1792' (*PW* i:324). It grew directly out of his experience of revolutionary France and its millennial hopes for man; and like so many of the century's written accounts of Continental tours, it is a comparative study of the different kinds of human life sustained by the political, geographical and cultural conditions of the different countries it describes: France (45–79), Italy (80–175), Switzerland (176–679), Savoy (680–739) and finally France again (740–809). Wordsworth's aim, however, is to do more than to instruct and delight his educated readership with accounts of foreign manners, history, arts and politics; his aim is to radicalise them. *Guerre aux châteaux! Paix aux chaumières!* – *Descriptive Sketches* embraces the force of this revolutionary slogan, albeit with reluctance, and focuses its concern exclusively upon the cottage life of the poor in order to judge the economic and political conditions of the countries they inhabit.

Formally, the poem is an imitation of Goldsmith's *The Traveller* (1764); and this fact alone should guard us against the almost universal assumption that the poem is 'largely conventional in both matter and devices'.[1] Wordsworth wrote a radical imitation of a conservative poem because he wished to explore the new political consciousness which he found appropriate to a new historical age. *The Traveller*, we remember, having surveyed all Europe with extensive view in search of

> Some spot to real happiness consign'd,
> Where my worn soul, each wand'ring hope at rest,
> May gather bliss to see my fellows blest,
>
> (60–2)

21

had come quickly to see the vanity of its own proceeding. We must search not without but within, for 'that bliss which only centres in the mind' (424). Goldsmith would have thought it betrayed an avariciousness of hope (cf. 51–8) to long for the new world of a millennium, and at the end of the poem he made himself come home in renewed self-dedication to the old self and the old world from which he had formerly fled. Dr Johnson's lines, incorporated into the poem, were decisive in encouraging his return:

> Still to ourselves in every place consign'd
> Our own felicity we make or find:
> With secret course, which no loud storms annoy,
> Glides the smooth current of domestic joy.
>
> (431–4)

Most men, remote from the power of political mischief, are free to live their lives in happiness and virtue; and the structure of *The Traveller*, with a balance that demonstrates this restraint of judgement that Goldsmith tried to teach himself, argues the universality of this truth. Each European country has the related weaknesses of its own particular strengths, and life is everywhere much the same . . .. But what was simple realism to Goldsmith and Johnson must have seemed, to a radical readership, an irresponsible compliance at the political heart of the poem; and Langhorne had already challenged it here on its first appearance.

> We find that what is the object of public attention in one reign, is totally changed in another; and that as interest, power, and caprice prevail, political sagacity is for ever varying its principles and practice. The character of a people is not always the same:[2]

The aim of *Descriptive Sketches* too is the development of such a historical sense, so that we can recognise, besides the thousand natural shocks that flesh is heir to, those avoidable political ills that need to be ruthlessly cut away (see the epigraph from Virgil) if the thinking mind is to flourish in relationship and peace.

The poet's desire is declared in his opening line: 'a spot of holy ground'. The sacred character that this pastoral desire held for Wordsworth throughout his life has commonly been recognised; already since *An Evening Walk* it has deepened and developed.

'The Journey has become a Quest', as Geoffrey Hartman
succinctly puts it; and yet something is omitted if we think of that
quest as only 'an Idea of Nature in search of a nature adequate to
it'.[3] Donald Wesling makes the same omission when he writes that
'Wordsworth is more interested in the landscape than in people.'[4]
It is John Beer, I think, who gives the right emphasis: the quest, he
says, is for 'a place of civilisation which might be adequate to
human needs'.[5] This emphasis upon civilisation is important, for
Wordsworth is primarily in search of the same 'domestic joy' that
The Traveller claims to have found. But his quest has quite opposed
results.

> In the wide range of many a weary round,
> Still have my pilgrim feet unfailing found,
> As despot courts their blaze of gems display,
> Ev'n by the secret cottage far away
> The lily of domestic joy decay;
> While Freedom's farthest hamlets blessings share,
> Found still beneath her smile, and only there.
>
> (719–25)

The pleasures of cottage life are tainted by political tyranny; and
what is true of domestic joy is certainly true of the joy in
landscape. For what we see is a function of what we are, and only
the free mind can see freely: it is liberty that adds a precious seeing
to the eye. If Wordsworth did not get as far as the tropics of
Huxley's essay,[6] he saw enough of Europe to know that men's
perceptions of nature were inseparably bound up with their
cultural and political formations; and it is this knowledge that
enabled him in *Descriptive Sketches* to open up for our examination
the ideological basis of the whole pastoral tradition. For the poem
is the first of those many critiques of pastoral that Wordsworth
was to write, in his wish to redeem the traditional idealism of the
genre from the kind of compliant retreat with which, in *An Evening
Walk*, he was finally obliged to be content.

The poem opens, with the reservation of its subjunctive mood,
upon the convention it is to criticise. The long introductory
paragraph (1–44) shows an orthodox Sentimental Traveller
journeying in search of that talismanic spot whose power to

alleviate pain acts like grace upon the soul. A holy separated spot
. . . these opening lines draw on the language of the picturesque to
create several such spots where a man may surely find Nature
sufficient to his human needs. So great would be the power of
a perfect pastoral spot, or (alternatively) so attentive the
ministrations of Nature to the traveller who must move on, that he
would immediately find himself at home in alien surroundings.
The imperfections of the old world would vanish in the perfections
of the new. He would mix freely with the poor, the young, the
virgin, he would find friends in the brooks and luxury in the cloud
that covers the midday sun. . . . The paragraph becomes a texture
of natural and human blessings inseparably interwoven to create
the imaginative plentitude of pastoral.

But the brief second paragraph of the poem (45–52) moves at
once to an individual test of these general literary fancies; and it
does so in a language whose specificity and tone suggest how
Descriptive Sketches, in its own way no less than Sterne's *A
Sentimental Journey*, is driven to separate truth from self-deceptive
vanity.

> Me, lur'd by hope her sorrows to remove,
> A heart, that could not much itself approve,
> O'er Gallia's wastes of corn dejected led,
>
> (45–7)

The seeming innocence of pastoral fantasy is tested against the
all-too-familiar guilty dejection of real life. The causes of
Wordsworth's self-disapprobation remain partly private, and
later lines in the poem (632–43) suggest that such a condition is
typical of adult life – pain, poverty, disease, grief, labour, age,
remorse between them extinguish all possibility of hope, each of us
(the image is an organising one in the poem) is silently bleeding to
death. But Wordsworth's dejection has a public aspect too, for it is
bound up with those wastes of French corn through which he
walks. France is at war; and it is important to realise that the
poetic search for 'a spot of holy ground' meets first with an image
of desecration in the sacking of the Grande Chartreuse (53–79).
'The cloister startles at the gleam of arms' (60): Mary Moorman
has shown how Wordsworth fused what he read of the 1792
military occupation of the monastery with his own first-hand
experience of it in 1790,[7] and evidently he did this at the start of

Descriptive Sketches in order to establish at once the minor key of the poem. For this paradoxical sense of a France desecrated by the sacred fight for liberty will brood over the search that follows, perplexing the poet with the energies of the guilty hopes it rouses in him.

The innocence of pastoral hope, therefore, has yielded to a guilty recognition of reality; and this pattern will recur throughout the poem in each of the countries that Wordsworth visits. The detail of the pattern is movement, of course, but I have described that detail elsewhere[8] and will content myself here with a summary. An amorous pastoral upon the peaceful beauties of Italy (80–147) yields to an alternative recognition that political servitude under the Austro-Hungarian empire has caused a sensuality of culture (148–61) which, reluctantly, the poet must leave. Two long sections then explore the 'tyrant Genius' (608) of Switzerland, where the human spirit is broken by the poverty of natural resources. The first is set in Uri (243–413) and passes from a contemplation of William Tell's memorial to a picture of a chamois hunter bleeding to death alone amidst a vacant, hostile landscape. The second is set in Unterwalden (414–631) and passes from a fancy of a mountain-dweller's idyllic existence to an old cottager's account of how poverty drove his sons away from home to become mercenaries in the service of Holland and France. In each case, the poet must face the fact that the proud tradition of military independence so dear to radicals is unable to withstand want. Nor does Savoy satisfy him better (680–739): despite its Elysian beauty, it is 'the slave of slaves' (706), a small despotic kingdom under the protection of the Austro-Hungarian empire and aligned with it against the revolution in France. In each of the countries that he has visited the particular geography, history and literature have sustained Wordsworth's pastoral imagination in appropriate fantasies of perfect earthly happiness – but only until the mind is recalled to the claims of its shared humanity. Neither the eye nor the fancy cheats the heart so well as it is famed to do. For Wordsworth has raised the tactic of the picturesque (the mind sees this *and* that) into a study of the mind's dialectical pursuit of truth – a dialectic which here he cannot synthesise but which has kept him restlessly on the move in search of that reconciling spot which he had pictured to himself.

It has been a mixture of remediable and irremediable evils that has prevented the realisation of Wordsworth's pastoral dream;

and certainly either poor soil or political tyranny, sickness or servitude has the power to expose that dream as, commonly, the idle luxury of leisured imaginations (cf. 590–607). But the co-presence in *Descriptive Sketches* of these two categories of evil is a measure of Wordsworth's dejection, of the struggle he is having with the fatalistic resignation of *The Traveller* that life is not susceptible of radical improvement. Everywhere his hopes are baffled, in a poem whose echoes, cross-references and contrasts only serve to throw his mind back upon its own separate, dissatisfied consciousness. *Descriptive Sketches* bears perfect witness to the rootlessness of the radical imagination in its need to make its own history. Wordsworth cannot yet, at this stage of his life, secure himself in the face of the natural and political evils that threaten him; and so he fluctuates between despair and a talismanic longing for that spot whose objective existence alone will be able to compose his subjective self, soothe his wayward moods and house his wandering imagination.

Hence the urgency of that last address to France. It is divided into four parts: a description of present-day France (740–55), a description of what the past has proved (756–73), a prophecy of what the future will show (774–91), and finally an impassioned prayer that France will first defeat and then liberate its enemies (792–809). The first part recalls the paradox with which we began, that the village life of the one European country sacred to liberty is desecrated by preparations for war. But nevertheless, the poem continues, although France has no Elysian fields, it still bears a hope founded in historical fact – that 'Freedom spreads her pow'r / Beyond the cottage hearth, the cottage door' (756–7). The cottage now is no longer the object of retreat from the world that it was in *An Evening Walk* but the centre of its liberating impulse. It seems that Freedom, with the breakup of the *ancien régime* and its stranglehold upon property, is lifting a curse that had lain upon the whole of creation:

> All nature smiles; and owns beneath her eyes
> Her fields peculiar, and peculiar skies.
>
> (758–9)

The journeying poet senses an improvement in the quality of life, of which his own sharper, more joyful perceptions are part. Only the villagers themselves, perhaps, at their hearths and doors are

not smiling; for it is a happiness not yet humanly realised that
Wordsworth pictures in his 'long long dreams' (768).

The impetus of his need, however, gives his hope prophetic
strength; strong rhetorical writing seeks to bridge that dangerous
gulf between imminent war and its desired end, the final triumph
of Liberty over the pandaemonium of an embattled Oppression:

> Lo! from th' innocuous flames, a lovely birth!
> With it's own Virtues springs another earth:
> Nature, as in her prime, her virgin reign
> Begins, and Love and Truth compose her train;
>
> (782–5)

It is a prophecy of the dawning of the millennium and the
perfection of the State of Nature; and then, in an image whose
power would itself sweep aside the allied enemies of France,
Wordsworth turns to prayer, urgent for the waters of liberty to
cover the face of the earth, drowning the old world and ushering in
the new, where man's pastoral hopes will finally be perfected.
Formally these closing lines are in imitation of the end of *Windsor
Forest* (413–22), where Pope celebrates the liberty and peace that
will flow with the waters of the Thames around the world and bind
the forces of discord firmly in hell. Pope's confident, even suave
trust in the power of British civilisation to dispense universal
liberty through its trade, religion and military force is strongly
contrasted by Wordsworth's desperate hope in the French
revolutionary forces. Pope is proud of what Britain over seven
hundred years has become, but Wordsworth shows no such centre
to his faith. Indeed perhaps the most remarkable feature of
Descriptive Sketches is its total disregard for Britain; except for one
glancing reference to his 'native mountains bleak and bare' (714),
Wordsworth is conspicuously silent. His hope is in France, in the
revolutionary war to end all wars.

The poem, however, ends in a deliberate anticlimax which
punctures the rhetoric of his hope.

> To-night, my friend, within this humble cot
> Be the dead load of mortal ills forgot,
> Renewing, when the rosy summits glow
> At morn, our various journey, sad and slow.
>
> (810–13)

Wordsworth's cadence here seems to echo the closing lines of
Paradise Lost, where Adam and Eve 'hand in hand, with wand'ring
steps and slow / Through Eden took their solitary way'; it reminds
us that we still inhabit the world of Adam Unparadised, where the
cottage provides us with no more than a temporary respite against
the evils of life. Paul Sheats argues that the poem embodies
'integrity, vision, and hope',[9] whilst Leslie Chard II finds in its
conclusion 'a full and fairly specific political credo';[10] but such
readings ignore the poem's structure, the way that style is baulked
by style as the poet tests his hopes against the realities of world
and self. The anticlimax of the poem's ending enacts
Wordsworth's failure to find any language, philosophy or politic
sufficient to his needs; there seems to be no Archimedean spot of
any kind from which he might move the world. He sees the need
for what Paine called a total 'Regeneration of man',[11] but he
cannot trust the revolutionary wars to bring it about; he remains
true to the pastoral dream and the sympathies which it promotes
towards man and nature, but he cannot find the place in which to
realise it. Those glowing rosy summits of the end of the poem
recall, in the language of landscape, the unattainable hope that we
felt at the end of *An Evening Walk*; and they cast long shadows
down the despondent valleys through which our journeys lie.
There is still in this later poem a gulf between man and his desired
future, a dissociation between the real and the ideal, a desperation
of hope that was for Wordsworth always an affliction; and it is
recognised both here in the bareness of that transition into the last
four lines and, years later, in *The Prelude*.

> Shall I avow that I had hope to see,
> I mean that future times would surely see
> The man to come parted as by a gulph,
> From him who had been,
>
> (xi:57–60)

Substantial hope is no nearer at the end of *Descriptive Sketches* than
it had been at the end of *An Evening Walk*.

    Yet it seems to me that the later poem shows a significant
advance in consciousness upon the earlier. De Selincourt thought
An Evening Walk the more artistically successful because, he said,
Descriptive Sketches 'is based less exclusively on the poet's own
observation, and draws more on literary sources' (*PW* i:325). But

of course it is deliberately a literary poem, as Wordsworth tests some of the literary modes of his own century precisely against his own observation; and it is this tactic of testing style against style that gives the poem its curiously modern, unaccommodated feel. He scrutinises in particular the lure of the pastoral which he had embraced in *An Evening Walk*, and he no longer finds it sufficient to protect his sensibility. Now he has a bolder political requirement, grounded in a deeper understanding of his alienation; for now he sees that full self-articulation necessitates the *sharing* of a spot, a *shared* culture based upon the public benefits of political liberty rather than upon the private pleasures of a cultivated correspondence – and therefore he must engage himself with the world. The difficulty there is in reading, and enjoying, *Descriptive Sketches* seems to me bound up with the strenuousness of that engagement. Wordsworth cannot find the spot either inside or outside himself to integrate either himself or his world. Nor in the strenuousness of his quest, having abandoned the retreat of *An Evening Walk*, can he yet imagine that area which is neither within nor without (though related to both), that play-area of the mind which Winnicott calls 'the location of cultural experience' and in which 'relaxed self-realisation'[12] may occur. The poem is commonly upon the stretch, more violent and more disturbed than *An Evening Walk*, and unable to find a place of satisfactory relaxation. Deeper energies are at work, enriching the poetry but, in their final thwarting and turning in upon the self, producing a despondency much deeper than the melancholy of the earlier poem. Wordsworth is not yet fully conscious of the power of poetry to accommodate self amidst the natural and political evils of life; that is to say, he has not yet fully appreciated the value of human creativity – what we may call the 'holy ground' of our mental life – where inner and outer are enabled to play together, both in sickness and in health. It is the business of this second section of my book to trace that gradual development in self-consciousness, which is also a process of self-integration, until its emergence in the fully assured poetic of *Adventures on Salisbury Plain*; and I shall proceed by exploring the nature, and adequacy, of the ideas of political sickness and health that Wordsworth expressed in his *Letter to the Bishop of Llandaff*.

3   A Letter to the Bishop of Llandaff . . . by a Republican (February–March? 1793)

Wordsworth was provoked to write his *Letter* by the well-publicised defection from the revolutionary cause of the liberal bishop Richard Watson. In a piece chiefly remarkable for its poverty of argument and its ostentation of rhetoric, Watson had attacked the regicide, the abolition of the nobility, the forcible sequestration of church property and also the lawless violence with which he believed these measures had been implemented in France. By contrast, he had glamorised the British constitution, whose balanced powers of monarchy, nobility, church and judiciary he declared himself determined to protect against the threats of uneducated, unpropertied 'peasants and mechanicks' – for, he wrote, republicanism is 'the most odious of all tyrannies', where the people must suffer 'the tyranny of their equals'.[1] Watson's work, published (appropriately enough) as an appendix to his sermon 'The Wisdom and Goodness of God, in having made both Rich and Poor', was shoddy ware indeed, written with the angry sentimentality which is characteristic of defection; and its tone must have aroused Wordsworth as much as its content. His reply, he tells us at once, is written in 'a republican spirit' (20), and it has a strong prose coherence which, as it shames Watson, glories in its own capacity for heroic resistance. For we should not forget that Wordsworth's *Letter* attacks the British constitution and approves the course of the Revolution in France at a time when the two countries were at war. It was a bold enterprise to engage with Watson, and perhaps the *Letter* is left incomplete because either its author or its intended publisher came to find the enterprise imprudent. But the heroic tone of the writing is new in Wordsworth: the hour has proved the man, and 'the friends of liberty congratulate themselves upon the odium under which they are at present labouring' (681–2). The hope and despair which alternated in the alienated poet of *An Evening Walk* and *Descriptive Sketches* have here for the moment found a vigorous synthesis in the bold proclamation of a threatened faith.

My aim here is twofold: first, to explore the ideological ground of Wordsworth's republican beliefs, chiefly as revealed in the metaphors and images he uses, and second, to assess their sufficiency to the world they seek to measure. They are beliefs quite typical of the radicalism of the time, expressed in the paternalist manner of middle-class dissent rather than with the direct popular appeal of Paine; and their aim is uniformly to lessen that inequality between rich and poor for which Watson so humbly thanked his God. They are as follows: universal male franchise, accountability of government through frequent elections and referenda, brief periods of office for public officials, abolition of hereditary nobility and (presumably) the monarchy, abolition of the law of primogeniture, discontinuance of reward for public service by title or emolument; and general legal reform to make punishment more proportionate to crime, to simplify and cheapen legal procedure, and to dismantle all the monopolistic legislation that favoured the landed interest over labour. Wordsworth specifically rejects available theories of common ownership; he does not wish to abolish inheritable private property, and is presumably content with the consequent inequality in the belief that it will increasingly reflect the merits of talent and industry. Underlying all these articles of belief is his larger vision of a whole regeneration of man – of man raised from the blindness, narrowness and passion of partial self-interest to the contemplation of the general good. In such 'a fairer order of things' (114), inequality itself would be fairer; plain open government would replace the 'disciplined treachery and hoary machiavelism' (298) which is Wordsworth's version of Burke's 'science of government';[2] and society would no longer be constituted in the 'indissoluble compact of a dead parchment' (633–4) but in the daily experience of reason and the reasonableness of fellow-feeling, fulfilled through the particular lives and general will of the people.

The ideological ground of these republican beliefs that

Wordsworth holds is a confidence in the substantial unity of the true and the insubstantial multiplicity of the false – a confidence whose roots lie over a century deep in the religious and scientific consciousness of dissent. He has a vision of health and sickness, of social harmony and discord, of 'the open field of a republic' and 'the shade of monarchy' (160–1) that we might epitomise in the central imagery of *Paradise Lost*: whilst God dwells eternally in the courts of Heaven, Satan is doomed to improvise the impermanent and unsatisfactory parody of Pandaemonium. The body of truth, says Milton in *Areopagitica*, is 'homogeneal, and proportional';[3] and Wordsworth's *Letter* is very much in the spirit of *Areopagitica*, challenging Watson that the contest between truth and falsehood might be held in the open.

> For who knows not that Truth is strong next to the Almighty?
> She needs no policies, nor stratagems, nor licensings to make
> her victorious, those are the shifts and the defences that error
> uses against her power.[4]

To Wordsworth, the mere assertiveness and ostentation of Watson's work were such shifts and defences of error against truth; and his own piece by contrast is conspicuously developed as an argument in order to demonstrate 'that fatality by which the advocates of error furnish weapons for their own destruction' (174–5).

Plain speaking automatically produces a true politic . . . . Paine's work was particularly irradiated with this common radical faith: 'The American constitutions were to liberty, what a grammar is to language: they define its parts of speech, and practically construct them into syntax.'[5] To Paine the illogic of Burke's *Reflections* was political illiteracy. He did not see how its very resistance to order embodied Burke's sense of the implication of each part of the constitution in each other; how its richly poetic life embodied his sense of the rich historical life of the nation; or how its seemingly endless refinements, restatements and qualifications embodied his faith in the checks and balances of the constitution he defended. To Paine, quite simply, Burke's genius was itself 'without a constitution'.[6] Similarly, Wordsworth in his *Letter* presents the rhetorical ill-discipline of both Burke and Watson as an infatuated drunkenness, an attempt by defectors to compromise in 'business on both sides of the road' (676); and he tries, by the sober logic of his own plain prose, to institute the true discipline that will give directly upon a republican future.

Many are the traditional dissenters' images in which Wordsworth apprehends that mystification of truth which is the peculiar triumph of the ruling classes in denying man his rightful future. He taunts Watson, for instance, as Paine taunts Burke, with popery; he scorns his reprobations and 'anathemas of a republic' (167–8), and at one point ironically compares him with 'the incendiary of the crusades, the hermit Peter' (669–70). The point of such taunts is twofold: to chastise the worldliness of a church anxious for its economic and political power, and to condemn its usurpation of the universal right of man to exercise his own reason in matters of conscience. Again, he finds in Watson (as Paine in Burke) a superstition of false poetry, an idolatry of the imagination in his high evaluation of the 'fictitious superiority' (481) attached to the badges of office and rank; and like Paine again, he draws on the barbarous language of heroic tragedy to illustrate how 'we are taught from infancy that we were born in a state of inferiority to our oppressors, that they were sent into the world to scourge and we to be scourged' (190–2). Throughout his *Letter* Wordsworth struggles to expose those deceptions of language and those superstitions of the imagination that keep men from the singleness of truth. He tries to meet the mystification and theatre of public life with the educative clarity of a prose that aspires itself towards a science (rather than an alchemy) of politics.

This radical opposition between truth and superstition took deep hold on Wordsworth's mind. We can see it still in the *Imitation of Juvenal*, on which he sporadically collaborated with the Anglican clergyman Francis Wrangham between 1795 and 1797; for here he derides the barbarous superstition of the whole administrative structure of British government under George III, that king whom Paine in *Common Sense* had dismissed as 'the hardened, sullen tempered Pharoah'[7] of England.

> Is Common-sense asleep? has she no wand
> From this curst Pharaoh-plague to rid the land?
>
> (15–16)

The whole poem, comparing this Pharaoh-plague with the heroes of the British parliamentary movement and the American

Revolution, bears the stamp of Paine and the radical tradition; and nowhere more so than in its sense of language. Wordsworth's fine couplet on James I emphasises how much he longed for 'plain blunt sense' and real 'subtlety of thought' (8):

> To patient senates quibble by the hour
> And prove with endless puns a monarch's power,
>
> (111–12)

Punning is the Satanic pursuit; and like Satan, James spends his time ignobly 'not in fitting words to things (which would be a noble employment) but in fitting things to words'.[8] Like Rivers too, in *The Borderers*, 'he is unable to suppress a low hankering after the *double entendre* in vice.'[9]

Sound thinking, therefore, is the right naming and honouring of really existent things: we are dealing here with something more than 'the old antithesis between nature and art'[10] which M. H. Abrams says Wordsworth shared with other eighteenth-century primitivists. We are dealing with a cultural formation which is characteristic of dissent, where the definition of the unnatural lies somewhere between the religiously unreal, the politically insubstantial, the psychologically sick and the scientifically nonsensical. We can sense something of the power of this formation in Paine's impatience with all the theoretical defences of the British constitution:

> it will always happen, that the nicest construction that words are capable of, when applied to the description of some thing which either cannot exist, or is too incomprehensible to be within the compass of description, will be words of sound only, and though they may amuse the ear, they cannot inform the mind.[11]

As Leslie Chard has argued,[12] the tradition of radical dissent gave rise to a potentially revolutionary theory of language; and Wordsworth's lifelong wish to make his verse 'deal boldly with substantial things' (*Prelude* XII:234) has its roots in that tradition, where the complexities of reality were to be honoured by simplicity of expression.

I want to approach the question of the sufficiency of
Wordsworth's republican beliefs to the world around him through
some well-known sentences from the start of *The Eighteenth
Brumaire of Louis Bonaparte*, where Marx with characteristically
witty shifts of perspective expresses his reservations about
republican theory during the French Revolution.

> The tradition of the dead generations weighs like a nightmare
> on the minds of the living. And, just when they appear to be
> engaged in the revolutionary transformation of themselves and
> their material surroundings, in the creation of something which
> does not yet exist, precisely in such epochs of revolutionary
> crisis they timidly conjure up the spirits of the past to help them;
> they borrow their names, slogans and costumes so as to stage
> the new world-historical scene in this venerable disguise and
> borrowed language. . . . The social revolution of the
> nineteenth century can only create its poetry from the future,
> not from the past.[13]

Marx's ironic sympathy should serve to keep before us
Wordsworth's courage in dissociating himself during increasingly
dangerous times from the dominant ideology of his society. We are
accustomed to think of his poetic dissociation from eighteenth-
century culture, but his political dissociation preceded it and was
its necessary precondition. However, Marx's lines remind us too
that the models for eighteenth-century republican thought were
all archaic or inappropriate (the classical or the Swiss city-state,
the political writings of seventeenth-century theorists), and that
these models served in crucial ways to blind men to the world they
wanted to confront.

I want now to suggest three ways in which this is true of
Wordsworth, beginning with a passage that seeks to clear the
Revolution of the charge that it has merely replaced one form of
tyranny with another:

> a philosopher will extend his views much farther; having dried
> up the source from which flows the corruption of the public
> opinion, he will be sensible that the stream will go on gradually
> refining itself. I must add also that the coercive power is of
> necessity so strong in all the old governments that a people
> could not but at first make an abuse of that liberty which a

legitimate republic supposes. The animal just released from its
stall will exhaust the overflow of its spirits in a round of wanton
vagaries, but it will soon return to itself and enjoy its freedom in
moderate and regular delight.

(272–80)

'Truth is compared in Scripture to a streaming fountain,' says the
Areopagitica; and yet, in fact, such metaphoric intimation of the
perfectibility of the people served Milton no better than
Wordsworth.

For, first, Wordsworth's understanding of the concept of the
people was too abstract; he saw no real need of subtler class
distinction than that between oppressors and oppressed,
aristocracy and people, a distinction corresponding precisely to
that between the self-destructiveness of falsehood and the
integrity of truth. But such antithesis inhibited perception of the
multiplicity of interests in France. 'The nature of man is intricate;
the objects of society are of the greatest possible complexity,'
wrote Burke;[14] but it was this sense of intricacy and complexity
that Wordsworth attacked in his *Letter*, and he was led as a result
into too enthusiastic a hope in the accessibility of the general will
of a society.

Second, this idealisation of the people blinded him to the
essential divisiveness of bourgeois capitalism, which in practice
determined the limits of most radical ideology, both populist and
paternalist. In its hostility to the interventions of monarchical and
aristocratic government, eighteenth-century radicalism believed
itself to be perfecting the revolutions of the seventeenth century;
but in retrospect it is clear how much it anticipated the
laissez-faire economics of the nineteenth. Wordsworth was in no
doubt that wealth of all kinds contained 'an oppressive principle'
(436), but nevertheless he (like Watson) justified the existence of
government in the need to preserve private property 'against the
depredation of the necessitous' (433–4); and although he included
the right to labour in his definition of property, and believed that
government should moderate inequality, he saw no contradiction
between a republican faith and the protection of predominantly
bourgeois capital. To be sure, disillusion was not long in coming:
the pastoral poetry of 1799–1800 shows, as we shall see, a
prolonged attack upon the principles of political economy that the
radicals had all accepted. True still to his respect for private

property, Wordsworth was then to attempt the same powerful idealisation that Shakespeare had turned into romance with *The Merchant of Venice* – the distinction between property and property in terms of the spiritual value it might hold for the individual in his community. But in 1793 Wordsworth was not yet conscious of the contradictions of a radical capitalism; he was still confident in the companionship of his fellow friends of liberty and the reasonableness of their cause.

For, in the third place, behind his idealisation of the people lay an equally inadequate idealisation of reason. We should remember that neither *An Evening Walk* nor *Descriptive Sketches* had idealised reason in the manner of the *Letter*; rather, they had shown it to take its colouring from the various moods of the mind, to be a function rather than an independent arbitrator of our lives. *Descriptive Sketches* in particular had shown something that Wordsworth was never to forget, and that makes his alleged 'Uniformitarianism'[15] more complex than is often allowed: namely, the importance of culture and locality to the nature of what we see and understand. Thus, although the heroic prose commitment of the *Letter* affords a fresh perspective upon the alienated poet of the early poems, the poems in turn help us to see the unsatisfactoriness of a political philosophy which – in the words of *The Prelude* – 'promised to abstract the hopes of man / Out of his feelings' (x:808–9). For, to return to Wordsworth's own image, from a variety of causes the horse did not soon return to itself and enjoy its freedom in moderate and regular delight: both man and his society were to prove more complex than the radicals, with their trust in human reason, had supposed.

It seems to me that Wordsworth's greatness is inseparably bound up with his own recognition of these inadequacies in his early republicanism, and with the strength of his need to meet the challenges they offered him. Both inner and outer worlds were soon to fall into disintegration, as the collapse of revolution in France and the growth of reaction in England dissipated both his faith in the self-sufficiency of reason and his faith in the possibility of organised radical resistance. His *Letter* was written at almost the last moment possible before that disintegration set in; indeed, it was perhaps abandoned because of it. It was written at a moment, too, when changes that had long been at work in British society were about to manifest themselves in a new political configuration which was to make the capitalist rather than the aristocrat the chief target for radical attack. The republican tradition, that is, was to disintegrate still further as its economic base was increasingly identified and opposed; and Wordsworth was in the forefront of this process, remaking old criticisms of agrarian capitalism and commercial enterprise with a new force directed against the free market praised by the political economists.

Wordsworth's challenge was to remake radicalism in an unpropitious time, to integrate inner and outer worlds in a refashioning of the paternalist dissent which he had adopted. I do not think he ever found a satisfactory new synthesis – it is hard to imagine what such a synthesis at such a time might have been – but we shall follow the progress of his search through the poetry up to 1800. For once again the gulf between the man who had been and the man who was to come was opening up in front of Wordsworth; poetic despondency and prose optimism needed to be reconciled and – to avoid the lure of rhetoric and the desperation of hope, to achieve the substantial universal language which is perhaps the aim of all radicalism – he felt the need to make good in himself, as far as possible, the nature of that man who was to come. But that was not yet: it was to be an even deeper despair that first prompted him to reshape the world, in poetry, and thus to discover the particular importance of its play-area to the long process of social transformation.

4   *Salisbury Plain* (1793–4)

Wordsworth wrote in *The Prelude* that the British declaration of war against France in February 1793 caused his mind to take 'a stride at once / Into another region' (x:241–2); British alliance with the enemies of the country that had promised the universal regeneration of man caused 'most unnatural strife' (x:251) in his heart. His next poem, begun in consequence of a pedestrian expedition across Salisbury Plain in the July and August of 1793, was also a stride into another region: for with *Salisbury Plain* Wordsworth for the first time achieved an authentic tragic intensity as he explored the unnatural strife aroused in him by the obdurate unregenerateness of mankind.

The journey of *Salisbury Plain* is more than the display of poetic sensibility paraded in *An Evening Walk*, more than the quest for pastoral perfection undertaken in *Descriptive Sketches*. It is a 'dark descent'[1] into 'night-terrors' (st. 14), a hunger of the unaccommodated mind to image and if possible to master the full extent of its own alienation. It is a journey into time as well as space, a journey whose distances are danger; for Wordsworth is compelled to test himself against the violent extremes of human experience, and to keep those extremes alive in himself as authentic measurement of all the injustices of man's political history. *Salisbury Plain* is, to the best of my knowledge, the first of many Romantic and post-Romantic journeys to the uttermost. It confronts and appropriates the appalling truth that (in the words of Conrad's Marlow, from the account of a similar journey in *Heart of Darkness*) 'the mind of man is capable of anything – because everything is in it, all the past as well as all the future.'[2] Salisbury Plain is Wordsworth's Congo; and his Kurtz, the image with which he returns empowered upon the present, is Stonehenge. It is an image of the barbarous dependence of all so-called civilised societies past and present upon superstition and human sacrifice.

It is important to recognise both the subjective and the objective nature of Wordsworth's exploration; for the poem is a historical analysis undertaken by a self-analytic imagination, history proved upon the pulse. Most critics have concentrated upon the objective nature of the exploration. They discuss the poem as social protest, illustrating Wordsworth's 'views' of the 'political and social cancer'[3] of injustice. If the tone of the poem is mentioned, it is commonly referred to the critical stage of Wordsworth's own life – to the 'enormous amount of unconscious guilt'[4] that he felt, perhaps, as an Englishman supporting the national enemy France where his lover and illegitimate child waited inaccessibly. Thus 'views' dissolve insensibly into biography and evade the challenge of what was meant. Geoffrey Hartman, on the other hand, characteristically emphasises the subjective nature of the poem's exploration; he speaks stimulatingly of it as a Night Journey, but thinks (oddly enough) that its 'humanitarian or political emphasis does not succeed in being central.'[5] This too evades the full challenge of the poetry; for the apocalyptic terror of the imagination upon which Hartman dwells is a truth within human society, and the truth about that society is measured precisely by its effects upon the imagination. Both ways of talking, we shall see, involve a serious distortion of the nature of Wordsworth's renewed attempts to integrate inner and outer reality.

If the search of *Descriptive Sketches* was geographical, here in *Salisbury Plain* it is historical; and its historical analysis is organised according to a common radical pattern. The poem takes us chronologically through four main periods of history: the age of savage rule (the introductory stanzas 1–4); the age of superstitious rule (stanzas 5–22, in which both the traveller's imagination and his conversations with the vagrant are haunted by the Druid history of the plain); the present age of unjust power sustained by military force (stanzas 23–47, in which the vagrant tells her tale of natural rights usurped); and the future age of reason, into which the poem's concluding stanzas urge us to pass. A parallel analysis, though omitting the savage period, is found in *Rights of Man* where Paine reviews 'the several sources from which governments have arisen, and on which they have been founded'.

> They may be all comprehended under three heads. First, Superstition. Secondly, Power. Thirdly, The common interest of society, and the common rights of man.
> The first was a government of priestcraft, the second of conquerors, and the third of reason.

When a set of artful men pretended, through the medium of oracles, to hold intercourse with the Deity, as familiarly as they now march up the back-stairs in European courts, the world was completely under the government of superstition. The oracles were consulted, and whatever they were made to say, became the law; and this sort of government lasted as long as this sort of superstition lasted.

After these a race of conquerors arose, whose government, like that of William the Conqueror, was founded in power, and the sword assumed the name of a sceptre.[6]

Savagery, superstition, power, and the age of reason to come: such is the objective framework of historical understanding in *Salisbury Plain*, and through it Wordsworth dramatises both the increased expectations and disappointments that civilisation has hitherto brought to the poor. History has been simultaneously progress and decline, and we might find an emblem of Wordsworth's mixed feelings towards what was commonly a matter for self-congratulation in that 'naked guide-post's double head' so eerily lit up by lightning in stanza 12.

The mention of Wordsworth's mixed feelings about historical progress, however, brings us to the subjective framework of the poem; for through that 'most unnatural strife' aroused in him by the betrayal of his revolutionary hopes, Wordsworth was beginning to develop a deeper, more specific understanding of the subjective experience of alienation. In *Salisbury Plain* he consistently shows the alienated mind to be tossed between opposed extremes of mood, lost amongst discordant images which it cannot harmonise – and his own mixed feelings about history, of course, are one small expression of this. Enid Welsford, in a sensitive appraisal of the poem, has drawn attention to its organisation upon the principle of contrast, which she refers with some reason to the influence of Spenser. She speaks of 'an undulating rhythm of alternating light and darkness, peace and perturbation,' and adds:

Like Spenser, Wordsworth makes considerable use of contrast: the contrast of night and day, past and present, war and peace, domesticity and vagrancy, hope and despair, love and cruelty; all of these contrasts being summed up in the contrast visible both to the outward and inward eye of Salisbury Cathedral and Stonehenge.[7]

What we must add is that Wordsworth's literary technique of contrast is the hermeneutical tool of the new psychology which he was evolving and which was to substantiate all of his future work. It reaches its culmination, perhaps, in the great insight of *The Prelude* that 'there is a dark / Invisible workmanship that reconciles / Discordant elements' (1:352–4): in health, that is, the mind is mysteriously able to harmonise the opposites to which in sickness it succumbs.

But Wordsworth, like many students of the mind, only came to his understanding of health through the long and painful diagnosis of sickness. It must have been his own experience which chiefly taught him; for after the melancholy harmonics of *An Evening Walk*, the unintegrated extremes of hope and despair in *Descriptive Sketches* reveal a discordant spirit which was then to be jarred still further by the events of February 1793. We have already seen the roots of this self-understanding in the platonism of the British dissenting tradition from Milton to Paine – and perhaps we should add, with Enid Welsford, in the platonism of Spenser. But, equally importantly, with *Salisbury Plain* we come to the question of the influence of Shakespeare upon Wordsworth. *Hamlet* had helped him in the first two poems to explore a recurrent mood of world-weariness; but from now on the two great feudal tragedies of *King Lear* and *Macbeth* were to be as important as *Hamlet* in helping him to image the potential harmony of social life and the most unnatural strife aroused by its betrayal. Over the next few years, and especially in *The Borderers*, Wordsworth was to develop Shakespeare's feudal imagery into a radical critique of precisely the long continuance of feudal oppression. He transformed the Shakespearean language of reciprocity from a feudal into a fraternal ideology; and he did so by concentrating upon the potential harmony of village rather than court society.

'I love your Majesty / According to my bond; no more nor less': Cordelia's words to her father say it all (1:1:91–2) – only the *bond* of her relationship can save her from those irreconcilable and limitless extremes of 'more' and 'less' into which Lear will later fall. Her reason cannot save her, we should note; for the bond of which she speaks is not a social contract signed by reason but a relationship constitutive of her deepest life, bound up with the primary feelings upon which her reason depends and determined in its nature by the more general traditions of her society. Wordsworth's interest in Shakespeare coincides with his growing dissatisfaction with the familiar radical model of society as a kind of joint-stock company, in whose business each individual is free to participate or not according to the judgement of his reason. Inner and outer realities are neither so neatly divided nor so easily related as that. In *Salisbury Plain* I believe that Wordsworth is beginning to see how fundamentally our social experience is constitutive – how the quality of our life depends upon the relationships into which we are born, and upon the way in which they subsequently fare, determining our capacity to symbolise in that intermediate area where inner and outer blend. He is beginning, I believe, to think more naturally in terms of health rather than of reason: that a just society will tend to create healthy relationships and an unjust society – as here in *Salisbury Plain* – will tend to create unhealthy relationships that alienate the individual and disturb his capacity to symbolise. It is for Wordsworth a question of feeling at home or not feeling at home, and he concentrates once again upon the possibilities of independent cottage life. Hence, of course, the importance of that extraordinary emblem from the central acts of *King Lear* – the emblem of the unaccommodated man, alone upon the heath, desolate, with no relationship to man or nature to discipline his mind and save it from its own extremes. This is the emblem that informs *Salisbury Plain*, helping Wordsworth to bring his objective sense of history into play with his subjective sense of the suffering mind.

The landscape of the poem is sublime, associated throughout history with the terrors of the elements and the many forms of human misery: homelessness, hunger, unproductive labour and war. In no period, savage, Druid or Christian, has man been able to relax there and make himself at home in time and space. It is the disturbance of this capacity that was perhaps the occasion of the poem's historical inquiry (I am thinking of the usurping power of that image of Stonehenge) and that now forms its subject. I want to explore it here, not in relation to the savage and Druid periods, which I have described more fully elsewhere,[8] but in relation to the vagrant's story, where Wordsworth's verse is significantly at its best.

The vagrant considers herself – the phrase is an echo of *King Lear* (iv:7:63) – 'robbed of my perfect mind' (st. 43); and she begins her tale by trying to recreate the perfection of the relationships she had once enjoyed.

With thoughtless joy I stretched along the shore
My parent's nets, or watched, when from the fold
High o'er the cliffs I led his fleecy store,
A dizzy depth below! his boat and twinkling oar.

(st. 26)

The intricately interwoven syntax suggests beautifully the interwoven fabric of her life, binding together the distances of time and place. It is a fabric composed of many threads, the coherence of the whole depending upon the presence of each of the parts: hereditary cottage and communal village life, filial love and friendship, labour and holiday pleasure, worship and secular song. At 'the central point' of the circle of her joys,[9] harmonising these potential opposites, is the image with which her tale begins – her father's cottage, her home. It is the place from which the balanced habits of her life reached out affectionately into her community, sharing its memories, activities and hopes. The past sanctified the present, which in turn brought hope for the future and gave to death both a place and a meaning in the midst of life (cf. st. 30). In Macduff's phrase, the time was free: and so was the place.

Or so it seemed. But the whole delicate fabric of her life is irreparably torn apart when she and her father, after initial harassment, find their property seized and themselves evicted from their cottage by the uncomprehended forces of Oppression. Now we see why she spoke of her earlier joys as thoughtless; for her experience of the power and pride of the rich has permanently embittered her, and given her life the antithetical cast of before and after. All the relationships of her life are affected; her religious faith is inhibited and, despite the apparent reintegration of her maturer life in marriage, she finds herself unable to enjoy her children without strange fits of depression. 'I sighed / And knew not why' (st. 33) . . . a life where all had been known is falling into confusion and nostalgia. She tells the images of her early life superstitiously, as though they were beads on a rosary, but her memory has ceased to be creative enrichment and has become instead a bitter self-division. Nor is Oppression yet finished with her. War breaks out with America, trade languishes and her husband's loom lies idle until, in the violent hopelessness of frustration, he flies to join the army, squandering his labour to support his family. They sail, as the woman comes to see, 'a poor devoted crew' (st. 34), sacrificial offerings to the power of the rich; and it is here that Wordsworth's poetic journey to Stonehenge is fulfilled in his picture of the imaginative terror of the war where the woman lost her family.

The cycles of night and day, storm and calm, which shape the action of *Salisbury Plain*, bring changes of mood to its central characters. But these changes are no more than changes, alternations. Nothing substantially new happens to them; opposite moods are not integrated, and there is no dialectical advance in consciousness. Calm succeeds storm, storm succeeds calm endlessly, each implicit in the other but unable to enrich it. So the vagrant's nightmare vision of the terrors of war (st. 41) is succeeded by an equally sinister trance of peace aboard the boat home.

> And oft, robbed of my perfect mind, I thought
> At last my feet a resting-place had found.
> 'Here will I weep in peace,' so Fancy wrought,
> 'Roaming the illimitable waters round,
> Here gaze, of every friend but Death disowned,
> All day, my ready tomb the ocean flood.'
> To break my dream the vessel reached its bound
> And homeless near a thousand homes I stood,
> And near a thousand tables pined and wanted food.
>
> (st. 43)

The voyage had a port, the mariner had a home – but the vagrant has the discipline of neither home, friend nor purpose. Her moods are beyond her control, possessing her and tending always to a boundlessness like that of the sea or plain itself – a boundlessness in which, despite her fancy, 'the imagination has no rest'[10] and therefore no capacity to build a reciprocal relationship, either with nature or her fellow men. Neither the sunrise nor the presence of a listener can really warm her, we might say. Indeed, the chilling silence into which she falls at the end of her story marks the tragedy of an unfinished life which is a completed tale. Her narrative has brought neither energy nor true relief; it has merely reinforced the harmfully retrospective habits of her mind by one further indulgence of them. Her one hope remains death, not as part of the pattern of infinitely renewing life but as termination.

Wordsworth has from the start of *Salisbury Plain* identified himself as a poet with the poor of his civilisation, with the vagrant and the traveller, and all those many others 'of comfort reft, by pain depressed' (st. 3) whose tragic extremities of mood express their bitter experience of social inequality. He has travelled to the uttermost in his night journey, like Marlow in *Heart of Darkness*, in order to reach these extremities; and now, as the vagrant ends her tale, the sunrise brings the parting of the ways. The image is a potent one in radical thought. 'The revolutions of America and France have thrown a beam of light over the world, which reaches into man'[11] – so Paine was able to prophesy the irresistible illumination that the dawning of the age of reason was about to bring to all men. The sunrise in *Salisbury Plain* focuses Wordsworth's longing for the same millennial dawn (st. 37), but in 1793–4 he was pessimistic where Paine in 1791 had been optimistic:

> reason's ray,
> What does it more than while the tempests rise,
> With starless glooms and sounds of loud dismay,
> Reveal with still-born glimpse the terrors of our way?
>
> (st. 48)

He turns to meditate upon the worldwide injustice of which his tale has been a local epitome, and finds everywhere oppression, mystification and superstition. In prosperous nations old and young are starved to death, brutalised by labour or deceived into blessing their oppressors for a 'charity' which is no more than superfluity; and such usurpation is not merely domestic but international.

> From the pale line to either frozen main
> The nations, though at home in bonds they drink
> The dregs of wretchedness, for empire strain,
> And crushed by their own fetters helpless sink,
> Move their galled limbs in fear and eye each silent link.
>
> (st. 50)

The extraordinary Gothic intensity of these lines suggests beautifully the extremism of the human imagination alienated under imperialism, and Wordsworth goes on particularly to indict the savagery of Spanish imperialism in Peru and perhaps of British imperialism in India.

At the heart of his disillusion with reason, of course, is the Parisian Terror; for in Paris Wordsworth saw men who believed in the power of war to create peace, punishment to create wisdom, execution to create justice and legal repression to create liberty (sts 57–8). The French Revolution seemed to have proved a false dawn, plunging the world back again into the contradictions of those dark ages that had preceded it; and these contradictions have their natural expression once more in the desperate hope of Wordsworth's conclusion, as he screws despondency into passionate indignant appeal.

> Heroes of Truth pursue your march, uptear
> Th' Oppressor's dungeon from its deepest base;
> High o'er the towers of Pride undaunted rear
> Resistless in your might the herculean mace
> Of Reason; let foul Error's monster race
> Dragged from their dens start at the light with pain
> And die; pursue your toils, till not a trace
> Be left on earth of Superstition's reign,
> Save that eternal pile which frowns on Sarum's plain.
>
> (st. 61)

Here Wordsworth is attempting to master everything that the poem has confronted, to image the discipline of all the anarchic powers arising from his contemplation of Stonehenge and, in so doing, to turn history, memory and imagination to a fully creative use. He is attempting to meet tragedy with hope; and yet the hope is desperate.

There are two interrelated reasons for this. First, the mastery of the poem's conclusion is to be achieved only vicariously, if at all, not in the personal experience of the poet himself (who is, we remember, 'by pain depressed') but in a projected image only – the image of those unnamed 'Heroes of Truth' to whom the last stanza is addressed. Second, these sages and heroes are idealised figures in a way that the 'friends of liberty' of the *Letter* were not. Events in France and repressions in England had finally destroyed the actual political societies and social friendships that were once Wordsworth's hope, and left him (it seems from an incomplete manuscript) to compose his great men into an imaginary company of his own constitution. They must achieve what he himself with his self-divided imagination cannot: they must dispel error with reason, compose the bitterness of anger with gentleness, establish political and economic justice, and by the power of their imaginative harmony make a peace that will finally conclude those wars – psychological, civil and international – which so faithfully express the injustice and inequality of contemporary society. It is indeed a desperate hope, as Wordsworth in his hectic use of the transformational devices of romance shows himself to be aware: the rhetoric of his poetry communicates the poverty of its political theory. For despite its plethora of poetic figures, the poem's conclusion has no home-born image of power 'to melt into our affection(s?), to incorporate itself with the blood & vital juices of our minds.'[12] Wordsworth cannot find for himself in the present what he imagined for the vagrant in the past – a home, a resting-place where strenuousness may sometimes relax, an image sufficient to bind the mind into time and place and save it from its own unaccommodated extremes. He cannot find a hope to constitute his mind in healthful relationship with the world, as increasingly he sees that he needs; and thus the poem, perhaps for this cause never completed to his satisfaction, falls back into the rhetoric of a rationalism that, paradoxically, perfectly expresses his despair.

In the retrospect of the 1805 *Prelude*, Wordsworth thought that his experience on Salisbury Plain was his first self-conscious initiation into the power of his imagination to transform the natural world in obedience to the passionate impulses aroused in him by that world. This is so; but we should not let the rather playful passages where that experience is recollected (xii:320–53) blind us to the painful nature of the transformation which we see in *Salisbury Plain*. In the summer of 1793, Wordsworth had been unable to travel to France, where he most wanted to be. The British declaration of war against the revolutionary armies, having first betrayed his hopes of a general European liberation, now kept him ashore; and his despondent journey across Salisbury Plain followed a month's observation of the battle preparations of the British fleet off the Isle of Wight. The poem inspired by that journey, *Salisbury Plain*, is indeed a stride into another region. It is the inner journey of a man with nowhere in the outer world to travel to. It is a solitary research into the iconography of the terror which is a true measure of Wordsworth's civilisation; and its master image of Stonehenge enabled him to articulate the different kinds of self-division into which political inequality had thrown the mind at other periods of its history too – and which only a future age of fraternity would be able to reintegrate. The break from descriptive poetry is complete and final; for in the painful betrayal of his hope for political transformation of the world, Wordsworth is discovering the means of its poetic transformation. Imagination, the poet's capacity to see 'a new world' (*Prelude* xii:371), was discovered in the night-terrors of the revolutionary's failure to make one; and although that discovery remains incompletely realised in *Salisbury Plain*, where the transformational power of that image of Stonehenge proves too disruptive to integrate, it is fully realised in its successor, *Adventures on Salisbury Plain*. Here for the first time Wordsworth found himself free to let inner and outer play together in the new world of his verse.

5 Adventures on Salisbury Plain (1795–9?)

The shaping idea of *Adventures on Salisbury Plain* is that the healthy development of mind is dependent upon meeting satisfaction in its sense of justice, and that the causes of crime and perversion lie in the sense of betrayal experienced when this satisfaction is denied. It is the shaping idea too of Godwin's *Political Justice*:

> A neglect of justice is not only to be deplored for the direct evil it produces; it is perhaps still more injurious by its effects in perverting the understanding, overturning our calculations of the future, and thus striking at the root of moral discernment, and genuine power and decision of character.[1]

With real sympathy Godwin presents the reforming radical's case against injustice: that 'the poor man will be induced to regard the state of society as a state of war, an unjust combination, not for protecting every man in his rights and securing to him the means of existence, but for engrossing all its advantages to a few favoured individuals, and reserving for the portion of the rest want, dependence and misery.'[2] The threat here to those who accept the conventional Hobbesian formula is precise and consciously polarised: the poor, in opposition to the rich, will consider the state of society to be a continuance rather than a composition of the state of war which existed before, and will act accordingly.

Adventures on Salisbury Plain apprehends as an actuality what Godwin had only entertained as a future possibility, for, to the sailor and the soldier's widow who are its central characters, the state of society really has been a state of war. They are the neglected victims of wars waged by the rich and powerful, and the poem traces the gradual process of the embitterment which is caused by their unjust neglect. 'Oh! what can war but endless war still breed?' Wordsworth had asked in *Salisbury Plain* (st. 57). Similarly here, in his new poem, he shows how injustice breeds injustice and betrayal breeds betrayal, even in the best of minds, until the sailor is driven to murder and the soldier's widow to vagrancy and theft. These aggressive acts against life and property are partly provoked by need; but they are also inseparably bound up, as we shall see, with those responses of resentment and revenge in which the poor attempt to reconstitute their outraged sense of justice – and which, of course, in their turn provoke the revenge of the rich. It is a vicious circle in which the whole of society is implicated; and the rich have the upper hand. Hence the new emblem with which Wordsworth replaces the Stonehenge of *Salisbury Plain*: the gibbet, image of the pharisaical justice by which society institutionalises and compounds its injustices, and condemns itself to the continuing self-division of civil unrest.

The poem, however, sets out to break this vicious circle of revenge; and it does so by the new kind of concern it calls into play. Gone is the urgent historical scheme and the heroic strenuousness of *Salisbury Plain*, with its hunger to storm the Bastille of the future. Instead, we have an expansive, spacious poem, measured like the verse of Chaucer and Spenser, and reflecting Wordsworth's growing conviction that history must be wooed, not ravished. It is a triumph of pace, at home with time; and if *Salisbury Plain* could not integrate the disruptive energies aroused by its own image of Stonehenge, the image of the gibbet is easily accommodated here. Paul Sheats is surely mistaken in his sense that the poem is disorganised by the displaced energies of Wordsworth's unadmitted feelings for Annette Vallon, by 'the decay of love into fear, guilt, and hate'.[3] The contrary seems true to me, and a sentence from Winnicott gives my point the necessary emphasis:

> The word 'concern' is used to cover in a positive way a phenomenon that is covered in a negative way by the word 'guilt'.[4]

The development of the capacity for concern, he argues, belongs to the self becoming integrated in time and able to turn its primitive sense of guilt to constructive ends of reparation. *Adventures on Salisbury Plain* shows Wordsworth perfecting this capacity in his poetry for the first time. He has found a way to liberate the mind from the vicious circle of those emotions that imprison it – from guilt and from vindictiveness, where the imaginative hunger for justice is expressed as aggression against the self and against others, and also from those unintegrated extremes of hope and despair that had bedevilled his earlier work. It is the turning-point of his career; and as he settles to concern himself with the sufferings of others, we may notice that for the first time his own alienation does not provide the central drama of his poetry.

Formally the poem is an imitation of the popular criminal biography, most familiarly known perhaps in the collection of *The Newgate Calendar* which Godwin had used in writing *Caleb Williams*. It is a literature commonly of crime, remorse and repentance, a form which – pandering to sensational delight in crime under the cloak of moral disapproval – reinforces that double standard of guilty desire and punitive revenge under which we still languish. The undemonstrative pace and the avoidance of climax which characterise *Adventures on Salisbury Plain* should be understood in relation to the immediate but contradictory gratifications offered by such popular fiction; and its imitative tactic is one particular example of a more general concern: to search out the contradictions created by political injustice amongst the various cultures and counter-cultures of the poor. Wordsworth's interest is in vagrants, gipsies, small tenants and freeholders, discarded members of the armed forces and criminals on the run – in the underprivileged, the dispossessed and the unpropertied, who according to the constitution have no political right in their own country. He has written a poem full of meetings, missed meetings and partings, of casual and accidental encounters, which bring out perfectly the contradictions and strangled possibilities of the lives to which the poor are condemned.

The poem itself, however, is created as a play-area exempt from such restriction, where contradiction may be temporarily resolved. It constitutes an idealised alternative society for its reader, where we need not rush to judgement. Instead, our understanding and sympathy may unfold at the pace of the poem, free from those disruptive emotions that risk tightening still further the vicious circle of injustice – emotions such as bitterness, anger and indignation, which according to *The Prelude* 'works where hope is not' (x:967). Clearly, of course, unlike the criminal biographies which it imitates, *Adventures on Salisbury Plain* is not written as a popular work which the poor will read. Yet although

Wordsworth's sense of political intervention remains paternalist we should notice that his imaginative commitment to the poor has the power, as E. P. Thompson has observed, radically to transform the 'paternalist sensibility'.[5] The sympathy aroused by the poem is far more challenging than that aroused by *Political Justice*, for instance, and not least because Wordsworth is now regularly dramatising the inner life of his characters. It is this seriousness of imaginative commitment that validates his idealism, not only in the play-area of this poem but of the poetry to come; it gives to his poetry its power to enrich significantly – if not, in terms of political change, sufficiently – the understanding and the sympathies which we bring to the contradictions of the real world where we find ourselves.

The terror accommodated in *Adventures on Salisbury Plain* is that a good man may be brought to murder, that the slow growth of a lifetime's habits may be overthrown in the pleasure of a moment's recklessness. Wordsworth offers no motive for the murder, only history – history of a man who, on his way home after two years in the Navy, had been press-ganged into many further years of armed service and who, finally on his release, had been turned away penniless by the government officials who should have paid him:

> and now towards his home return'd,
> Bearing to those he loved nor warmth nor food,
> In sight of his own house, in such a mood
> That from his view his children might have run,
> He met a traveller, robb'd him, shed his blood;
>
> (st. 11)

It may be that the ugly recklessness of mood in which the murder was committed had expressed the sailor's vengefulness, or perhaps a bitter hatred of himself and others was fuelled by the proximities of his home and family – for we learn that 'he had done the deed in the dark wood / Near his own home!' (st. 85). But it is important that we admit the difficulties of describing mood and ascribing motive, for they are difficulties characteristic of the new poetry that Wordsworth is now beginning to write. It is a poetry whose creative hold upon the imagination lies in its suggestiveness, drawing our sympathetic curiosity to consider matters which otherwise we might outlaw. It is poetry that invites us to play, and it is poetry that makes us work, so that our understanding of the sailor is simultaneously a startled recognition of ourselves: 'What hearts have we!' (st. 73). We are implicated by the very act of our understanding; and thus, in the open court of the poem, the temptation to blame is averted, the criminal is reclaimed for our fellow-feeling, and his crime is contextualised in ways critical of that faith in individual responsibility upon which the whole edifice of law and punishment stands.

The aim of *Adventures on Salisbury Plain* is that of any criminal biography – to bring the criminal to justice, if possible by virtue of his own remorse. Accordingly, Wordsworth has structured his poem upon the plan that he was later to use again in *Peter Bell*: he has invented a series of remarkable coincidences, events and encounters during the course of which his hero becomes increasingly unable to live with his sense of guilt. There are five main episodes in the poem: the sailor's friendly meeting with an old soldier, unknown to him his father-in-law (sts 1–5); his solitary terror before the gibbet on Salisbury Plain, at night in stormy weather (sts 6–22); his meeting and night-long conversation with the vagrant (sts 23–67); their joint encounter next morning with the father who beats his son (sts 68–74); and lastly his unexpected meeting with his dying wife and his subsequent confession (sts 75–92). Enid Welsford has criticised this scheme for its 'clumsy duplication of persons and incidents',[6] and she found the repeated use of the device of the autobiographical tale particularly awkward. Yet these recurrent patterns are crucial to the poem in two ways. First, they enact the widespread and repetitive nature of the injustices that the poor actually suffer (and here we should understand that the tradition of relating one's life history expresses both the wish of the needy for something to give and also the wish of the ill-treated for the justice of sympathy); and second, they do not only duplicate but they also exacerbate the sufferings of the poem's central character, the sailor, intensifying the contradictions that he feels until he is driven to surrender himself to the law.

From the very start of the poem Wordsworth has made us aware of the difficulties experienced by the sailor in negotiating the extremes of his own emotions. He is torn between love and fear, between social feeling and sublime passion, between those kindly sympathies that draw him towards his fellow men and those guilty terrors that drive him away; and in consequence he can never enjoy more than the 'short-lived fellowship' (st. 4) in which initially we see him. Each succeeding episode in the poem serves to tighten the screw of these contradictory emotions upon him until finally, faced with his dying wife, he cries out in both love and terror together for her forgiveness. It is a moment that normally in such a work would recompose moral and social disorder into the harmony of justice. But not here: the sudden release of violent feeling consoles the sailor no more in remorse that it had done in murder – and indeed, its results are similarly fatal, for it overwhelms the failing constitution of his wife, and she dies. Typically of this poem of transitory and unfulfilled encounters, the sailor is so absorbed by the strength and perhaps by the dangerousness of his own emotions that he cannot be comforted by the forgiveness which the poet detects on the dead woman's lips. Instead her death increases his anguish and, when her funeral has been undertaken by the kind pair at the inn, he goes to a nearby city where he gives himself up, is duly executed and his body exposed on a gibbet.

Why does he give himself up? It is tempting to look for moral tags with which to label the poem's end tidily in our minds. Enid Welsford, for instance, talks both of the sailor's penitence and his remorse.[7] Yet penitence, with its root sense that a crime may be made good and a wrong repaid by sorrow, seems wholly inappropriate here. Remorse is a more accurate term, with its tragic intimations of the ultimate impossibility of adequate repayment; but no single word will do. Wordsworth's reluctance here to ascribe motive is an acknowledgement of the strangeness of those contradictions into which the sailor has been betrayed. If we speak of his remorse, we should also speak of his despair at injustice; of his heartsickness at the thought of human law; of his weariness of the extremes of fear and terror; of the sinister pleasures that lie in self-punishment; and of his wish to be dead. He has been hounded out of the creative possibilities of penitence and out of the sharp focus of remorse, into a state of confusion which he cannot reconstitute upon the principles of justice. It is a vicious circle from which, in terms of the society of the poem, there seems to be no escape.

The sailor's experience is emblematic, repeated (as I have said) throughout the breadth of the poem. Nowhere amongst the cultures and counter-cultures of the poor that Wordsworth searches does he find an extensive sympathy unperverted by injustice. Two further examples will suffice here. First, there is the grim perception with which the poem ends, when we see the kind couple at the inn, excited by their suspicion of the sailor's behaviour, decide despite their pity to surrender him to the law. The insidiousness of injustice, wearing its familiar mask of law, perverts their feelings and clouds their minds until they abandon the contradictions of their experience to the higher power of state justice for resolution. Such pharisaism, penetrating even the kindest of hearts amongst the class the sailor and the vagrant themselves come from, expresses in miniature their whole society – a society which Wordsworth finally images in the repressive power of the gibbet and its dominant place in popular culture.

> They left him hung on high in iron case,
> And dissolute men, unthinking and untaught,
> Planted their festive booths beneath his face;
> And to that spot, which idle thousands sought,
> Women and children were by fathers brought;
>
> (st. 92)

So the gibbet insinuates the callousness of the rich man's justice into the heart of the families of the poor; and the vicious circle of vindictiveness remains intact.

Second, there is the new treatment of the episode of the vagrant. Though now more capable of hope and affection than she was in *Salisbury Plain*, Wordsworth has multiplied the injustices from which she has suffered. We read in detail of conditions in the armed services, of coldness in state hospitals and finally of a mind reduced into the outlawry of gipsy life in the hope of relief from penury, loneliness and the chill hazards of beggary. ' "I have my inner self abused" ' (st. 61) – Wordsworth has transformed the tragic innocent of 1793–4 into a criminal, a thief and vagrant to match the criminal status of his new hero, and in so doing he has indicated precisely the limitations of that gipsy counter-culture that was interesting so many contemporary writers in their search for alternative forms of social organisation. The vagrant had been lured by a politic that promised her the reciprocity for which she had longed, a politic where ' "all belonged to all, and each was chief" ' (st. 57). Of the three stanzas in which she describes her impressions of the gipsies (sts 57–9), the first two are full of warmth, colour, joy, music, activity, ease, company and a life apparently with its own seasonable pieties and its own human kindness. Only the third stanza, where colour yields to the darkness of midnight theft, reveals the truth behind the blandishments of first impressions: it is a life of disguise and fear dedicated to the betrayal of trust and faith. The ideology of gipsy life proves to be no more than a parasitic inversion of the culture which it claims to supersede; its vagrancy is financed by the property of others, and its daytime ease is stolen by the nightly labour of theft. Its characteristic vacillations between the extremes of kindliness and terror connect with the disturbed lives that the sailor and the vagrant still live outside the law; and although its practical communism bears testimony to spiritual needs unsatisfied elsewhere, it is unable finally to do more than fuel further the reciprocities of revenge. Tragically, here as elsewhere in the poem, the poor – vagrant and gipsy alike – are doomed to fail in their attempts to make the justice which they cannot find.

The question of Godwin's influence on Wordsworth has been much discussed, and I want to say a little about it in conclusion. Usually it is discussed in an all-or-nothing fashion, as though the curious blend of necessarianism, rationalism and perfectibilism in *Political Justice* were only to be accepted as a whole or not at all. I want, however, to isolate three important features of Godwin's thought that perhaps influenced and certainly must have confirmed the trend of Wordsworth's thought. First, as we have seen, Godwin believed that the healthy growth of mental power depended essentially upon the sense of being justly done by. Second, he believed that such growth was best secured in the slow culture of habits of mind that build up what in *The Old Cumberland Beggar* is called the 'mild necessity of use'. Third, he believed that the growth of mind in good habits might create hitherto unimagined powers within a wholly transformed society. It seems to me that these three beliefs were shared by Wordsworth, and that they lie at the heart of the hope in all the great poetry of the next decade.

But the difference between the two men is important too; for although both saw that the idea of justice was integral to the mind's organisation of its experience, Godwin defined that idea in terms of rational principles whilst Wordsworth defined it in terms of the reciprocities of feeling. It is the origin and nature of the *sense* of justice, rather than its rules, that interested Wordsworth in his growing conviction of the primary emotionality of mind; and his work of 1795–7 was to be a still further exploration of those creative or perverse feelings through which the mind develops its sense of justice – feelings of forgiveness or revenge, of grief or guilt, of love or bitterness. *The Borderers* and *The Ruined Cottage* lay bare with wonderful accuracy the different ways in which the mind may accommodate, or fail to accommodate, the treacherous experience of injustice.

It is in *Adventures on Salisbury Plain*, however, that Wordsworth discovered what he wanted to do. This is his first fully self-confident poem, in which for the first time the quest for justice that had begun with *Descriptive Sketches* does not sink back into despondency and despair. The poet has found a way to break out of what Robert Osborn calls 'the vicious round of betrayal, crime, guilt, and punishment perpetuated, as Godwin had argued, by the self-righteous quest for justice in an unjust society';[8] and he has achieved this by the exercise of his craft. *Adventures on Salisbury Plain* is as tragic in conception as its predecessor *Salisbury Plain*, but Wordsworth's conception of tragedy has developed. The desperate hope and strenuous indignation of the earlier poem has matured into a capacity to grieve – a grief which is not submission, expressing a pity which is not patronisation, but which instead challenges the reader by the unassertive rigour and comprehensiveness of its understanding. The vagrant at one point had confessed to the bitterly vindictive impulse to obtrude her dying body 'in the streets and walks where proud men are' (st. 43). Wordsworth's poem is a purification of this impulse, unyieldingly meek in its determination to tell its tale and be heard; it is intent to do justice to the lives it describes by articulating them in the fullness of their relationships, rescuing them from the morality of the ruling classes and reconstituting them in a republic of genuine sympathy.

Hence the new simplicity and austerity of Wordsworth's language. It is not yet as metaphorically rich as the best of his work, and not yet wholly free of its Gothic trappings, but nevertheless it shows that he has already chosen his means to strengthen the feelings that bind men together. *Adventures on Salisbury Plain* depicts a society which perverts and alienates these feelings; and it is to rectify this process that Wordsworth, in the belief that no man is wholly good or bad, addresses our sympathies in plain republican language. For this is one thing that poetry can do: it can mend the sensibility. It has a power more substantial and more permanent than might be conceived from the contemplation of descriptive verse or rhetorical incantation; it can provide the mind with an imagined but really existent world, with its own particular laws, its own particular time and space, where sympathies may be redisciplined – for, to quote Winnicott once more,

> playing and cultural experience are things that we do value in a special way; [they] link the past, the present, and the future; *they take up time and space*. They demand and get our concentrated deliberate attention, deliberate but without too much of the deliberateness of trying.[9]

Descriptive Sketches and *Salisbury Plain* were both marred by the deliberateness of trying, by a rhetoric which seems a form of self-address, of self-conviction. But *Adventures on Salisbury Plain* shows a new hope and a new purpose, a new poetic which is also a new politic (not, I think, necessarily opposed to political activism). It is both a certainty and a possibility: that poetry is a reconstitution of the world that may reconstitute the world.

Part III
The Borderers:
The Poet and Justice

6 *The Borderers* (1796–7)

(a) THE PLAY AS IMITATION

Coleridge in 1797 pronounced *The Borderers* to be 'absolutely wonderful' and went on: 'There are in the piece those *profound* touches of the human heart, which I find three or four times in "The Robbers" of Schiller, & often in Shakespere – but in Wordsworth there are no *inequalities*.'[1] Wordsworth's own mature judgement of the play, given in 1843 and reprinted in the Osborn edition which I use here, is even more striking:

> my care was almost exclusively given to the passions & the characters, & the position in which the persons in the Drama stood relatively to each other, that the reader (for I had then no thought of the Stage) might be moved & to a degree instructed by lights penetrating somewhat into the depths of our Nature. In this endeavour I cannot think upon a very late review that I have failed.   (p. 814)

If neither Coleridge's enthusiastic praise nor Wordsworth's considered verdict of the play's success in sustained power of psychological insight has evoked an answering response from modern criticism, the cause is perhaps twofold: a sense of its theatrical clumsiness, and a sense of its youthful derivativeness. Enid Welsford's judgement is representative: 'Wordsworth was no dramatist and his attempt to convey genuine psychological insight through the medium of a curious blend of "Gothic" melodrama, Godwinian argument and Shakespearean tragedy was bound to end in failure.'[2]

About Wordsworth's improficiency in the skills of the theatre I have little to say; I propose to deal with the play as Wordsworth came to think of it, as closet drama to be staged in the theatre of the mind. We should remember, however, that each of our major Romantic poets wrote plays or fragments of plays. They were interested in the money and the audience that theatre could

command, and also in the capacity of dramatic form to do justice
to the powers of the human mind. Their hope was to renew and
rival the dramatic achievements of Shakespearean England; and
if the author of so dramatic a poem as *Adventures on Salisbury Plain*
did not labour to acquire theatrical skill, we should not seek
explanation only in his diffident personality or his exclusively
poetical vocation. Bourgeois theatre, with its small number of
licensed theatres, its powerful managers, its unadventurous
audience and repertoire must be held responsible too in forming
that personality and its sense of vocation. Through Wordsworth's
hopes and fears for his play with Sheridan, and his final
conclusion about 'the deprav'd State of the Stage at present' (see
EL 197 n. 1), we can see him grappling in those dark years of
radical dispersal with his abiding problems: What is a Poet? To
whom does he address himself?

It is the dismissal of the play for its derivativeness that concerns
me here. Coleridge does not make this mistake; like Wordsworth
he had been brought up in a literary tradition which cultivated the
historical sense through imitation, allusion and quotation, and
therefore understood quite naturally that *Die Räuber* and
Shakespearean tragedy were the defining context within which
Wordsworth wished to establish his meaning. Since 1793 and the
betrayal of his faith that history was the handmaiden to the
necessary progress of mind, Wordsworth had begun to
understand more subtly the complex reciprocity between man
and his past. Whilst *Descriptive Sketches* had imitated *The Traveller*
in order to place Goldsmith's wisdom firmly behind it as a thing of
the past, *The Borderers* understands that history may equally well
be loss as gain, and that the powers of the past may be needed fully
to articulate the losses of the present. The play's newness is not a
means of disowning the past but of recovering it for the present, of
establishing in time and place a living and sympathetic
relationship between them. Wordsworth's use of the imitative
method is thus in itself a particular enactment of the more general
moral position that we shall see argued within the play: that
justice includes the debt of gratitude to all that is good in the past.

First, the imitation of Shakespeare. When Enid Welsford
described Wordsworth's discovery that 'human nature is more
effectively illuminated by William Shakespeare than by William

Godwin',[3] she rightly meant that he found in Shakespearean tragedy an adequate poetic realisation of the challenge presented by human evil to the harmonious conception of a divinely ordered Nature. But we need to understand precisely the evil that Shakespeare portrayed. We have already seen in discussing *Salisbury Plain* that the vulnerable societies of *Macbeth* and *King Lear* had depended for their goodness not upon reason alone but upon the reciprocity of traditional bonds in which love and duty strengthened one another. When Wordsworth wrote in the prefatory essay to *The Borderers* of 'the milk of human reason' (p. 64), he echoed *Macbeth* because he saw in the metaphoric richness of Shakespeare's poetry an acknowledgement of the need for reason to be kind if the single state of man and his society is to be preserved. He saw a vision of a feudalism quite the opposite of Godwin's Protestant individualism, a vision that – to quote Enid Welsford once more – 'we are members one of another'.[4] The evil in Shakespearean tragedy is the denial of this sense of kind; it is the struggle of men for reasons of fear, bitterness, jealousy or deep malice, to deny all that they have ever truly known of kindness, both in themselves and other people. The bold speculative reasonings of Macbeth, Edmund and Iago too prove to be so dangerous because, as they seem to cut the individual free from his bonds to pursue his future, tragically they deny his debt to his past, to whatever there may be of goodness still alive in him. It seems to me that what Wordsworth found in Shakespeare was an iconography of evil as betrayal and self-betrayal; and it is this knowledge, epitomising how we really belong to time and place, that Wordsworth wished to recover for the cause of radical perfectibility.

For an imitation is not a copy. Wordsworth did not take from Shakespeare his precise historical curiosity interesting itself through the tragedies in the variety of men's social structures, the inner contradictions by which they perished and the irrecoverable loss through which they have left us to know the present. Instead, he has written a tragic parable, intent like *Adventures on Salisbury Plain* to act upon history by reforming the sympathetic understanding of its reader. It is ironic, therefore, that his parable should have been so often misunderstood. Carl Woodring, for instance, writes that 'except for traces of humanitarian sympathy and complete skepticism concerning subtlety of intellect, *The Borderers* has no democratic bias';[5] whilst more recently Marilyn

Butler seems to have characterised it as a reactionary piece, with Herbert 'a father-figure who might stand generally for the *ancien régime* or more specifically for Louis XVI himself'.[6] Such a provocative reading, of course, by mistaking the man for the class or one individual for another, refuses the point of Wordsworth's parable altogether: namely, that there are Herberts and Cliffords together and that the difference between them matters, that (although Rivers tries to usurp the words) 'there is no justice when we do not feel / For man as man' (II:3:172–3). Justice abstracted out of the mercy that contemplates the individual is as terrible in *The Borderers* as in *King Lear* or *Othello*; and yet because Wordsworth wants to reclaim the poetry of feudalism for the radical cause, the play is urgent beyond anything in Shakespeare for the reconstitution of our sense of justice.

This brings us to the imitation of Schiller, himself of course deeply read in Shakespeare. *Die Räuber* had created a stir in England similar to that which *Faust* was to create in the following generation. It stimulated an episode in *Caleb Williams*, Southey planned a tragedy entitled *The Banditti*, whilst Coleridge wrote a powerful early sonnet, *To the author of The Robbers*, imitated its plot in *Remorse* and continued throughout his life to praise the play as a young man's success. But Hazlitt's testimony is the most remarkable of all:

> There is something in the style that hits the temper of men's minds; that, if it does not hold the mirror up to nature, yet 'shews the very age and body of the time its form and pressure.' It embodies, it sets off and aggrandizes in all the pomp of action, in all the vehemence of hyperbolical declamation, in scenery, in dress, in music, in the glare of the senses, and the glow of sympathy, the extreme opinions which are floating in our time, and which have struck their roots deep and wide below the surface of the public mind. We are no longer as formerly heroes in warlike enterprise; martyrs to religious faith; but we are all the partisans of a political system, and devotees to some theory of moral sentiments.[7]

Die Räuber was so popular, Hazlitt says, because it gave voice to the passion that had newly entered political and moral debate. It is a play vibrant with images of greatness and heroism, with the energies of men grappling in their souls with destiny and damnation in order to replace the old corruptions of the world with new justice and new authority. Schiller had been drawn to Shakespeare, perhaps, because he wished to restore the poetic imagination to its true power in the mind, to shame the pharisaism of his bourgeois audience and to embody in tragedy the consequences of the injustice that he found in the uniquely repressive conditions of his own society. Wordsworth was drawn in turn to Schiller, perhaps, because he too felt the hunger of the poetic imagination after greatness and heroism, and also its hunger to create an authentic counter-culture with strength to shame the spiritless legalism of bourgeois society. *The Prelude*, as we shall see, shows the satisfaction of these desires; but they are already present here in *The Borderers* where Rivers, imperfect speaker though he be, is the first of Wordsworth's poets sown by nature. Yet his poetry is perverse and the play ends, like *Die Räuber*, with the tragic self-perpetuation of injustice.

The myth embodied in Schiller's play, that is, is one that the degeneration of the French Revolution into the Terror was to make dominant in Romantic and nineteenth-century literature of all genres. It is the myth we might epitomise in Blake's little poem *In a Mirtle Shade*: that the violent resistance of oppression perpetuates injustice. As Geoffrey Hartman puts it, it is the myth of 'the revolutionary discovering once again that a New Order cannot escape a founding crime'.[8] Godwin's *Caleb Williams*, Byron's *Cain* (and most of Ibsen's theatre after him) explored the myth as tragedy, Shelley's *Prometheus Unbound* resolved the tragedy into love. It seems a secular revision of the old myth of original sin, where evil is transmitted not through our inherited humanity but through acquired experience of social injustice. The vicious circle of revenge and guilt that we saw in *Adventures on Salisbury Plain* has tightened still further as the impossibility of a fresh start was brought home to Wordsworth; he saw, in that phrase of Ibsen which summarises the whole tradition, that we sail 'with a corpse in the cargo'.[9] Furthermore, it is something of value in us – our resistance to injustice – that makes us vulnerable to corruption. As Wordsworth put it in 1842, meditating over his play and its commentary upon events in France,

The study of human nature suggests this awful truth, that, as in

the trials to which life subjects us, sin and crime are apt to start
from their very opposite qualities, so are there no limits to the
hardening of the heart, and the perversion of the understanding
to which they may carry their slaves.   (p. 813)

There are no limits. . . . The tragic business of *The Borderers* is with
those boundless and contradictory extremes into which Rivers
and Mortimer fall, as they discover – like the heroes of *Die Räuber* –
that all things are possible except the recovery of lost innocence.

But once again an imitation is not a copy. Schiller's tragedy is
anarchic, melodramatic and fatalistic in a way that faithfully
reflects its Germanic background. It is a play that cannot image
virtue, and its characters all live at the extremes of their
experience, pulled like puppets by the wires of irresistible master
passions. But Wordsworth has written a very English tragedy
whose difference from *Die Räuber* is part of its meaning. He has
seriously occupied his imagination with the greatness and
heroism of goodness; and the fatherly figure of Herbert provides a
moral centre to the play which is not discredited by his defeat. For
Herbert knows that, if all men are both good and bad, just and
unjust, all justice must be tempered with the mercy of individual
consideration; and he knows too that the capacity for such justice
in each man depends upon the disciplining power in the present of
goodness enjoyed in the past. It is a knowledge whose didactic
purpose within the play distinguishes Wordsworth from either of
the two authors he chiefly imitates. For *The Borderers* steers its own
course between the bygone feudalism of *Macbeth* and *King Lear* and
the hopeless anarchy of *Die Räuber*. But it does so,
characteristically, by submitting to the discipline of what is good
in each of its models. Its radical hunger for a new justice is tempered
by its recognition of the importance of the old bonds; power does not
overturn tenderness.

(b) HERBERT AND MATILDA

Herbert is an old man in a play whose other central characters are
young. Old, blind, dispossessed and poor, he is a grotesque
dramatic emblem of the most painful separations and injustices a
man may suffer. Yet whilst the younger people in the urgency of
their purposes are impatient for action to remedy the injustices
they see, Herbert in the frailty of age is patient. His sufferings are

in part the common inheritance of old age, but even more they are the particular consequences of accident and injustice; and yet they do not alienate him in bitterness or vindictiveness. Instead, they enrich his capacity for trust, and in so doing facilitate the reciprocities of kindness in others.

> And such a man – so mild and unoffending –
> By obvious signal, to the world's protection
> Solemnly dedicated –
>
> (v:3:46–8)

Herbert is the first of those extraordinary old men with whom Wordsworth's poetry is so reverentially full; and he shows Wordsworth grappling again with the question that had left him so despondent in *Descriptive Sketches*: how may a man accommodate (if at all) those sufferings and injustices, both natural and political, that are (unequally) our common experience of life? How may the vicious circle of the unjust resistance to injustice be broken? The answer here lies in the nature of Herbert's patience; and the quality of that patience lies in his hold upon the goodness of his past and present relationships, chiefly within his family. Wordsworth, we remember, showed only a precarious hold upon the lost goodness of his childhood in the nostalgia of *An Evening Walk*.

It is in particular the good relationship between father and daughter that is the battleground of the play's action. Rivers must destroy it to liberate Mortimer from what he considers the empty ceremony of traditional morality, whilst Herbert again and again must recreate it to keep freshly alive that gratitude which is the heart of the moral memory of mankind. The first act establishes for us the mutuality of debt between father and daughter. The narratives in which they ritually recount events of the immediate or distant past both express and reinforce their bond; and the courtesy with which they habitually listen and talk to each other, at length without interruption, is the perfection of that sympathy which can adapt to the different pace of others in their different journeys through life. So Herbert tells of the fire in Antioch where he lost his sight in saving Matilda's life, and she – lovingly anxious to hear the story again – must needs respond in the grateful love of present concern. It is a relationship rich with flexibility; now one is the protector and now the other, now one bears the blame and

now the other, now they are father and daughter and now as
twins, now they live in the past and now the present. Yet both are
conscious too of the limits of their love, neither abuses the
responsibilities of power: so there is space for disagreement
between them – as over Matilda's love for Mortimer, Herbert not
tyrannically forbidding her the man she will not offer to give up.
The bond between them is so secure because grounded in a true
sense of self and other; and it is enriched and made more valuable
by the sufferings they have been through. As Herbert says to
Mortimer, 'you are young; forty years must roll over your head ere
you can know how much a father may love his child' (II:3:102–4).
Pain and injustice, it seems, are behovely, inescapably our
common lot (if unequally distributed) and justified if we can turn
them to purposes of love and active sympathy.

Herbert's sense of goodness is not confined to personal
relationships, however; it is extended into a faith in the ultimate
goodness of the universe. *The Borderers* is Wordsworth's first work
to be seriously interested in the quality of religious experience;
and if the writing that describes Herbert seems unusually biblical
and old-fashioned for Wordsworth, it may be that he is once again
honouring those past forms of culture in which men have found
the necessary perspective to harmonise pain and evil. In times of
joy, as Robert Osborn says, Herbert has 'the mystical sanctity of a
man whose "life is hidden with God" ' (p. 26). He is confident in
the providence which God has bestowed upon the innocent and
helpless, and compares himself to Elijah – a teacher and prophet
amidst unbelievers, driven by superstition from his just place in
society and yet protected in the wilderness. He can even on
occasion, he says, as he walks with Matilda along the British
roads, momentarily compose a small community around him out
of the habitual war of their society, so that 'armed men / Met in
the roads would bless us' (III:3:73–4).

It is important, however, not to etherealise Herbert's character;
he has to struggle throughout the play to keep hold of his sense of
goodness. Since *An Evening Walk* Wordsworth has always
characterised mind by the variousness of the moods in which it
habitually experiences the world, a variousness which he feels
harmonious in health and contradictory in sickness. Herbert,
anxious both for himself and his daughter, is deeply conscious of
his changeableness of mood:

> Therefore I bless her: when I think of man
> I bless her with sad spirit; when of God,
> I bless her in the fulness of my joy!
>
> (iii:3:113–15)

This act of blessing, so important to Wordsworth and Coleridge in these years, is Herbert's way to struggle for balance of mind between sadness and joy. It is an enactment of Christ's commands in the Sermon on the Mount: love your enemies, bless them that curse you, do good to them that hate you. We may think of a blessing as a verbal gift, a benign dedication of mental power to make its object invulnerable to harm in the mysteries of God's protection; and it is in particular this sense of mystery that Herbert values. His injunction to Mortimer, that he should learn 'to fear the virtuous, and reverence misery' (iii:3:81), is central to the play. For only such awe before the mysteries of goodness and suffering can save the mind from the impetuous self-assertiveness of reason, coding the moral universe in its own desires. Herbert's awe and his patience are his struggle to acknowledge the real existence of a good world, not always comprehensible, lying beyond the self:

> Merciful God! thou has poured out the phials of thy wrath upon my head – but I will not murmur – blasted as I am thou hast left me both ears to hear the voice of my daughter and arms to fold her to my heart – I will adore thee and tremble!
>
> (ii:3:130–3)

So he fights to maintain his meekness, his firmness of purpose free from the assertiveness of ego; and his allusion to the Book of Revelation suggests his readiness to wait patiently upon God's good time for the descent of a new heaven and new earth. It seems indeed, in his capacity to meet injustice with meekness, treachery with faith and cruelty with blessing, that he embodies prophetically the promised future reserved for man.

Yet he is left to die; and his death opens up a breach through which the powers of violence and vindictiveness are freed to pour. Lured into mortal danger by the wind-blown bells of a ruined chapel, Herbert can no longer sustain the religious harmony of his mind. His last ejaculations are the broken syntax of a fractured personality; and although, alone in his extremity, he retains the habits of meekness and faith and blesses his daughter, the solitary death he endures proves unendurable to the contemplation of those who survive him. Its terror is best expressed by Margaret in her fear that – by what René Girard calls the *mimetic* infection of violence[10] – her husband's desertion of Herbert in his dying hour will surely repeat itself.

> Oh! Robert, you will die alone – you will have nobody to close your eyes – no hand to grasp your dying hands – I shall be in my grave. – A curse will attend us all –
>
> (IV:3:71–3)

Her fear of being accursed expresses perfectly the violence she feels in contemplating Herbert's death; her fear of revenge is already realised in the guilty fear itself. The vicious circle of fear and revenge starts up again. Even Matilda, whose eye had the power to create peace in troubled hearts (III:3:59–61) and who well remembers her father's command 'to bless all mankind' (v:3:61), falls to her knees and curses his murderer:

> Hear me, ye Heavens! (*kneeling*) may vengeance haunt the fiend
> For this most cruel murder – let him live
> And move in terror of the elements –
>
> (v:3:64–6)

This mercilessness, nourishing the violence of revenge within her, is a dreadful perversion of her father's faith. Blessing becomes a curse; and it is pronounced with such youthful ferocity that it blasts utterly the future possibilities of love and forgiveness between her and Mortimer. She herself faints at the recognition of the violence she has done to her love; and the vital energies of her mind seem doomed to such obsessive circling as that of the girl seduced and abandoned by Lord Clifford, who could only pace round and round the lost hopes and buried goodness in her baby's grave. The loss of Herbert's discipline is absolute within the world of the play; and the reciprocities of revenge against which he had struggled reassert themselves.

(c) RIVERS

The character of Rivers is a study in hubris, in that pride and ingratitude which sets a man against both God and his fellows.

Almost the first we hear of him is his inability to admit his debt of gratitude to Mortimer for having saved his life; and the subsequent plot of the play is the history of his desires, both conscious and unconscious, to avenge himself upon the discipline of love which he so resentfully feels inside himself when faced with Mortimer and Herbert. It is the familiar satanic compulsion 'out of good still to find means of evil', secularised by Wordsworth out of the theology of *Paradise Lost* (i:165) in order to explore the self-contradictory perversities of psychological sickness and social evil. Rivers might echo Satan's words in Eden:

> the more I see
> Pleasures about me, so much more I feel
> Torment within me, as from the hateful siege
> Of contraries; all good to me becomes
> Bane,
>
> (ix:119–23)

Cynical hatred is the tribute forced from him by his own recognition of human goodness; and every thought and action only serves, as with Satan, to involve him more deeply in the toils of this self-contradiction.

The hubris of Satan, of course, like that of Macbeth before him, is so centrally subversive because it threatens all the relationships of an existent paternal justice, in order to code a new moral law in the personal caprice of a dependent. It has the quality of a parricide; and so does the hubris of Rivers, who significantly dreads his father's ghost (ii:3:328), who has already murdered the captain of his ship at sea and who now is compelled to duplicate the crime in his hatred of the paternal bond between Herbert and Matilda. For the father embodies *pietas*, that mixture of love and duty in social bond which in a patriarchal society binds men together in the continuities of time and place; and the parricide, in René Girard's words, 'strikes at the most fundamental, essential, and inviolable distinction within the group. He becomes, literally, the slayer of distinctions.'[11] Rivers, obsessed with male relationships and contemptuous of 'compassion's milk' (ii:1:83), jealously desires the death of the good father with whom he is locked in unresolvable conflict; and the violence of his cynicism against Herbert, 'this old venerable grey-beard' (ii:3:226), testifies to the distinctions he has already destroyed (and which, of course, continue to haunt him) – distinctions that express his true connections with the past.

If Rivers' history seems obscure, it is because he himself distorts it; but the truth is clear. 'His master passions are pride and the love of distinction,' Wordsworth wrote in his prefatory essay (p. 62): it is as with Falkland in *Caleb Williams* – we are dealing with a man mistakenly educated in the meaning of honour, with a false self organised by the anxieties of approval and disapproval. As a young man Rivers had lived in the mirror of other minds, finding himself only in the image they seemed to return to him: 'I was the pleasure of all hearts – the darling / Of every tongue – as you are now' (IV:2:6–7). It is wholly characteristic that he should see Mortimer (quite inaccurately) as an image of his former self; for his mind is haunted by the insubstantial poetry of mirror and echo. The people around him are the supporting cast for his own heroic drama, fantasy projections without real independence; in so far as they are perceived to be independent, he must hate them. It is not surprising that so self-regarding a man, so prone to think himself enviable, should be so easily betrayed, and that being betrayed, he should feel no remorse – for he lacks the faith in the goodness of the world necessary to trust himself to begin the process of reparation. Instead, he retreats into paranoid delusions:

> I now perceived
> That we are praised by men because they see in us
> The image of themselves; that a great mind
> Outruns its age and is pursued with obliquy
> Because its movements are not understood.
> I felt that to be truly the world's friend,
> We must become the object of its hate.
>
> (IV:2:151–7)

When threatened with the reproach of dishonour, he internalises his principle of honour so that the people whose admiration he had formerly sought become contemptible and he alone the just standard of excellence, confirmed in his quality by the very reproaches that had threatened him. He still walks the obsessive circle of his own self-admiration but in the contrary direction now; he has become his own mirror. There is no trace of sympathy for the captain's suffering; and the difference from Herbert here, in parallel experiences of rejection, dispossession and dishonour, is at the heart of the play. Betrayal and injustice confirm Rivers in the callousness of his false self even whilst they enrage him inside, leading him into that contradiction which Burke detected in Rousseau and considered typical of the whole revolutionary enterprise: 'benevolence to the whole species, and want of feeling for every individual'.[12]

Driven to idealise solitude as a necessary proof of virtue, Rivers nevertheless feels his loneliness and cleaves to Mortimer. He wants two quite contradictory things of him – an ambiguity which, as Robert Osborn beautifully says, 'reflects the paradox implicit in the act of satanic appropriation' (p. 29). On the one hand he wants Mortimer to be his equal in friendship; he arranges the murder of Herbert to parallel his own murder of the sea captain so that the two of them might enjoy together their liberation from conventional morality. On the other hand he wants Mortimer to be his slave, subject utterly to him; and viewed from this perspective his plot against Herbert expresses his wanton desire to recommit the crime that obsesses his imagination, his envious hatred of innocence in all its forms and his need to undo the figures in authority over him. His predicament is that of the lonely bully who thrills with excitement and contempt at his power over other people even as he tries to engineer the friendship that, being engineered, can never satisfy him. All the while he tells that extraordinary tale to Mortimer in Act IV, in hypnotic rhythms that show a memory obsessed with the past chances of his life, he must also watch and manipulate his audience to prevent independent reactions hostile to his present purpose. He never dare relax; and when finally he fails, as fail he must, to secure either Mortimer's friendship or his subjection, he retreats once more into contemptuous delusion:

> If I pass beneath a rock
> And shout, and with the echo of my voice
> Bring down a heap of rubbish and it crushes me,
> I die without dishonour. – Famished!
>   (*Smiles exultingly, his eyes fixed upon* MORTIMER
> A fool and Coward blended to my wish.
>
>   (v:3:252–6)

It is an extraordinary way to die, like a broken Coriolanus

affirming his honour to an unheeding world – a world perceived
by him as no more than a cosmic echo-chamber, thrilling to his
every word.

His attempt on Mortimer, culminating in that watchful recital
of Act IV, has been a desperate gamble on which he has staked his
all and lost. As Satan (like Macbeth) had sought renewal in the
'hazard huge' (II:473) of heroic deeds, so too has Rivers sought in
the immediate excitements of danger compensation for the loss of
the gentle returns of love. It is an enterprise doomed to failure in
the facts of his own nature and the real world; and even at the
height of his hubris he seems haunted by the contradictory fear of
impotence. It is truly the contradictoriness of the compulsive
gambler that we see in Rivers, his conception of personal heroic
risk (where success would bring the highest approval) shadowed
by the cynical fear of the malevolent chanciness of things.
Mortimer finds these shifts of mood bewildering: 'that a man
. . . / Should thus so widely differ from himself – / It is most
strange' (III:5:89–92). But Rivers' need to gamble is a superstition,
a fetishism, derealising the world and its inhabitants into private
symbols whose purpose is precisely to disguise the true conflicts of
his mind. It is a ritualised anxiety of play which, like that of Peter
Bell, quite lacks the relaxation and trust which characterise
genuine playfulness. Wordsworth's preface describes him exactly:
he is 'a speculator in morals' (p. 65).

Wordsworth has Rivers draw his moral and political speculations
from amongst those 'extreme opinions' which Hazlitt said had
struck their roots 'deep and wide below the surface of the public
mind': there he finds a philosophical attempt parallel with his own
to establish 'a substitute for all the principles which hitherto have
been employed to regulate the human will and action'.[13] These
words of Burke are sarcastic, of course, but Wordsworth is drawn
seriously and sympathetically towards the problem of
establishing a counter-culture because it is a problem he shares;
and he has created in Rivers a parody of himself, a man who
embodies his own impatience, turbulence and love of
disobedience but who lacks an inner good self to discipline them.

We must first reckon with the style of Rivers' mind if we are to
assess the worth of his speculations. 'He is generally too much on
the stretch, and his manner has little variety. We cannot rest upon

any of his works' [14] – Burke's criticism of the literary style in which Rousseau developed his 'paradoxical morality' is relevant here. For whilst Herbert's language is harmoniously rich with the mystery of his reverence for goodness and suffering, Rivers' language is confused and confusing because always on the stretch to rationalise crime and repress remorse. At his very first entrance he praises medicine which 'while it is / Strong to destroy, is also strong to heal' (I:1:18–19); and ever thereafter he shows himself addicted, with a gambler's recklessness, to bold antitheses whose aim is to destroy the badness of the past and usher in the new millennial future. His cast of mind is oppositional rather than reconciling. He projects his own bad qualities rather than integrating them; and the boldness of his antitheses is his attempt both to mask and to master the fundamental contradictions in which this involves him.

Eighteenth-century radicalism, in the absence of oppositional institutions significantly involved in the life of the state, was by and large confined to the theoretical exposition of a counter-culture grounded in reason, nature and religion. Rivers appeals to all three (he cannot, within the terms of the play, appeal to history and the incompleted revolutions of the seventeenth century): and in each of the three we find him riddled with self-contradiction. First, reason. Rivers' basic tenet is that man is born free but is everywhere in chains: he alone, his antithesis runs, by virtue of a murder which all other men in their slavery condemn, has broken his chains and enjoys true intellectual liberty. Almost any radical author of the late eighteenth century might have taught Rivers the terms in which he praises Mortimer on the supposedly parallel occasion of his murder of Herbert:

> To day you have thrown off a tyranny
> That lives but by the torpid acquiescence
> Of our emasculated souls, the tyranny
> Of moralists and saints and lawgivers.
> You have obeyed the only law that wisdom
> Can ever recognize: the immediate law
> Flashed from the light of circumstances
> Upon an independent intellect.
>
> (III:5:26–33)

Of course, as is commonly noticed, Wordsworth is taking issue

with Godwin here, demonstrating that the intellect is not wholly
independent but that it is both formed and sustained by those
feelings that relate us to our individual and cultural past. The
root of Rivers' self-deception is not that he has been denied the
truth but that he has been famished of good feeling. Yet the
challenge of this insight is not confined to *Political Justice*. It extends
far into radical thought, whose characteristic strength lay in
critical exposure of the ideological bases of law and morality
rather than in constructive grasp of developmental psychology.
The *Essay on Morals* generalises the point succinctly:

> these bald & naked reasonings are impotent over our habits,
> they cannot form them; from the same cause they are equally
> powerless in regulating our judgments concerning the value of
> men & things. They contain no picture of human life; they
> *describe* nothing.[15]

His chosen ideology was so liberating to Rivers because it helped
him to evade the discipline to his feelings that Herbert provided.

Second, Rivers occasionally appeals to nature to justify himself.
He argues, for instance, that 'the institutes / Of nature' (III:5:95–
6) confer the right to kill a man as readily as a snake, as though the
value of a life were to be measured on a Godwinian scale of utility.
Yet the nature he sees is not simply the passive reflection of his
own callousness; for, in recounting his voyages through the
sublime landscapes of Syria and Lebanon, he attributes his
hunger for intellectual greatness (it is characteristic that he
specifies *intellectual* greatness) to the power of nature active upon
him:

> In these my lonely wanderings I perceived
> What mighty objects do impress their forms
> To build up this our intellectual being,

(IV:2:133–5)

It is not quite right, I think, to construct an antithesis between the
theological and the epistemological views of nature in the play, as
Paul Sheats does, between its pictures of 'nature's indifference to
man' and 'the potentially benign psychological influence of
nature, considered as epistemological object'.[16] *The Borderers*
shows a nature with power to act upon man according to the

feelings that he brings; and this is the heart of Wordsworth. What is good in Herbert and Matilda feels cheerful at the sights and sounds of nature and is won into a sense of harmony with creation (I:117–22); whilst Rivers, fostered by fear but not by beauty, can only be aroused to a malign sublimity which is meanness to his fellow men and contempt for the animal creation. Disordered feeling has produced in him a vicious understanding of the enablements that nature brings; and once again we are left to ponder the fact that the book of nature is a book without pictures in so much radical work.

Third, Rivers appeals to religion, to a God (perhaps to many gods) made in his own image – a sublime God who rules in the majesty of darkness and tempest, and uses 'the wholesome ministry of pain and evil' (II:1:73) to effect the purposes of benevolence. At the heart of his faith is the powerful myth of his own messianic role in history:

> Three sleepless nights I passed in sounding on
> Through words and things, a dim and perilous way;
> And wheresoe'er I turned me, I beheld
> A slavery, compared to which the dungeon
> And clanking chain are perfect liberty.
> You understand me, with an awful comfort
> I saw that every possible shape of action
> Might lead to good – I saw it and burst forth
> Thirsting for some exploit of power and terror.
>
> (IV:2:102–10)

The gospel according to Rivers is a history of betrayal, of descent to harrow the hell where all the slaveries of past and present are chained, and of final resurrection into an emancipated future where he will be the saviour of mankind. It is a gospel in which he seeks to procure a universal meaning for his own suffering; for unlike Herbert he does not reverence the suffering of others, he makes a fetish of his own. Nietzsche, whom Rivers uncannily anticipates, comes to the same point in his *Beyond Good and Evil: Prelude to a Philosophy of the Future*: 'Profound suffering ennobles; it separates'.[17] For Herbert the contrary is true: what is valuable about suffering is that it may bind men together. It seems to me that Herbert's (and Wordsworth's) reluctance to separate pain from injustice, unavoidable natural ills from avoidable political

ones – two categories which are separate and yet which run into
each other – is an attempt not to mystify but to root the motives for
political change in that sense of common suffering which flows
naturally into sympathetic action. It is an attempt to evade the
reciprocities of violence. Rivers, on the other hand, only concerns
himself with avoidable political ills and is quite unable to
integrate the antithesis between suffering and action which he has
drawn up in the history of his own descent and resurrection.
Therefore he will choose (believing himself free to choose) actions
that provoke violence and further suffering, in the belief that he
too may work 'the wholesome ministry of pain and evil' for the
purposes of goodness. It is the ultimate in self-contradiction,
hubris, blasphemy: that he may usurp the moral causality of the
world and make evil means yield good ends.

   Behind Rivers' ideology lies that well-known passage of satanic
ideology, quoted by Osborn (p. 29), where Satan bids farewell to
heaven and welcomes hell:

> Receive thy new possessor: one who brings
> A mind not to be changed by place or time.
> The mind is its own place, and in itself
> Can make a heaven of hell, a hell of heaven.
>
> (ɪ:252–5)

Rivers, in his own descent into hell, similarly tried to sever the
bonds between words and things, and free the mind from the
bonds of place and time; he tried to build a counter-culture in the
conveniently abstract language of the radical thought that
Wordsworth gave him. But his wish to control the future is really a
repressed wish to change his own past; and as he anxiously
believes himself to be entering a new world, that anxiety proves
him damned in the old. He cannot relax in time or space; he
cannot feel at home; and because he lacks what Erikson calls 'basic
trust',[18] his mind swings wildly between the extremes of
unrealistic hope and cynical despair. His sense of justice, too, is
perverted into an excessive self-esteem and a raging need for
revenge upon all that opposes him (including his own goodness).
Wordsworth traces these perversions and contradictions through
to their bitter deluded end because he sees the truth they conceal –
that the powers of reason, nature and religion may only be fully
brought into play in the creation of a counter-culture by a mind

that is in touch with its own goodness, that can feel concern and realise its sense of justice in the imagined picture of real human suffering. It is Mortimer's tragedy as the leader of the borderers that he loses his hold of just such a picture.

(d) MORTIMER

Mortimer, the 'amiable young man' of Wordsworth's preface (p. 66), was praised – perhaps overpraised – by Matilda at the play's start for his 'deep and simple meekness' (i:1:137), for the integrity of his mind before the threat of violent feeling. He had that strong gentle power over others that Herbert and Matilda also have, disciplining them into social harmony by the force of his character. Clearly he is well suited to his position as leader of the borderers, preserving justice in troubled times. Wordsworth, however, meditating upon events in France, is aware of three perils that beset him: first, he is a young and inexperienced man, particularly prone to impatience; second, he is a leader, romantically prone to the hubris of believing himself uniquely responsible for the administration of political justice; and third, his leadership is military, prone to the temptation of those sudden bold conceptions that seem to be the be-all and the end-all of our hopes. It seems initially that these perils will be countered by Mortimer's compassion. When he tells Rivers that Matilda's childhood tales of her father's sufferings were 'the beginning of my love' (i:1:68), he appreciates how the compassionate experience of pain may flow enrichingly back into the creativity of life, binding man to man and generation to generation; it seems he may prove Herbert's heir, able to fulfil in the strength of his personal qualities the political role from which Herbert is now disqualified.

There is, however, Rivers, the false mentor; and the competing powers of Herbert and Rivers in Mortimer's mind reflect Wordsworth's own experience of the French Revolution as a time of initiation, of education turned seduction, of perversion of those paternal and quasi-paternal bonds in which innocence and experience may maintain their mutually respectful conversations. Rivers pursues his seduction, like Iago, by obeying the deepest compulsion of his own nature: the compulsion to desecrate the holy. He juxtaposes lewd images of aristocratic power and sexuality with those images of parental and sexual love which Mortimer holds sacred, in the sure knowledge that such extreme juxtaposition will provoke precisely that violence which the concepts of sanctity and taboo have evolved to contain – that violence which, as Girard says, 'exists at the heart of the sacred'.[19] For, we remember, 'sin and crime are apt to start from their very opposite qualities'.

Yet not until Act III can Mortimer bring himself to act. His sense of Herbert's living presence and the realities of the natural world restrain him time after time from that sudden glory of action in which Rivers tempts him to cut the Gordian knot of indecision:

> Is not the depth
> Of this man's crimes beyond the reach of thought?
> And yet in plumbing the abyss of vengeance
> Something I strike upon which turns my thoughts
> Back on myself – I think again – my breast
> Concenters all the terrors of the universe,
> I look at him and tremble like a child –
>
> (II:3:59–65)

The manly leader and the dependent child: these are the psychological extremes between which Mortimer swings as his sense of the real fatherly presence of Herbert is put under increasing strain. Slowly, however, compassion and fear of his own violence succumb to horror and the wish for revenge. The delicate but firm subtleties of the real world begin to disappear; its objects and inhabitants lose their home in time and place and become (as Othello too experienced) symbolic puppets in the cosmic melodrama of his own aroused passions – and perversely, as his inner violence and its accompanying cynicism increase, so too does the need for revenge that fuels them further. He must meet injustice with punishment, or chaos will come again . . . and so the reciprocities of violence reestablish themselves.

Rivers in effect has stopped Mortimer talking to Herbert; he has stopped that open conversation between man and man where justice may be mitigated by mercy in the recognition of the mixture of good and evil in all of us. The judicial equivalent of such a conversation in the play is open trial by jury, which as C.B. Cone has shown[20] was enjoying in this decade a renewed popularity amongst radicals in their fight against aristocratic privilege; and this too Rivers is determined to stop by the independent prosecution of an act of private revenge. He sneers at the very idea of trial by jury (II:3:188–9), for he prefers to think of law and the judicature only as tools of the rich; he will not see their function in preventing the endless feuds of revenge and counter-revenge that occur when men take justice into their own hands (though ironically he himself will die by an act of such revenge). The strength of *The Borderers* seems to me to lie in the thoroughness with which it pictures the disturbances which may be brought about in the open court of conversation, as in legal procedure, by the perversion of the sense of justice. Conversation sinks into talk of blame, guilt, revenge, curse, sacrifice; whilst judicial processes degenerate, or threaten to degenerate, into show trials by ordeal or the hugger-mugger imprisonment and torture of which Robert is already a victim. Mortimer himself, in his inability actually to put Herbert to the sword, has recourse to a trial by ordeal. This is a kind of lottery, a barbarous parody of Herbert's grateful trust in providence, and grounded in a superstition that the pure element (in this case God or Nature) will cast out the impure. When Herbert blessed those that cursed him, he showed himself able to *accept* the evil and unjust in himself, in others and in life itself. But Mortimer is too horrified and must cast it out – a pharisaical response that leads him to forget that Herbert is both body and soul: he forgets to leave the food without which he dies of exhaustion.

The introduction of Robert into the play here seems to me a wonderful invention. First, he reminds us of the realities of social injustice when we might begin to assume complacently that there is no injustice in the world other than Mortimer's presumption. Second, he enriches our understanding of the variety of human responses to suffering; for whilst Herbert accepts it meekly, and Rivers regards it as a challenge to his manliness, Robert is unmanned and becomes cravenly vindictive. Third, Robert's difference from Mortimer yields to a deeper similarity as, in grotesque comedy, they both pharisaically protest their innocence of physically assaulting a man they both have left to die. For one brief moment Robert is to Mortimer a mirror of his own and Rivers' inhumanity. 'We shall howl together', he says (V:2:57); and yet it is out of the shadows of Rivers' empty mastery and Robert's vindictive cowardice that we finally see Mortimer reclaim himself.

It is a tragic self-reclamation, for he casts himself out, he dedicates himself to a perpetual exile from his fellows. It had

seemed at the end of Act IV and the start of Act V that he was
doomed like a latter-day Orestes to a lifelong flight before the
vindictive furies of his own self-loathing. But now he masters his
destiny, he becomes tragic in the voluntary assumption of the role
that he and his band had earlier allotted to Herbert – the role of
scapegoat, assumed also by that other parricide whom
Wordsworth surely had in mind here, Oedipus. Mortimer takes
upon himself the pain of Matilda's curse, of Herbert's fate and (in
forgiving him) of Rivers' perversity; and then he banishes himself
to a lonely life and death in the wilderness. Girard observes that
'sacrifice is primarily an act of violence without risk of revenge',[21]
and Mortimer's self-sacrifice is an act of self-violence which seems
to him the only way left to break the vicious circle of revenge into
which he has brought his world. Yet it is an imperfect solution,
with the imperfection of all substitutionary atonement; for
although Mortimer leaves behind him a monument to record his
history, his hope for the community lies in his own despair as an
outcast individual – suffering, injustice and evil are to be
banished, not integrated in mercy and self-forgiveness.

The Borderers is Wordsworth's monument to much that he had seen
and experienced in France. It does not, of course, anathematise
the injustice and the evil it depicts, but it integrates them into a
compassionate work of art only with a very chastened hope; for the
play is a tragic parable of the terrible self-contradictions into
which our sense of justice falls when 'we do not feel / For man as
man'. Yet it is a parable and not an allegory – that is, it is neither a
description of the world nor a direct political intervention in it, but
a reconstruction of the world in play. And here lies the heart of its
hope – a chastened hope indeed, for when we see Herbert for one
brief moment reconstitute a body of armed men into a peaceful
society, we see just how little a good man or a good play may do.
But that little seemed worth attempting. In the play-area of a
work of literature, a poet may feel himself to be a man speaking to
men, able to offer pictures of life which may make something new
out of his readers' old thoughts and feelings. In Rivers
Wordsworth has drawn a picture of perversity – of a man who,
unable to integrate his own past, is driven into deeper and deeper
isolation by the compulsions of his behaviour and the
rationalisations of his thought. In Herbert, with less poetic vigour,

he has drawn a picture of health – of a man whose past sufferings enrich his capacity for present concern. But Rivers and Herbert are extremes, and the words we need are large words: health and sickness, creativity and perversity, justice and injustice. Like all parables the play challenges us with pictures; it does not preach, for it is not didactic in that sense – its concern is not with the letter but with the spirit of justice. And with that Wordsworth *would* have us reckon, in our own contribution to the play which he has initiated.

Part IV
The Ruined Cottage:
The Poet in Mourning

7 *The Ruined Cottage* (1797–8)

(a) THE MIGHTY DEBT OF GRIEF

Rivers in *The Borderers* was unable to integrate his violence of feeling against the sea captain whom he deserted; and Margaret in *The Ruined Cottage* is unable to integrate the violence of feeling aroused in her by the experience of desertion. The subject of Wordsworth's new poem is the nature of the capacity to mourn; and he has chosen a heroine who, because of the cruel circumstances of her husband's disappearance and her continuing uncertainty as to his whereabouts, finds herself too disturbed to mourn. Like Rivers, she finds herself torn between past and future, between the extremes of hope and despair, in a way that prevents her from relaxation in the present; and grief depends finally upon such relaxation for the relief it brings. In *The Vale of Esthwaite* Wordsworth wrote:

> For much it gives my heart relief
> To pay the mighty debt of grief,
>
> (430–1)

He understood that the relief which is brought by mourning is a way of doing justice to the past, and that elegy is a creative response to loss because it reestablishes the bond of relationship between past and present, other and self, in a way that liberates both. But Margaret cannot mourn and falls into melancholia.

Freud, in his essay *Mourning and Melancholia* whose terms I borrow here, has drawn attention to the deep similarity between the two states of mind. Both show, he says, 'profoundly painful dejection, cessation of interest in the outside world, loss of the capacity to love, inhibition of all activity'.[1] But he draws a crucial distinction: 'In mourning it is the world which has become poor and empty; in melancholia it is the ego itself.'[2] This sense of dereliction in the self belongs to that which is unconscious in melancholia, Freud argues, the denial and repression of violent feeling; 'the patients usually still succeed, by the circuitous path of self-punishment, in taking revenge on the original object and tormenting their loved one through their illness, having resorted to it in order to avoid the need to express their hostility to him openly.'[3] It is to Margaret's guilt, and her unadmitted hostility against her husband, that we must look to understand that long 'sore heart-wasting' (699) of her life. We must remain aware of the continuity of Wordsworth's thought and understand her kinship with Rivers, who also in his own way found himself obliged by his past to avenge himself continuously on all that was good in his life.

However, as in *The Borderers* Wordsworth offered the example of Herbert to counter the incapacity of Rivers to deal with the suffering aroused by an unjust betrayal, so here in *The Ruined Cottage* he offers the pedlar to counter the incapacity of Margaret to mourn. From its very early stages, as Wordsworth developed his interest from the tale of Margaret's tragedy to include the character of its teller, the poem was designed to explore the contrast between health and sickness, between the capacity to mourn and the failure to mourn, between the creative excursiveness of the pedlar's mind and the perverse wanderings of Margaret's; and it is for this reason that, despite Wordsworth's own doubts and difficulties over his design, I have chosen to work from the Ms.B version of the poem published by Helen Darbishire in the fifth volume of the *Poetical Works* (pp. 379ff). I recognise the problematical status of this version as what Jonathan Wordsworth calls 'a working-manuscript in which the poetry has not yet taken its final shape'[4] (although the question of a final shape, or even of a temporary resting-place, is problematical in itself with this poem); but I choose it because it shows Wordsworth working out the contrast that lay at the heart of his own chosen version in *The Excursion*. For I believe that the lines about Margaret and the lines about the pedlar only reveal their fullest meaning when considered together: and I disagree with Jonathan Wordsworth, and the more recent critics that have followed him, when he writes that 'in critical terms there can be little doubt that each benefits from being considered alone'.[5] Together, they show Wordsworth's first attempt to tackle the question that had been facing him since the completion of *Adventures on Salisbury Plain*, the question posed by his own poetic

success: what habits of mind may enable a man to face the
injustice of tragedy undaunted? how may a man mourn and not
fall into melancholia?

For the pedlar can contemplate the sufferings of passion,
mischance and misrule, name them for what they are, and yet
retain his mind in 'a just equipoize of love' (Ms.B 15ᵛ). His
habitual bonds of affection enable him (like Herbert) to break out
of the vicious circle of the unjust resistance to injustice:

> for the man
> Once taught to love such objects as excite
> No morbid passions no disquietude
> No vengeance & no hatred needs must feel
> The joy of that pure principle of love
>
> (Ms.B 46ʳ)

The pedlar fulfils the paternal bond that Herbert could not fulfil,
not only in the elegy he recounts for one whom he loved 'as my
own child' and who always in return gave him 'a daughter's
welcome' (345–6), but also in his relationship with the young poet
who – as the older poet now – is imagined to reenact his discipline
in the writing of the poem. What Lionel Trilling said of Jane
Austen is equally true of the pedlar: he is 'committed to the ideal of
"intelligent love", according to which the deepest and truest
relationship that can exist between human beings is pedagogic'.[6]
It is against this paternal bond, and this ideal of intelligent love,
that we offend in separating 'father' from 'daughter' in our
consideration of the texts. We lose the fulness of the language of
health and morbidness that we need if we are to give to Margaret's
melancholia the justice of the pedlar's grief.

Some verses dating from the same period that saw the completion
of *The Borderers* and the first sustained work on *The Ruined Cottage*
will help us to establish the understanding of sickness which
Wordsworth was developing: the fragment entitled *Incipient
Madness*, the fragment known as 'The Baker's Cart' (both work
towards *The Ruined Cottage*) and the completed poem *Lines left upon
a seat in a Yew-tree*. We shall watch Wordsworth evolve the old
radical opposition between truth and superstition into a new and

subtle psychology, concerned for the manner of our object-relating and our symbolisation processes.

Incipient Madness describes a man obsessively drawn night after night to a broken pane of glass in a ruined cottage, longing to see it glitter on the earth in moonlight. It is a superstitious ritual born in a depression which cannot grieve; and the power with which the glass attracts him is ambivalently shadowed with a violent fear, suddenly realised one night when he hears the chains of a hobbled horse rattle in the cottage amidst the stormy noise of rain outside. The pane of glass is a fetish, irresistibly attractive, irresistibly repellent, and between these self-contradictory motions the narrator himself is hobbled by a habit that inhibits the creative excursiveness of his mind. He speaks of a 'strange incontinence' (17) which he cannot articulate; his heart is fastened to a dead thing that only seems 'akin to life' (7). Some extraordinary lines suggest something of what lies at the origin of this human need to symbolise:

> There is a mood,
> A settled temper of the heart, when grief,
> Become an instinct, fastening on all things
> That promise food, doth like a sucking babe
> Create it where it is not.
>
>   (7–11)

Here we need to make a delicate, but crucial distinction. The baby, relaxedly sucking perhaps on its thumb, may begin the long process of symbolisation of the world through the medium of its own body – a process that initiates its future capacity to play and create, and its ability to find pleasure and worth in the world. On the other hand, the same moment repeatedly robbed of its relaxation and its benign illusion may lead to an anxious strenuousness of endeavour to be forever making the hope which it cannot find – and it is this kind of psychic greed, this strange incontinence, that the narrator in *Incipient Madness* discloses in himself. The distinction is between creation and counter-creation, between creation that in general works 'in alliance with the works / Which it beholds' (*Prelude* II:274–5) and counter-creation that in general works 'in a devious mood, / A local spirit of its own, at war / With general tendency' (*Prelude* II:383–5). Coleridge wrote in *The Statesman's Manual* that a symbol 'always partakes of the Reality which it renders intelligible; and while it enunciates the whole, abides itself as a living part in that Unity, of which it is the representative'.[7] But there are perverse symbols too, that do not make for unity or intelligibility and that do not enunciate the whole in the part; and such is that broken pane of glass in *Incipient Madness*, reflecting the moon in heaven in its own fragmentariness. For love of its reflected light *displaces* love of the real, and alienates the narrator from general creation in pursuit of the private hieroglyphics of his own suffering.

'The Baker's Cart' similarly describes the counter-creations of sickness in a mind which – long starved of its daily bread, 'the common food of hope' (20) – has also become lost in the extravagance of private superstition. 'That wagon does not care for us' (16): the woman's words as the baker's wagon passes her home express the need for fellowship that lies at the heart of all withdrawal from society, but her need is expressed in a way that discourages the direct response of such fellowship. She is caught in the same perverse trap as Rivers, for she too has lost her hold upon the goodness in her past that might have enabled her to relate creatively to the world. Her good habits have been

>   by strong access
> Of momentary pangs driv'n to that state
> In which all past experience melts away
> And the rebellious heart to its own will
> Fashions the laws of nature.
>
>   (21–5)

She has been driven, like Rivers, to recreate the world in her own image and to code its ordinary happenings in her own betrayed sense of justice. The primary function of the symbolisation process by which we gradually make ourselves at home in the world, learning to love or resist first this then that, has become precisely inverted: instead of familiarising the alien, it alienates the familiar.

The *Lines left upon a seat in a Yew-tree* perfect this analysis of health in a poetry that is for the first time fully mature. They explore again the way that the mind's instincts for survival may be brought in self-defence to work against its fundamental health, this time in the sickness of misanthropy. A young man, who with something of the grandness of a knight-errant had (not unlike

Rivers) prepared himself to enter upon the world and eclipse all
envy of his virtues, found himself with insufficient love to tolerate
neglect and turned away with 'rash disdain' (19) into solitude.
Once more we see the damaged mind fall into contradictory
extremes which it cannot reconcile. On the one hand, with 'his
downward eye' (27) the young misanthropist loved to trace in the
nearness of the barren landscape 'an emblem of his own unfruitful
life' (29); on the other hand, he fed himself in the distance on
'visionary views' (41) of an unreal self-created beauty which,
unheartened by the reciprocities of human love, was empty of that
'kindred loveliness' (38) which the good man finds in nature.
What we see is a function of what we are: both barrenness and
beauty, both self-contempt and nostalgia are the counter-
creations of a man 'whose eye / Is ever on himself' (51-2). His
relationships in time and space are disturbed, so that he cannot
make a home in the world; and the symbols he forms serve only to
trap him fatally between extremes which ensure that nothing new
can ever happen to him.

It is wholly typical of Wordsworth that his first fully mature
poem should be an elegy, rescuing the past from this weight of
dead loss and setting out to break the vicious circle of
self-contempt and nostalgia into which the young man had fallen.
He finds his true poetic voice through his development of the
inscriptive genre, with its familiar opening wish to arrest the
traveller and adjust the movement of his mind, so that new things
may begin to happen to him. We should not despise that barren
landscape:

> if the wind breathe soft, the curling waves,
> That break against the shore, shall lull thy mind
> By one soft impulse saved from vacancy.
>
> (5-7)

The pace, the richness of the affectionately teasing tones, the
lightness of touch, above all the verse's embodiment of the poet's
responses to the relationships of the natural world – all these serve
to waken in the reader those new feelings that may transform our
seeing. For the first time Wordsworth has written a poem which
dramatically enacts the meditative processes of a healthy mind in
the fulness of its relationships with world and reader; and its
business is not with such extraordinary men and events as we saw

in *The Borderers* but with the health and perversity that we may detect in the daily motions of our own thoughts and feelings. The poem aims to act upon those thoughts and feelings with the same soft impulse as the wind itself; it aims to be a disciplinary power akin to nature, working in alliance with the works it beholds. The poet is to be nature's minister; the poem is to be a sacramental symbol of the compassionate love that may be won out of suffering; and the reader is to be the communicant – the man perhaps 'whose heart the holy forms / Of young imagination have kept pure' (44–5) so that he may respond truly 'in the silent hour of inward thought' (58). Yet if Wordsworth's aim is pedagogic, it is not didactic. If he is to do the created world the justice of intelligent love, he must do it by reawakening in his reader those feelings that connect with the best of his own past life – those tender playful feelings that lie at the root of our capacity to symbolise and feel concern.

(b) MARGARET

The story of Margaret is the story of the decline of a mind's natural excursiveness into sick extravagance. It is the story of the fracturing of ordinary hopefulness into extremes of reckless despair and unrealistic hope; the mind once nourished by 'the common food of hope' becomes hungry with sickly appetites that famish the organism they should feed. The tale is offered to us as both fact and symbol: that is, it enunciates the whole reality of man, and yet abides itself as a living part in that Unity. This is important; for whilst we recognise in the conception of the poem – a family overthrown, a 'wife and widow' (698) abandoned at home whilst her husband is at war – the power of ancient epic and heroic archetypes, that literature is disciplined to a new radical perception of the brotherhood of man. Margaret is no Penelope, and her garden is a cottage garden rather than the courtly garden or the aristocratic estate of our own literary tradition. The story reminds us that gardening – in fact as well as in the fictions of literature and theology – is a type of the labour we are born to, a joy rather than a curse, where one day's doing is consciously and unconsciously bound up with the hope of future fruition; and it reminds us too that the overgrown garden – actually in a cottage economy as well as archetypally in literature – is a symbol of all human dereliction. But it reminds us only by recreating those fraternal feelings that make it so – those feelings which suggest that it is only in the radical sensibility, where the part truly partakes of the whole, that we shall see the perfection of those symbolisation processes at work in all life and in all literature.

In happier days the cottage of Robert and Margaret was their focus, the focus of their hopes as of their labour. The pedlar says that 'two pretty babes / Were their best hope next to the God in Heaven' (379–80), but we should not let his respect for the pieties of their lives mislead us into formulating a hierarchy of hope in which such distinctions make living sense. In discussion we may isolate their religious faith, their children, their mutual love and pride in each other, their labour; but the story emphasises the delicate strength of the interwoven fabric of all these hopes together – hopes which centre on their home but which radiate outwards, connecting them (as through Robert's work and Margaret's hospitality) with the larger worlds of time and place beyond.

Robert's unemployment is the cut thread that unravels the fabric of their lives. The social nature of labour, whose reciprocal bonds of production and exchange have far more than merely market value, banishes the unemployed man into a kind of exile – an exile felt most acutely by Robert at home, the place of his labour, where he can no longer play the man's part in maintaining his wife and children. Suddenly lost in time and place, he tries with an uneasy self-consciousness to replace the pleasures that have hitherto sustained him. He busies himself with idleness, whistling mirthless fragments of merry tunes, carving grotesques . . .. He idles with what was business, blending the different tasks of different seasons 'with a strange / Amusing but uneasy novelty' (416–7). Even like Rivers, 'he finds his temptation in strangeness . . . his thirst after the extraordinary buoys him up';[8] and like Rivers still, his dissatisfactions draw him deeper into delinquency. Burdensome good humour turns to sulky irritability that drives him away to the town or to wander the fields. His home ceases to be the natural gravitational centre of the excursive energies of his life; their harmonious ebbs and flows are perverted into irreconcilable drives which, like polar opposites, both attract him towards his cottage and repulse him from it. What is more, his relationship with his children shows the same disturbed ambivalence: on the one hand he talks cynically of them, and on the other he plays with them in a spuriously extravagant pleasure which disturbs them in turn.

Once again we glimpse the violence and self-violence, the cruelty and the guilt which bedevil the mind betrayed in its sense of justice; and the culmination of Robert's revenge comes when he sells himself in secret into the army, leaving his bounty behind him at night on the cottage window-sill and disappearing forever from his wife's knowledge. 'He left his house' (516): Margaret believes he lacked the heart to say goodbye in case she and her children followed him and died. It is not cynicism, however, but a measure of Robert's alienation that makes us remember the perversity in his earlier pleasures and suspect that she holds fast to the kindest, self-kindest interpretation of his behaviour. We need to recognise more than just a 'terrible miscalculation about what his wife really needs';[9] the lucidity of the verse permits us to look down into the often unadmitted depths of our nature, into the strange contemptuous pleasures of punishment and self-punishment in which we express our anger and try to right injustice.

Margaret is quite unable to cope with the manner of her husband's desertion – hence the kindness of the motive she imputes to him. It is an act of betrayal so crucial that it unravels the whole texture of her life, so bitter that she dare not admit the violence of feeling it arouses in her; and thus the history of her decline traced in the pedlar's four visits is the story of a woman who dare not mourn her loss. When the pedlar first knocks at her cottage door and enters, just two months after Robert's disappearance, she bursts into bitter tears at the sight of him. Wordsworth does not explore the strangeness of those violent tears: the disappointment, the humiliation, the guilt, the anger, the self-anger of an abandoned woman, deserted in a cruel uncertainty which inhibits the capacity to mourn as it breeds the temptation to hope. Most obviously, she weeps in reaction to the sudden wildness of hope that the visitor might be her husband; and then in another change of mood she turns upon the pedlar with new clinging fervency of love. Formerly so hospitable to visitors, she now depends upon them for a knowledge which never comes her way. She is losing what Erikson calls the capacity to feel 'reasonably at home in a predictable world,' the capacity

to be central in [her] sphere of living rather than peripheral and ignored; active and effective rather than inactivated and helpless; selectively aware rather than overwhelmed by or deprived of sensations; and, above all, chosen and confirmed rather than bypassed and abandoned.[10]

The impotence that the pedlar feels in the face of her suffering is a testimony both to the limits upon which all friendship rests and also to Margaret's need to stretch those limits in order to force from him the comfort which she cannot find for herself. Together, indeed, the former habits of their relationship return and enable them to build up 'a pile of better thoughts' (534). But ominously Margaret's farewell blessing only 'seemed the very sound of happy thoughts' (543): what happened to Robert proves to be infectious, the authentic feeling is once again becoming its own simulacrum.

The pedlar's second visit is in harvest-time, when nature everywhere is fertile in response to human care – everywhere, that is, save in the increasing wildness of Margaret's garden. The borders now are overgrown and the pedlar, desolate and restless in the detail of his perceptions, feels the alien power that lies in an undisciplined unloved nature. Neglecting the near – her crying baby inside the cottage, for instance – Margaret has begun like Robert to wander far afield. The cottage that once had focused the integrity of her hopes now drives her restlessly to wander away from it and restlessly to come back. It is both the place where Robert deserted her and the only place to which he might return, an emblem both of despair and hope – for the disturbance of her capacity to feel at home has also been a disturbance of her capacity to symbolise. If it is true (as David Pirie nicely puts it) that 'people are home-builders and they are travellers',[11] then it is also true that home is where we start from; the processes of symbolisation whereby we gradually invest the world with value and meaning depend crucially upon the values and meanings that we find at home, both in our beginning and in our going on. So now we watch Margaret fashion her home in the image of her own guilty self-neglect, losing the sense of its otherness in a new sense of its alienation.

Everything has been overthrown in her husband's betrayal: her relationships with her garden, house, friends, children, her own mind and body, and of course her religious faith.

> 'I am changed,
> And to myself,' said she, 'have done much wrong,
> And to his helpless infant. I have slept
> Weeping, and weeping have I waked; my tears
> Have flowed as if my body were not such
> As others are, and I could never die.
> But I am now in mind and in my heart
> More easy, and I hope,' said she, 'that heaven
> Will give me patience to endure the things
> Which I behold at home.'
>
> (602–11)

This hope of Christian patience is a remembered piety at whose heart, if we may trust the logic of her words, is a fatalistic willingness to die. Wordsworth creates vividly the inner distances of mind amidst which Margaret is lost to real time and space, and in which we follow the obsessive excursions of a fantasy desperate to correct the injustice of its enforced separation. Her absence of mind, her subdued body, her low voice, her downcast eyes, her listless actions, her distant disembodied sighs: each remedy worsens the situation, denying the violent feelings whose admission alone could lead to creative mourning.

On the pedlar's third visit he finds her 'sad and drooping' (646) amidst the fresh growth of spring. The irony reminds us of the different natures they inhabit; and it is once more through her superstitious use of nature – the neglected apple-tree whose bark is nibbled round by sheep – that we trace Margaret's 'reckless' (731) degeneration. ' "I fear it will be dead and gone / Ere Robert come again" ' (675–6): her words show the hunger of her mind for emblems of its fate. The apple-tree is a self-image born in her deep sense of guilt and worthlessness, an image of the slenderness of hope in the teeth of a remorseless destiny; and all the relics which she guards – her husband's suit of clothes, his staff, his idle loom – wear this same double face of her single 'torturing hope' (739). They are the private symbols of a mind which is putting life (as a gambler does) to a ritualised test, to which everything else becomes subordinate; and certainly the maternal love she professes for her children has the ring once more of a remembered piety – not insincere but inauthentic.

The pedlar's final visit finds her alone: her friendless elder child had long since been apprenticed by the parish and her baby now has died; 'poverty and grief' (663) have stripped her down, as she wanted, to her single overmastering obsession. Heedlessly, in her need for fellowship that connects like a talisman with what she has lost and fears she will never find, she wanders with the pedlar down the muddy lanes of autumn, begging him always to inquire after her husband. After that they meet no more. It is a long and desperate heart-sickness which claims the remaining five years of Margaret's life. The overgrown garden around her and the tantalising length of road beyond her, together express perfectly her life in its excursions of obsessive fantasy:

> On this old Bench
> For hours she sate, and evermore, her eye
> Was busy in the distance, shaping things
> Which made her heart beat quick.
>
> (704–7)

With the trembling guilt of a debauchee she brings herself to beseech almost every passer-by for news, working in her garden where she can watch the road and leaving her seat each time a dog goes by, until finally the decay of the house – seemingly untouched since time stopped with Robert's betrayal – brings on her fatal illness and ends her long ordeal by self-neglect.

'Lord, we know what we are, but know not what we may be' (*Hamlet* IV:5:43–4): Ophelia's great cry expresses the tragic vulnerability of all men to betrayal in their dependence upon bonds whose heart is feeling – a vulnerability well encapsulated by David Pirie in the phrase he takes from the poem, 'the weakness of humanity' (448).[12] Margaret's suffering is beyond all reach of blame and, indeed, the pedlar quickly discovers the futility of even the kindliest of exhortations (639–42): her suffering, to return to Herbert's injunction, is to be reverenced. The tragic vision is close to that of *The Borderers*: that a mind may be betrayed into dissolution by its feelings of love, that such recklessness and dereliction as Margaret's may 'start from their very opposite qualities'. Her melancholia, moreover, has similar effects to the remorselessness of Rivers; it prevents her from doing justice to her past, it drives her into a vicious circle of compensatory violence and self-violence (what De Quincey pharisaically calls 'criminal self-indulgence')[13] and it damages the powers of symbolisation that had formerly made her at home in the world. Unable to mourn, she falls deeper and deeper into a system of private symbols that increasingly isolate her from the discipline of real relationship. Once again, as in 'The Baker's Cart', we see the rebellious heart fashion the world in its own image – a process to which the pedlar's account of gradually decaying house and garden is acutely sensitive. I want now to turn to the pedlar, in whom we may trace the development of Wordsworth's art from the parable of *The Borderers* to his most characteristic form of meditative elegy, in which a mourned past makes a home of the present.

(c) THE PEDLAR'S MEDITATION

The drama of the pedlar's narration originates in the state of excitement engendered by a meeting. When the young poet first espies the pedlar, he is stretched out upon a bench before the bare walls of a ruined cottage. 'His eyes were shut, / The shadows of the breezy elms above / Dappled his face' (304–6). The poet behaves with the natural restlessness of youth in the preoccupation of its own desires: thirsty from walking, he asks where he might find water and – being told – he clambers over the garden wall, finds a half-choked well in a dark cheerless corner, drinks his fill, clambers back and stands there hatless, cooling off and ready for adventure. But it is the unexpected that happens, as the pedlar suddenly breaks into passionate, even morbid speech:

> 'I see around me
> Things which you cannot see. We die, my Friend,
> Nor we alone, but that which each man loved
> And prized in his peculiar nook of earth
> Dies with him or is changed, and very soon
> Even of the good is no memorial left.'
>
> (325–30)

It is not difficult to intuit the complexities of the pedlar's mood. An old unmarried man, musing in the shade upon death and mutability, he sees in his young friend's heedlessness the oblivion that has befallen Margaret and that will surely befall himself; and a sudden pang reveals in her fate a symbol of the desperate condition of all humanity.

> 'Oh Sir! The good die first
> And they whose hearts are dry as summer dust
> Burn to the socket.'
>
> (346–8)

The superstitiousness of such despair may be only momentary, yet it shows how deeply Margaret's story has become his. Loving her as he does, he feels betrayed in the injustice of her loss as she felt in Robert's – and hence the acuteness of his sensitivity towards her. Indeed, his commonplace lament that the good die young implicates all of us in the common sense of life's injustice. We die, my friend . . ..

Meditation, as the *OED* makes plain, is a word with religious force: 'The continuous application of the mind to the contemplation of some religious truth, mystery, or object of reverence, in order that the soul may increase in love of God and holiness of life.' In traditional Christian practice the mind's excursiveness was to be disciplined in meditation either by the authority of external structures such as devotional texts or by the authority of internal faculties such as the will or reason. But Wordsworth's poetry sets out to create a new, more comprehensive meaning for the word, in line with his sense that reason and will are largely determined by our passions and feelings and that those passions and feelings are themselves experiences of the outside world. Meditation in Wordsworth is simply the everyday communing or self-communing of a mind adventuring upon itself and the world it sees; and all the moods, feelings, passions, fantasies and thoughts that make up such communion and self-communion have their place in the meditative process. All contribute to an excitement which will finally, if healthy, bind the mind more closely to reality or, if sick, drive it into isolation; but no authority can guarantee which way the adventure will lead, for the mind is always vulnerable when old habit meets with new experience.

The Ruined Cottage clearly contrasts the meditative sickness of Margaret's mind with the pedlar's meditative health; and if we ask why Margaret sank under her suffering whilst the pedlar regains the buoyancy of hope through his, there are many answers we might give. We might say that the real tragedy was Margaret's and only vicariously his; we might say that she was more vulnerable in marriage that he in bachelorhood; or we might

illustrate the more resourceful habits of mind formed in the
pedlar's education. But the need to make these distinctions should
not blind us to the essential kinship between the two of them. For
they both share in the common mystery of pain and they both
attempt to defend themselves against that pain in similar ways.
We should recognise the motions of Margaret's mind in the
pedlar's initial despair – a deep despair which momentarily
threatens his trust in the benign nature of the world – and in the
superstitious fantasies which express that despair and help to
control it:

> 'my spirit clings
> To that poor woman, so familiarly
> Do I perceive her manner and her look
> And presence, and so deeply do I feel
> Her goodness that a vision of the mind,
> A momentary trance comes over me
> And to myself I seem to muse on one
> By sorrow laid asleep, or borne away,
> A human being destined to awake
> To human life or something very near
> To human life, when he shall come again
> For whom she suffered.'
>
> (614–25)

Such a fantasy, born in the sometimes intolerable separation of
death, has much in common with Margaret's former fantasies of
Robert's return, and is perhaps in some sense caught from her.
Also, as befits a man whose youth was nourished by 'the
preternatural tale' (179), the pedlar is remembering Perrault's
Sleeping Beauty. Throughout his narration he sees Margaret's
gradual delinquency as a falling asleep, a withdrawal into an
inner world of dream; and it is natural for him now to resist her
death in fancying her asleep in her cottage amidst an overgrown
garden – she is not dead but sleepeth. These archetypal fantasies
of resurrection from Bible and fairy tale demonstrate a common
human response to a betrayal which is too terrible to grieve.

It is this recognition of kinship that gives fully human meaning
to the differences between the pedlar and Margaret – differences
which, despite the overlapping of mourning and melancholia,
focus upon the unconscious violence and the duration of

Margaret's suffering. The pedlar proves able, as Margaret was not, to trust himself to fantasy and superstition, to foolishness and despair, and to redeem them in a recovered balance of mind that turns them all to love. It is, he says in an important later addition to Ms.B, the characteristic activity of 'the Poets in their elegies and songs' (Ms.B 19^v). Their imaginings turn superstition and fantasy (and, we may add, the counter-creations of sickness and perversity) to creative purposes of love and, in so doing, vindicate the ways of life to man – a natural theodicy accomplished now by the pedlar himself, as his despair modulates into elegiac celebration.

'Why should a tear be in an old Man's eye?' (446): suddenly he becomes conscious that his mood has changed. The urgency of his initial passion with its edge of reproach has abated, until his own narrative comes to seem to him an uncreative 'weakness of humanity' (448), a self-destructive 'feeding on disquiet' (451) not dissimilar perhaps to that which killed Margaret. Suddenly he feels that his grief wrongs the season: and in turn the natural beauty of the time and place, to which he is now open in his newly relaxed mood, enables him to see the preposterousness of his despair, as it taxes divine disposal and threatens his harmonious hold upon creation. This counterpoising change of mood, simple as it is, is the key to the self-corrective health of his mind. It is partly a matter of will but only in so far as his will expresses the pre-existent tendency of his passions. As Cordelia had the grace to say 'no more nor less', so too has the pedlar the grace to say 'enough' (Ms.B 53^r); and though no doubt he will feel despair again, and perhaps be overthrown by it, there is in his present change of mood a further small strengthening of the habits of his mind in their just equipoise of love. When he continues his story in the second part of the poem, although moved by what he relates, he will have a much more pedagogic intent, wishing to cultivate in his young companion the same just balance between grief and hope.

The young poet had earlier comforted himself in his toiling across the moor with a very different fantasy of meditation from the unexpected form it was actually to take in the pedlar's narration:

Pleasant to him who on the soft cool grass
Extends his careless limbs beside the root
Of some huge oak whose aged branches make
A twilight of their own, a dewy shade
Where the wren warbles, while the dreaming man,
Half conscious of that soothing melody,
With sidelong eye looks out upon the scene
By those impending branches made
More soft and distant.

                                        (10–18)

The fact that *The Ruined Cottage* begins by reworking lines from *An Evening Walk* – the passage (53–84) where the poet withdraws at noon to nurse his melancholy sensibility in the shade of an artificial twilight – suggests the potency that these lines held for Wordsworth in their figuring of poetic vocation. The precise descriptive balancing of the earlier couplets is gone, however; instead, the rhythmic relaxation of enjambement and loosely connected clauses eases us free from the holds of time and place and recreates perfectly in us that mild blending activity which is the particular excitement and (we shall see) the danger of meditation.

It is a subtle picture; and it is only later when we meet the pedlar, similarly recumbent and withdrawn in meditation, that the youthfulness of the fantasy becomes obvious. Such carelessly dreaming seclusion amidst the works of nature is innocent of the injustice, suffering and mutability that grieve the pedlar; and the older man's concern in his new self-consciousness is to guide his innocent young listener into the experience of the tale which he began so passionately, whilst securing him in the same meditative habits that safeguard him. For he sees that in telling his tale he is exercising that power which an older personality sometimes acquires over the young, the power in which innocence is indeed initiated into experience, and he wishes to exercise it responsibly. He wishes in fact to share it:

            'we have known that there is often found
        In mournful thoughts, and always might be found,
        A power to virtue friendly;'

                                        (482–4)

Yet the conditional caution in these words is in part his debt of remembrance to Margaret's inability to perceive her grief as blessing. There can be no guarantee that suffering will enrich; for the mind is always vulnerable before those passions and feelings on which its development depends.

In each of the draft endings to *The Ruined Cottage*, excluding the very fragmentary third (see *PW* v:400–4), the young poet is particularly at risk because – turning naturally away from the pedlar in the privacy of passionate meditation – he finds things absent more real than things present. Margaret lost herself in self-preoccupation in the distances of such meditation; and so, in the version of the ending that Wordsworth was eventually to shorten and use, the pedlar allows his friend brief absence of mind and then recalls him to the present: 'My Friend, enough to sorrow have you given' (Ms.B 53^r). Wordsworth is acutely aware of the dangers that beset even the best intentions in literature as well as in life – dangers of flirtatiousness or debauchery, of 'vain dalliance' (478) with the sufferings of others or of that 'strange incontinence' in suffering which he had described in *The Borderers* (iii:4:10) and again in *Incipient Madness* (17). They are dangers that particularly beset the sentimental literature of the eighteenth century, but they are dangers too at the heart of the poetic life, and more widely of all human creativity in so far as it values the power of feeling and the inwardness of thought. The pedlar's check to his young friend's mood, therefore, is a lesson in balance which also expresses Wordsworth's own faith in the health-giving power of those feelings that connect the mind affectionately with reality, that maintain basic trust in a good-enough world. These were the feelings that Margaret had lost.

The success of the pedlar's initiation is shown in the quality of the poet's reestablished relationships with the real world, both of man and of nature. First, his fraternal relationship with humanity is deepened and extended when (in an addition to Ms.B that remained permanently in the poem) he blessed Margaret in his meditative abstraction 'with a brothers love' (Ms.B 51^v). The pedlar's elegy has done justice to the memory of Margaret, sorrowing and creating sorrow where sorrow is due, yet discovering through that sorrow a love true to everything that was best in her; and this elegy is reciprocated now in the work of the poet's own maturity, remembering his old friend remembering

Margaret. So her tragedy becomes a thread of the fabric and a symbol of the power binding generation to generation.

Second, his relationship with nature is deepened and extended when, as he seeks the 'secret spirit of humanity' amidst 'the calm oblivious tendencies / Of nature' (Ms.B 52^r), the pedlar provides him with the symbol he needs to reconcile humanity and nature – the weeds and the speargrass on the neglected garden wall. It is a symbol that captures a harmony more profound than that of the earlier symbol of gardening by virtue of the fact that it comprehends the experience of neglect. A glimpse of the tranquillity and beauty of nature had once recalled the pedlar from the anxieties of loss to that pleasure whose worth is not merely for one individual but for all mankind; and that glimpse, that revelation of hope, had become by its power an emblem of the potential harmony between man and man, man and nature, whose realisation is the highest achievement of meditation. It had freed him as if from a curse to walk his ways in happiness; and so too at the end is the poet freed by the friendship of the older man – love of man and love of nature substantiate and balance one another.

This ending to the poem has been curiously misrepresented in critical discussion, it seems to me, in ways that we may epitomise by David Perkins' epigram: 'Nature was loved as a reality, man as an idea.'[14] Paul Sheats writes of the pedlar's need to choose 'between relationship to man and relationship to nature' and argues that the choice of nature 'does not permit a full and generous response to Margaret's plight'[15] – and here, of course, is the reason for critical unease and attack: a sensed inhumanity in Wordsworth, a sense of imaginative and political withdrawal from the sufferings of his fellow men. A liberal critic like Cleanth Brooks professed himself unsure about the aesthetic and religious grounds of the pedlar's final comfort in the face of suffering,[16] whilst a radical critic like David Aers protests against the temptation to political quietism that lurks in Wordsworth's 'aestheticizing of avoidable human suffering'.[17] What was Wordsworth up to? I think his concern is more fundamental, and also more radical, than a concern merely for political injustice. It is a concern for the establishment of sane consciousness, without which we cannot do justice to political injustice. It is a concern for those relationships that might enable us as far as possible to confront pain and injustice without succumbing to the

melancholia into which Margaret fell. They are relationships that
would flourish best, he believes, in a republic – relationships with
man, nature, and God in which each symbolises and substantiates
the others, encouraging the growth of trust and spread of
affection, making men at home in time and place and yet leaving
them free to wander in both, enabling them to mourn tragedy and
liberating them from despair and the indignation that works
where hope is not. The poetry does not contain a programme for
social change but it does contain the challenge of a vision – a vision
whose unpredictable adventure upon the future is suggested
beautifully in some of the most memorable lines that Wordsworth
ever wrote:

> I turn'd away in weakness; and my heart
> Went back into the tale which he had told
> And when at last returning from my mind
> I lookd around, the cottage and the elms
> The road the pathway and the garden wall
> Which old & loose & mossy oer the road
> Hung bellying, all appeared I know not how
> But to some eye within me, all appeared
> Colours & forms of a strange discipline

(Ms.B 43ᵛ)

The strange incontinence of melancholia into which Margaret fell
is matched precisely by the strange discipline of mourning which
awaits the listener of her tale.

(d) THE PEDLAR

The hope that Wordsworth has embodied in *The Ruined Cottage* is
in nothing done or said. It is in the power of what the pedlar is – 'a
chosen son' (272). In reviewing *The Excursion* in 1814, Francis
Jeffrey was to attack Wordsworth for his 'provoking perversity of
taste'[18] in making a pedlar his hero, whilst Hazlitt complained
loftily that Wordsworth was inviting him 'into low company, and
company, besides, that we do not like'.[19] Wordsworth's own note
appended to I:341 makes it plain that they were right to be
provoked:

> At the risk of giving a shock to the prejudices of artificial society,
> I have ever been ready to pay homage to the aristocracy of
> nature; under a conviction that vigorous human-heartedness is
> the constituent principle of true taste. *(PW* v:411)

It is in the vigorous human-heartedness of his pedlar that
Wordsworth tried to ground a counter-culture sufficient to shame
the élitist culture and intellectual snobbery of readers like Jeffrey
and Hazlitt; and I want now, without anticipating later discussion
of *The Prelude*, briefly to explore the strange discipline of the
pedlar's education, following the five stages laid down in the
poem: boyhood (53–98, omitting 59–69); the transition from
boyhood to youth (98–118); youth (119–220); the transition from
youth to manhood (221–60); and finally manhood (261–300,
including the long passage footnoted in *PW* v:386–7). For what
education might enable a man to tell Margaret's story justly? It is
the question that Wordsworth's poem posed for him.

The pedlar was graced in early boyhood with moments of a not
unpleasurable terror, experienced through the imagery of a
sublime landscape and associated with the guilt that belongs
naturally in children to such terror:

> From that bleak tenement
> He many an evening to his distant home
> In solitude returning saw the hills
> Grow larger in the darkness, all alone
> Beheld the stars come out above his head,
> And travelled through the wood, no comrade near,
> To whom he might confess the things he saw.
>
> (70–6)

Clearly (to recall Erikson's words) 'feeling reasonably at home in
a predictable world' has become an increasingly complex
experience to Wordsworth since the vagrant spoke of her father's
cottage in *Salisbury Plain*; and the difference lies in his increasing
interest in the nature and origins of mental power – something
that the boy learned in his unearthly journeys through the
ordinariness of the woods, we should note, and not at school.

We might describe the value of the boy's experience in a number of ways. First, the natural imagery of the landscape enabled him to articulate and to externalise universal human feelings whose unmanageability often leads to their denial; it enabled him, that is, to begin to recognise the darker powers of his own nature. Second, the articulation of these emotions through the landscape helped to draw him more closely to the world, so that his intellect would be guarded against the barren abstractions of unfeeling. We might say that these lines, with their wood and their bleak deserted waste, redeem the landscapes of *Salisbury Plain* and *The Borderers*, for they integrate the experience of terror into a healthy mind. Third, the natural imagery had power to aggrandise rather than belittle the passions it evoked; and Wordsworth refers the extraordinariness of the pedlar's vigour at least in part to the fact that he had felt such greatness 'long before his time' (79). Fourth, the greatness of the power the pedlar felt was expressed through transformation of the physical world; it made possible the adult's perception that the significance of life is a spiritual question, to be pursued by the mastery of mind over matter and sensory perception. Also, it was the presence of such satisfying powerful experience, followed by its absence, that created in the boy the activity of mind to search by himself for such satisfaction amongst other natural images: the greatness of his vigour sprang from the greatness of his appetite. Last, the greatness the boy felt seemed at that time not an effect of subjective passion but an objective perception of the world's behaviour – a perception, however, whose relationship was so powerful and intimate as to seem a 'communion' (78). Wordsworth explores the boy's animistic sense of strange powers behind the world, and really present in it, with delicately ambiguous reference to the Eucharist, so that we cannot dismiss experiences which are the foundations of an adult religious faith as mere delusion – the boy's fear was a boy's response to the real world, and the adult later can only find himself in awe before the world by grace of the fear he had felt when young.

The transition between boyhood and youth is characterised in this spiritual biography by many hours' involuntary animation of the still objects of nature:

> Even in their fixed and steady lineaments
> He traced an ebbing and a flowing mind,
> Expression ever varying.
>
> (106–8)

It was a period of imbalance when the restless hunger for communion led him to fantasy, creating kinship where none was to be found – an enriching playful fantasy that preserves him in his unconscious faith that the living variousness of the world will suffice him.

The youth, at the next great upsurge of inner life in puberty, found once more his own potentially disturbing energies disciplined and enriched in intercourse with nature; the restlessness of earlier desires was more than met in the unexpected satisfactions of love.

> Oh! then what soul was his when on the tops
> Of the high mountains he beheld the sun
> Rise up and bathe the world in light. He looked,
> The ocean and the earth beneath him lay
> In gladness and deep joy. The clouds were touched
> And in their silent faces did he read
> Unutterable love. Sound needed none
> Nor any voice of joy: his spirit drank
> The spectacle. Sensation, soul and form
> All melted into him. They swallowed up
> His animal being; in them did he live
> And by them did he live. They were his life.
>
> (122–33)

A shepherd on the mountains, his communion no longer had the particularity of boyhood perception but extended through particular perception of the sunrise to the whole face of nature in its primary manifestations of sun, ocean and earth. The diffusion of self-consciousness, so characteristic of adolescence in its search for identity and embodied in the synaesthesia, anthropomorphism and blending of abstract and concrete in the poetry, created a feeling of universal harmony; subject and object interpenetrated with an intensity of emotion which inhibited the attribution of power to either one in isolation from the other. It was a harmony that seemed to extend across time as well as space, fostering an intuition into the immortality of all things in their motions. These ecstasies, of course, had an adolescent incompleteness; in their obliviousness to suffering, their thoughtlessness and their concentration upon divine creation rather than divinity, they were immature. Yet, once again, they were not unreal but the adolescent's response to the real world, his way of claiming kinship; without them the adult's faith would have tended towards mere dogma, his maturity towards compliance and his love towards a narrow partiality. Nor were they islands amidst a waste sad time stretching before and after; their absence disciplined him to a patience and humility in which he doubted not the world but himself. The boy's animism has yielded to the 'superstitious eye of love' (166) – a benign superstition in which the diffusion of the self over the world will enable the individual later to attain self-consciousness with unimpaired trust in creative relationship.

The transition between youth and manhood was a further period of imbalance. The satisfactions of youth broke down under the turbulence of growing powers: 'his mind became disturbed, / And many a time he wished the winds might rage / When they were silent' (224–6). We can sense the perverse possibilities of this period in the various stratagems that the pedlar adopts to appease his desires; and yet still he is not outcast, for still there are times when the world more than satisfies him – times when 'he felt the sentiment of being, spread / O'er all that moves' (242–3), when

> in all things
> He saw one life, and felt that it was joy.
>
> (251–2)

We have become so used to thinking now in terms of what Jonathan Wordsworth calls (my emphasis) 'the *doctrine* of the One Life',[20] taken over by Wordsworth from Coleridge, that we need perhaps to recollect that this passage, both here and in its final resting-place in the second book of *The Prelude*, describes experiences which characterise the imbalance of late adolescence – experiences which save the mind from its own perverse tendencies by drawing it closer to the created world and its creator, but which also by their weight help to break down the pedlar's 'bodily strength' (258) and drive him away from home.

The choice of life in which the pedlar exercises his manhood is uncommonly dangerous. The gloom of his father's fears suggests the financial, emotional and moral dangers that might beset so lonely a life; and the danger in his case lies chiefly in the turbulence of the homeless passions that determine his choice, in the urgency of his need to satisfy bodily restlessness, sensory appetite and mental curiosity. He owes his preservation both to the grace of circumstances and the established habits of his mind. In the uncommon situation of a single life, he is spared both suffering and misfortune and also the partiality of affection which contributed to Margaret's tragedy. Neither inner nor outer constraint inhibits the sympathetic excursiveness of his mind in his meetings with pain and vice; and so he accumulates the resources to mourn, 'to suffer / With those whom he saw suffer' (Ms.B 16ᵛ). It is only apparently a paradox that a man may develop sympathies in a solitary life; for solitude, in so far as it is not loneliness, enjoys the present sense of things absent. The pedlar's solitude is in fact composed of numberless relationships, both with man and with nature, and his individuality comprises all that he has been and known, so that he comes to seem 'a being made / Of many beings' (Ms.B 17ᵛ). Through the strange discipline of his education he has become able to hold together the worlds of nature and man in that harmony of an individual life which Wordsworth calls a just equipoise of love.

The Ruined Cottage, as I see it, traces the processes by which one mind comes to find itself accommodated in the world and another comes to find itself unaccommodated; it traces two extremes of the human condition in the knowledge of a common vulnerability. The pedlar has found himself at home in the world; by the grace of circumstance and the wealth of his own subjectivity, sustained in the bounty of nature, he has established relationships that bind him closely to nature, man and God. We cannot put these relationships in a hierarchy any more than we could with those of Margaret; and when Jonathan Wordsworth wrote that 'the ability to love is part of a total well-being',[21] he was drawing attention to their usual interdependence. They are consubstantial; they substantiate and symbolise one another. The pedlar, then, through the free play of his subjectivity under the strange discipline of nature, has developed a hope and love that give him a sense of worth in life, that enable him both to do justice to the

world and to mourn its injustices. His development witnesses
what Burke called 'that action and counteraction, which, in the
natural and in the political world, from the reciprocal struggle of
discordant powers, draws out the harmony of the universe'.[22]
Margaret, on the other hand, develops a diseased sensibility that
cuts her off from that harmony; her passions fall into
irreconcilable extremes of hope and despair, her fantasy becomes
what Winnicott calls 'the fixity of fantasying',[23] her faith becomes
superstitious and her creativity perverse. Her suffering proves too
great for her to grieve.

What Wordsworth has discovered is, in the words of Stephen
Prickett, that 'poetry was the "science" of the whole man',[24] or to
put it another way, he is trying to formulate (as we shall see more
clearly when we come to *The Prelude*) a science and a politic
grounded in the uninhibited right of the individual to develop his
subjective capacity to symbolise under the discipline of the
otherwise alien world of man and nature.

> Thus disciplined
> All things shall live in us & we shall live
> In all things that surround us.
>
> (Ms.B 50ʳ)

The pedlar in his idiosyncratic way has achieved this. 'He had a
world about him, 'twas his own / He made it' (283–4); and what
saves him from madness and superstition is the fact that he has an
eye alive to 'shades of difference' (291). Wordsworth states in the
Preface to *Lyrical Ballads* that upon 'the accuracy with which
similitude in dissimilitude, and dissimilitude in similitude are
perceived, depend our taste and our moral feelings'.[25] I think it is
his purpose here that, when we read *The Ruined Cottage*, we should
recognise the similitude between ourselves, Margaret and the
pedlar – for in that recognition lie the possibilities for the
education of a genuinely radical sensibility. It is also important,
however, that we should recognise the dissimilitude – for so we
may be alert to all those shades of difference in passion, feeling,
fantasy and thought which mark the delicate – but crucial –
distinctions between the realities and liberties of health and the
unrealities and restrictions of sickness, as we adventure through
the processes of symbolisation upon the world around us.

Part V
The Ballad Poetry of 1798:
The Poet at Play

8 *Lyrical Ballads* (1798)

Wordsworth's ballad contributions to the first volume of *Lyrical Ballads* are an exceptionally playful poetry dealing mostly with exceptionally painful material. Donald Davie has written of them as 'experiments in expressing glee and / or investigations of that state'; and he attributes the painful nature of the subject matter to a character trait which he believes that Wordsworth shared with Nietzsche – the Dionysiac self-delighting strength 'in which health seeks out morbidity'.[1] It is a poetry which we may epitomise in two lines from *We are seven*: 'Together round her grave we played, / My brother John and I'. The little girl playing – so indecorously – around her sister's grave is keeping alive her delight in relationship in the face of death; and the adult poet, in his greater self-consciousness and with his own particular poetic indecorum, is also responding with delight to the challenge of the greatest losses that he is capable of imagining – the losses of family or lovers, of property, health, sanity or life itself. For anxiety is never far from play: and Wordsworth, 'bold to look / On painful things' (*Prelude* x:871–2), was challenged by images of life *in extremis* to see if indeed the poet might carry *everywhere* relationship and love, and so prove like his pedlar that 'all things shall live in us & we shall live / In all things that surround us'. The ballads are full of meetings and meditations which challenge that faith and which fail to subdue it, until we come to find the poet too to be 'a being / Made up of many beings', binding together 'by passion and knowledge the vast empire of human society, as it is spread over the whole earth, and over all time'.[2]

Yet something is lost if we think of the play of the poetry as Dionysiac; for its power is compassionate and tender, in the spirit of a Herbert and Matilda rather than a Rivers. It is disciplined to respect the otherness of the world, concerned not for mastery but for fraternal relationship; and in its freedom from the anxiety and willed strenuousness of Nietzsche, it expresses a richer interplay between the subjective and objective worlds. For this is the area that interested Wordsworth – that play-area of the mind where we make our sense of life, that area where our feelings, faiths and values find their home and from where they adventure back upon the world. Clearly it is a vulnerable area; for as Marion Milner has said, 'the inner dream and the objective fact can never permanently coincide, they can only interact'[3] – and where there is possibility of interaction, there is also possibility of betrayal, loss and final isolation. Hence the proximity of anxiety to play, as Winnicott has suggested:

> Playing is inherently exciting and precarious. This characteristic derives *not* from instinctual arousal but from the precariousness that belongs to the interplay in the child's mind of that which is subjective (near-hallucination) and that which is objectively perceived (actual, or shared reality).[4]

There is a light which may go out: the play-area is also an area of illusion . . . . It seems to me that these two words, *play* and *illusion*, indicate precisely both the excursive confidence and the vulnerable fears which are expressed in Wordsworth's ballad poetry of 1798–9 and which, moreover, are embodied in the peculiarly precarious triumphs of the verse.

De Quincey wrote in 1845 in his essay 'On Wordsworth's Poetry' of the difficulties that bedevilled poets and critics alike in the absence of a scientific psychology: 'we must have a good psychology, whereas, at present, we have none at all.'[5] Wordsworth's work in the decade from the spring of 1798 onwards was largely devoted to the attempt to establish just such a scientific psychology – a radical religious precursor of what we now call object-relations psychology, tracing the development of adult creativity out of the earliest days of childhood play and focusing attention always upon the play-area where subjective and objective meet in relationship. *Lyrical Ballads* was part of this attempt; and its very title calls our attention to the way that the ballad's objective history of event and feeling is enriched by the lyric's subjective embodiment of the personal meaning of those events and feelings. It is a poetry crucially dependent upon the personality, and then upon the mood, of a speaking voice at a particular point in time and space; the knower is not to be separated from the known. It is a poetry too which offers us relationship in the terms that Wordsworth valued; for as we pursue the delicate tones and meanings, the delicate ambivalences and contradictions of characters at the extremes of their experience, the discipline of the poetry makes us work and leaves us free to play. It is remarkably open poetry, confident, trusting its reader and not abiding by decorum, and therefore unusually vulnerable to ridicule. Yet it invites us, if we like, to get to know it better, to extend our acquaintance; and this is what I now propose to do.

(a) THE CREDAL LYRICS

Geoffrey Hartman has written that 'surmise expresses the freedom of a mind aware of itself, aware and not afraid of its moods or potentialities';[6] and the fact that such surmise is, as Hartman says, a common mode of Romantic poetry has its roots in the recognition that our feelings and imaginations too have their hypotheses. Nothing adventured, nothing gained: the mind only comes into its 'liberty and expansiveness'[7] through cautious trust in itself. For surmise is the conscious play of the mind in the play-area of belief. We might make the point through two poems from *Lyrical Ballads* which predate the ballad experiments of 1798, and which I shall do no more than mention here, the *Lines written near Richmond, upon the Thames at Evening* and *Old Man Travelling*; for both poems wonder about the many possibilities for the necessary growth and perfectibility of mind, even beyond death, whilst retaining firm hold of the realities of suffering, decline and mortality. Surmise, that is, displays the intellectually unaggressive irony characteristic of Romanticism; it maintains contact between the different worlds which we inhabit, the objective world of often painful limits and the subjective world of hope that it might not be so – and it is the mode of Wordsworth's religious poetry in the spring of 1798.

The four credal lyrics – the *Lines written at a small distance from my House, and sent by my little Boy to the Person to whom they are addressed, Expostulation and Reply, The Tables Turned* and *Lines written in early spring* – are poems of particularly bold surmise which still do not silence the humble caution of the intellect. The basic common measures which they share with much English hymnal writing and psalm versification tap a tradition of Christian experience, but they do not tabulate a formal Christian creed. In their strong confidence of feeling and their doctrinal tentativeness before the limits of human ignorance, they too make their home in that unmapped territory between mere subjective fantasy and objective description where (in Keats' words) 'man is capable of being in uncertainties, Mysteries, doubts, without any irritable reaching after fact & reason.'[8] They appeal to the quality of a shared human experience in a natural creation on behalf of a belief which is part religious and part political; for if feeling cannot verify faith, it can at least authenticate it.

Lines written at a small distance from my House is typical of the group. Its theme is older than Christianity, as old and as common as the poetic spirit itself: the rebirth of the year in spring. The 'blessing in the air' which the poem describes, in a language somewhere between simple description of spring weather and overt religious statement, re-creates that universal feeling of the mysterious bounty of the world with which our sense of the worth of life is inextricably bound up. Each minute, says Wordsworth, is sweeter than before, and this moment-by-moment access of pleasure speeds up the urgent pace of the poem ('Make haste', 'Come forth') as Wordsworth seeks in turn to confer the blessing he has received. As the robin sings, as the air seems to yield joy to the trees and mountains, so too the poet writes a verse-letter to his sister to be delivered by his little boy: seemingly by necessity love spreads and seems for an instant to link together all creation. It is the *now* of the poem, the strength of the poet's subjective response to the real world, that necessitates its springtime dalliance with innocent superstition and demands that both feeling and faith be spread. It is what in *Michael* Wordsworth calls 'the pleasure which there is in life itself'.

'Come forth and feel the sun': and in *The Tables Turned* Wordsworth urges his friend to 'come forth into the light of things'. These phrases, with their distant echo of Christ's words to Lazarus, establish the contrast underlying all four poems: the contrast between the shadow-world of death and the substantial world of things, between compliance and creativity. 'Compliance', says Winnicott, 'carries with it a sense of futility for the individual and is associated with the idea that nothing matters and that life is not worth living.'[9] The letter killeth but the spirit giveth life. . . . Wordsworth's *Lines* invite his sister to come forth with neither book nor calendar but with her woodland dress and in *primavera* spirit; and the 'joyless forms' which he would have her leave behind include all those authorities – reason, law, religion or simply the sense of household duty – in which subjectivity so easily goes dead and which only the sense of inner creativity can authenticate.

In *Expostulation and Reply* the poet meets the friend who can least tolerate such subjectivity – Matthew, whose words seem to pour out of the anxieties underlying the purposive strenuousness of English Protestantism, out of the need to find the worth of life in intellectual mastery. The briskness with which Matthew exhorts and reprimands his idling friend, the very noise of his conversation, suggests the aggressiveness of a dominant religion recalling man to his duty: namely, to make full use of the precious gift of time to study and bring light into an otherwise forlorn mind. Even if his words imply no formal religious creed, they certainly imply a formal view of culture and the responsibility of the educated classes.

> 'You look round on your mother earth,
> As if she for no purpose bore you;
> As if you were her first-born birth,
> And none had lived before you!'

To set oneself up as Adam in an unfallen world is to Matthew the height of hubris; it offends his sense of the cultural tradition in which he finds himself. For he seems unable to trust to himself, and it is not hard to sense envy and fear of his friend behind the humorous aggressiveness of the attack. Similarly, he cannot trust to nature; the dramatic outburst of the first stanza suggests how its solitudes amaze and frighten him in his reliance on his own purpose.

The poet begins the discomfiture of his positive friend in an appropriately oblique way, with a single narrative stanza whose cheerful air of irresponsibility dissipates the force of Matthew's bullying questions:

> One morning thus, by Esthwaite lake,
> When life was sweet I knew not why,
> To me my good friend Matthew spake,
> And thus I made reply.

Disarmingly, Wordsworth cannot tell why life was sweet that morning, and in so saying he affirms a power in joy beyond the mastery of human purposes. The wind bloweth where it listeth:

the poet's apparent whimsicality expresses the deepest truth he knows. Moreover, William's actual answer to Matthew within the poem makes of the mind a far more interesting place than his friend can ever make. For his boasted self-mastery, William says, is moment by moment belied by the involuntary activity of his senses in response to the powers of the world; the whole world is a living language to whose sweetness and harmony Matthew is quite deaf. Like Casaubon in *Middlemarch* he is in danger by candlelight of forgetting the day. The accusation of hubris is reversed, and suddenly we feel the emptiness of Matthew's pride as he raises his voice above the sound of 'things for ever speaking'. Against the purposiveness and intellectual aggressiveness of his friend, William sets his own quiet receptiveness: there are times when it is wise to wait upon the unpredictable relationship between the objective powers of the world and the subjective idling of the attentive mind.

It is clear that Matthew finds his friend subversive, and rightly so; for a poet who cannot but believe that the trees and birds feel pleasure, that the heart in spring may make its own silent laws and that the lore of nature is more valuable than scholarship is clearly capable of an utter disregard for the authorities of church, state and education. The unpredictable and unproductive play of these four poems sets itself against the strenuous dutifulness and competitiveness of the busy world around it; and even when Wordsworth mourns that world and 'what man has made of man' in it, his grief still opens out for others to share. It has the confidence that – in the words of *Home at Grasmere* – 'joy spreads and sorrow spreads' (Ms.B 644). Such joy and such sorrow are common enough; and at their heart is the individual's delight in the trust which he feels in the benignity of the relationships which he is enjoying. It is this delight which the credal lyrics affirm, as the feeling upon which our healthy excursiveness of mind and our home-sense of the worthwhileness of life chiefly depend; but I want now to turn to three poems in which that excursiveness and that home-sense are threatened with inhibition.

(b) *WE ARE SEVEN*; *ANECDOTE FOR FATHERS*; *SIMON LEE*

Both *We are seven* and *Anecdote for Fathers* trace the cause and the effect of an educated adult's mild attempt to bully the simplicity of childhood through an exploitation of the delight and trust that

bind them together. In *We are seven*, educated poet meets cottage
girl, and there springs up at once between them an affection of
which their conversation is one expression. The poet from the
beginning feels the access of pleasure that comes naturally from
her beauty, her vitality, her wildness and her 'woodland air'; her
eyes seem to grow in beauty as he watches her, he is intensely
conscious of that plenitude in her which is so common to children
of her years. And so he begins to talk, and the child, wondering at
him across the gulf that separates their experiences, replies with a
fullness which, even in her growing obstinacy to the man's
persistence, expresses her own naturally outgoing trust in him.
Wordsworth said once it was the strength of her feelings of 'animal
vivacity' that prevented her admitting the notion of death as an
adult must (*PW* iv:463). However, we can hear in her words
something other than animal vivacity: we can hear too the words
in which her mother sought to reconcile her to loss.

> 'The first that died was little Jane;
> In bed she moaning lay,
> Till God released her of her pain,
> And then she went away.'

The educated poet seems ill at ease with the village culture which
sustains the child's continuing assertion that they are seven, and
he is blind to her natural capacity and need for fantasy which this
culture encourages. The poem creates beautifully the child's
world in which the business of life (knitting, hemming, eating
supper) is blended indistinguishably with the private and – to the
adult – inaccessible world of play.

> 'My stockings there I often knit,
> My 'kerchief there I hem;
> And there upon the ground I sit –
> I sit and sing to them.'

The child is not yet vulnerable to the common adult self-delusion
that objective reality may be separated entirely from subjective
fantasy, and in the free play of her fantasy (she does of course
'know' her brother and sister are 'dead') she bears witness to what
the pedlar in *The Ruined Cottage* called the 'strong creative
power / Of human passion' (Ms.B 19ᵛ). In her innocence she

enjoys with ease what the pedlar could only feel with trouble: the abiding enriching presence of the dead. It is, as Hartman observes, a presence imaged in the characteristic geography of the British village, in 'the closeness of the cottage to the churchyard';[10] and it embodies a familiarity that characterised the mother's account of their bereavement to her daughter.

The adult's persistent challenge of the young girl's play denies her the reconciling area of creative fantasy which is not only at the root of the plenitude he enjoys in her but also at the root of his own adult creativity. It is no wonder the girl reacts with stubbornness to the threatening behaviour by which he abuses her confidence, for he is striking at the healthy base of her liberty of mind and its security in the creative traditions of her home life. Perhaps, if he is moved by anything more than whim, he feels that the little girl is in danger of surrendering the real world wholly to fantasy; but if so, the rest of the poem is against him, for her outgoingness, his own joyous perception of her beauty, everything that passes between them convict him of the opposite danger, of surrendering fantasy to the objectivity of the world: and so a meeting rich in spontaneous pleasure ends in a stubborn polarisation that seems quite sterile. But of course the poem is wiser than its apparent writer, and the moment's inhibition which it describes becomes the agent of a deepening understanding. For the playfulness of *We are seven* embodies Wordsworth's recognition that the child is father of the man in that its capacity to play is the point of origin for later adult creativity.

Anecdote for Fathers, showing how the art of lying may be taught seems a companion piece to *We are seven*; it too shows a bullying abuse of the trust of love, for its heart is in the depth of the child's feeling for the man who seems to be his father – 'dearly he loves me'. It is another excursion of springtime joy; the lambs, the sunshine, the young boy in his slim beauty, the poet, all are full of their different but interrelated pleasures.

> A day it was when I could bear
> To think, and think, and think again;
> With so much happiness to spare,
> I could not feel a pain.

'My thoughts on former pleasures ran. . . .' The joy of nostalgia is a valuable but precarious mode of adult plenitude; lost in thought and testing the nature of his separation, he finds the buoyant play of his mind suddenly change into an anxious bullying of the child. Why? Perhaps from simple change of mood, perhaps from perverseness at not being answered after idle entry into conversation, perhaps from a sudden need for objectivity to rescue him from his own mind, perhaps. . . . But the loaded questions he asks the boy are heavy with adult anxiety and the need to control. Where would you rather be? Here at Liswyn? Or by the smooth delightful shores and green seas of Kilve? He has seized the boy by the arm, and he continues to hold him fast. The child, naturally unconscious of the fields of interest amongst which the adult wanders, gives in thoughtless love the answer he thinks expected of him – Kilve – and is utterly at a loss when the adult turns upon him with the threatening demand for explanation of his choice.

Things go from bad to worse in the child's guilt: he has given the wrong answer, he has failed when called upon, he has preferred Kilve to the woods and warm green hills around sweet Liswyn farm. The adult can play with alternatives as no child can, and the sudden glamorisation of Liswyn at the expense of the formerly glamorous Kilve is the undoing of Edward. He hangs his head in shame, tongue-tied, until suddenly he sees the weathercock – sees it and grasps its possibility: there was no weathercock at Kilve. What might naturally have delighted the boy is perverted from its natural place in the glittering spring morning to become an enforced emblem of his dislike, associated with guilt and shame. John Beer speaks rightly of this as an alien fantasy;[11] it is a superstitious image imposed upon the world as the boy's natural symbolisation processes are inhibited and the reciprocity of love becomes a reciprocity of aggression and defence. But such aggression is counterproductive; and Mary Jacobus' perception that both *We are seven* and *Anecdote for Fathers* are satires upon those eighteenth-century verses that instruct children in the fact of death or the immorality of lying[12] helps us to see just how thoroughly Wordsworth tried to purify his ballads of aggressive moralisation and replace it with the play of affection. For love is the only way to learn (as the poet here comes to see) those truths about love which are never fully learned but without which the mind falls into superstition or compliance.

Simon Lee, the Old Huntsman, with an incident in which he was concerned is another of the *Lyrical Ballads* to record a meeting which threatens to inhibit the mind's excursiveness but whose inhibition actually proves to be a liberation of subjectivity from conventional literary, moral and social prejudice. Nowhere do we feel this more strongly than in the surprise and openness of the poem's end:

> – I've heard of hearts unkind, kind deeds
> With coldness still returning.
> Alas! the gratitude of men
> Has oftner left me mourning.

John Danby, who wrote beautifully in *The Simple Wordsworth* of the way this poem playfully teases itself free of our expectations, wrote of these lines:

> we can hear the weariness, the impatience amounting to contempt, in Wordsworth's voice. He is conjuring up the whole sickening sphere of the moral and verbal cliché, the set-pieces of life and literature, the jejune dogmas that encase the mind, hardening it into impercipience.[13]

It is particularly against the clichés of a paternalist pity that *Simon Lee* is powerful.

The meeting which challenged the poem, in which the poet had helped the old huntsman uproot a tree, occurs at its end. ' "You're overtasked, good Simon Lee, / Give me your tool" ': one swift blow of the mattock, and Simon weeps his gratitude. The meeting was between the brusque energy of healthy youth and the decrepitude of age, between an educated man without financial worry and the 'poorest of the poor', scarcely able through infirmity to labour for his living. It was a meeting that cannot but make us aware of the deep gulf that may be between man and man – a gulf that the mere severing of a root, even when done (as we say) in common humanity, cannot begin to cross. No wonder the poet seemed appalled at Simon's tears and words of gratitude ('I thought / They never would have done'); such thankfulness for so casual a deed seems almost indecent, especially if we sense in Simon's tears the humiliating consciousness of dependency. In the face of pain, injustice and the mutability of human strength and joy, neither kindness nor pity is enough – Simon still has his life to live.

Yet the grief in which the meeting left the poet to mourn is not despair; it has 'a power to virtue friendly', it leads him in obedience to the strong creative voice of human passion to begin the poem (as the pedlar began his narration) in an attempt to re-create Simon's vanished past. Yet it is no easy task; for personal observation and conversation, hearsay and imagination provide but scanty material. The order of the poem's quatrains in 1798, so different from the neat chronological sequence in which they were left at the end of Wordsworth's life, has an interesting effect; it suggests a poet struggling to piece together scraps of information that might somehow get at the heart of Simon's life and do it justice. 'He says he is three score and ten, / But others says he's eighty'; 'a little man, / I've heard he once was tall'. . . . From these hesitant beginnings the verse gathers confidence, but still in its rapid shuttling between present and past it creates the special mode of this poem, its sense of casting round for an attitude or an image adequate to Simon's life. A contributory factor to this openness is the poem's deliberate abstention from the language of blame with which it tempts us: how easy to blame the pride and imprudence of Simon's youth, and how false to the glee he still feels at the barking hounds! If kindness and pity are not enough, blame is even more inadequate.

Simon Lee is a poem in which Wordsworth confronts the limits of his own poetic and political adventure of 1798, to bind together 'by passion and knowledge the vast empire of human society, as it is spread over the whole earth, and over all time'. Sometimes, perhaps particularly in the cases of the very young and the very old, the gulf between different human experiences may be too wide for even the most sympathetic imagination to cross. Sometimes, all that we can do by way of practical or sympathetic help for others may prove too little in the face of pain, injustice and mutability; and a life once known throughout 'four counties round' may indeed sink beyond recovery. Such seem the implications of the poet's grief at his meeting with Simon; and yet his grief is valuable to him. It does not inhibit him as it might. Instead, it liberates him in a play of subjectivity which is genuinely respectful of the inaccessible otherness, the glee and pain of Simon, and also subversive of those paternalistic clichés that had so often in the eighteenth century told poverty that charity was enough.

(c) *THE LAST OF THE FLOCK; GOODY BLAKE, AND HARRY GILL; THE COMPLAINT OF A FORSAKEN INDIAN WOMAN; THE MAD MOTHER; THE THORN*

Most of the poems in *Lyrical Ballads* trace the sufferings of minds tragically inhibited at precisely those moments in precisely those relationships where most they might have expected to reach outwards in love; they trace the superstitions of minds betrayed in their deepest sense of justice. The poet does not obtrude his own presence here. He still does not aim at ballad impersonality, for the speaking rhythms of his sympathetic understanding are still to discipline our responses, but the distance he maintains enables us to feel directly the suffering he describes – we learn, in Herbert's words, to reverence misery. We learn too to suspect the over-readiness of pity. Dr Burney said about *The Last of the Flock* that, if the author were a wealthy man, 'he ought not to have suffered this poor peasant to part with *the last of the flock*'[14] – yet such a reaction is grotesquely irrelevant to the spirit of the poetry. These poems do not seek primarily to arouse pity: pity, we have seen, is not enough. Reductive, self-consolatory and frequently paternalist, the clichés of pity in their narrow channelling of human response close down the creative spaces between men where the poems of *Lyrical Ballads* play; they prevent the possibility of fresh thought and fresh feeling about the world in which such suffering occurs.

The Last of the Flock epitomises the whole exploration of mind that we find in *Lyrical Ballads*. It opens upon the shepherd's memory of the gleefully expansive energies of his youth:

> 'When I was young, a single man,
> And after youthful follies ran,
> Though little given to care and thought,
> Yet, so it was, a ewe I bought;
> And other sheep from her I raised,
> As healthy sheep as you might see,
> And then I married, and was rich
> As I could wish to be;
> Of sheep I number'd a full score,
> And every year encreas'd my store.'

By the natural reproductive tendency of love, both family and flock increased together until there were fifty sheep and ten children. ' "They throve, and we at home did thrive" ' – the connection was a real one, both because they constituted one economic unit and because they each symbolised to the shepherd that the growth of his life was all one 'progress on the self-same path' *(Prelude* x:239). And hence, as Hartman has written, the particular terror of his betrayal:

> Lamb or child, there is no difference to his heart, because each loss is unique. Every new sacrifice is prophetic, and brings home the idea of separation, not only perhaps from his children, but from all that stands between the self and its nakedness. In this sense, certainly, property is a spiritual need, and like all *realia* . . . serves to keep imagination in check.[15]

'O! reason not the need' – Lear's words (II:4:266), as he faces a denudation similar to that of the shepherd, remind us how much a man's life lies in the extension of his love, and how vulnerable therefore he is to betrayal. The shepherd's bewildered sense of injustice discloses a sense of property founded in the pleasure, love and pride he has taken in everything he has made of his life; and he can only reconcile himself to the laws by which he loses that property through the perverse pleasures of self-punishment – a self-punishment shown in the poem by his counting backwards, which Hartman fascinatingly likens to 'primitive sacrificial rites'.

There are in fact two extremes of counting in *The Last of the Flock*: the objective computation of the administrators of parish relief, and the superstitious telling of numbers through which the shepherd impotently watches the appalling inevitability of his end. In between these two extremes lies the play of the shepherd's initial accumulation, a play with which the poem itself keeps faith – for abstaining like *Simon Lee* from the easy objectivity of blame and the superstititous excesses of pity, it opens out creatively upon the question which presses so hard upon the shepherd, the question of the competitive claims for resources. We are shown in the restless flickering of the shepherd's moods between guilt, shame, bitterness and recklessness the vicious circle of a mind unable to feed in health upon its sense of justice and driven instead to superstition (' "God cursed me in my sore distress . . ." '); but we are shown too the causes of that suffering in the conflict between a traditional peasant faith in accumulation (which may, however, as Hartman said, serve a genuine spiritual need) and the workings of a larger market economy. The play of the poem, that is, rises above the contradictions it depicts and liberates in us the desire for a future where the mind might not be inhibited in its excursiveness.

The same is true of *Goody Blake, and Harry Gill,* another fascinating picture of the superstitions into which the mind may fall in attempting to make the justice it does not find. Goody Blake begs for a curse from God 'that is the judge of all' upon the comparatively wealthy man who persecutes her:

> She pray'd, her wither'd hand uprearing,
> While Harry held her by the arm –
> 'God! Who art never out of hearing,
> O may he never more be warm!'
> The cold, cold moon above her head,
> Thus on her knees did Goody pray,
> Young Harry heard what she had said,
> And icy-cold he turned away.

The persecuted turns persecutor, and the oppressor in his own suppressed guilt finds himself unable to sustain the power of her hatred: he will never be warm again, they say. Revenge is a kind of wild justice, and the vindictive pursuit of justice merely perpetuates injustice: *Goody Blake, and Harry Gill* is a grotesque little poem on the same plan as *The Borderers.* In an English village we see how the grievance bred in the heartless upholding of unequal rights flashes into a sudden act of revenge. Wordsworth is quite clear that the love of private property may be the cause of the mind's inhibition, both for those who own it and those who want it, as much as the cause of its expansion; here it is at the heart of a familiar little vicious circle of spite.

Harry Gill vows in the rudeness of energetic youth that he will take vengeance on Goody Blake for pilfering wood from his hedge, and with extraordinary determination he spies and waits for her at night 'in frost and snow'. His succumbing to her curse is no modern miracle; his robustness (he has a voice 'like the voice of three' and an abundance of malice) has surely that over-excited edge which might easily be converted by the intense emotion of the vigil, the capture and the curse – all beneath that cold clear moon – into hysterical illness. Goody Blake's curse was her return

in kind for Harry's malice, the culminating expression of all her
long-suppressed resentments: of her poverty, her cold, her
hunger, her loneliness, her insomnia, her lack of light and
clothing, of all her self-comparisons with Harry Gill and his
hedge, his warm fire and clothes. It is her outcry too against the
law behind whose authority Harry can hide his meanness, her
own appeal to a higher authority. The pedlar's sense of the
immortal powers of the mind was part of the strength that
sustained him in the face of injustice; and Goody's superstitious
curse, uttered in a marvellous ecstasy of hatred, similarly sustains
her. It is a poem reminiscent of *King Lear* (' "Poor Harry Gill is
very cold" ') in its grotesque sense of what such vindictiveness can
do to the mind and of how it feeds back into the society that
nurtured it; it is a study of that paranoia which has for centuries
peopled English villages with witches – and the openness of its
final injunction to think invites us to consider ways of finally
laying such powers to rest permanently.

Perhaps the most delicate study of the superstition of the mind
in extremis in *Lyrical Ballads* is *The Complaint of a forsaken Indian
Woman*. The purpose of the poem, Wordsworth wrote, is to show
'the last struggles of a human being at the approach of death,
cleaving in solitude to life and society';[16] and indeed the very
sound of a voice articulate so close to death is moving testimony to
the mind's will to resist the final injustice of its own perishing. Not
even the traditions of a nomadic culture can reconcile it to the
terror of a solitary death – the terror that Wordsworth had already
explored in *The Borderers*. His chosen form here of the lament, with
its supposition of speaker and audience, expresses the woman's
resistance to that terror: the mind must people its solitudes, must
move outwards in search of fellowship, must compose itself
through the social medium of language into some relationship
with justice. It is as natural for the woman to talk aloud in the face
of death as it was for the child to play around the graves in *We are
seven*.

The lament seems spoken towards the end of night, as the
woman awakens from the play of dream to the distress of
actuality. During sleep she had transformed reality, as though in
the liberty of death (the allusion perhaps is to the Indian belief
that death was the journey of soul from body to sky). But now on
awakening she is disappointed to find that her consciousness has
not in fact dissolved into the strange beautiful powers of night, and

she begins at once to invoke that dissolution in the crooning rhythms of her speech. As she awakens further, her eyes look out upon the world, and her mind begins to fashion its meanings there; even amongst the embers of her fire despair seeks fellowship, superstitiously remaking the world in the image of its own needs. Fully awake and remembering the past, she reproaches her friends with their injustice in leaving her, and then by reflex she reproaches herself with lack of courage in the face of sickness. The little fantasy history of her illness since she was abandoned, in the last two lines of the third stanza, and the disturbed fantasy drama involving her child in the fourth, emphasise the depth of her will to live – to live in the others she has loved. The remainder of the poem flickers through a wide range of impulse, wish, reproach and sadness, following the excursions of a mind still at work in a frozen body to find the emotional and linguistic formula that will save her from the isolation of death – for to talk to oneself is to people the world. The *Complaint* is true to Wordsworth's practice in *Lyrical Ballads* of treating situations in which our primary passions and feelings are seen most simply in an unaffected complexity; it locates the fundamental urge of human consciousness in the need to reach out across the gulfs that separate us from other men and the world, in the play of a fantasy whose relationships constitute the health or sickness of our minds.

The Mad Mother also pursues the compensatory play of fantasy into superstition, caused here not by the extremity of death but by betrayal at the very heart of expectation. Wordsworth acknowledged the poem's debt to *Lady Anne Bothwell's Lament* in Percy. No doubt he was excited by the *Lament*'s insight into the damage done to maternal love by a husband's betrayal; for he too has written a dramatic poem full of the fear of violence and guilt, full of the fear of further betrayal by the child, and various in its impulse to achieve a truce between the warring factions of the mind. But the difference in tone is more remarkable than the similarity in subject. The *Lament* is tragic, the song of a woman able to carry her understanding into her pain, and, without hope, to articulate what she sees; but Wordsworth's poem is, in Stephen Parrish's words, 'far more passionate and distracted.'[17] Its manner, in fact, is closer in spirit to the play and holiday humour of *As You Like It* than to Percy – and yet the play and the glee are perverse, compulsive. It is because the mother cannot grieve that she must sing; and in following the songs of her intricately sick fantasy, attempting to justify itself in the midst of pain, we recognise in her the simulacrum of Wordsworth's own cheerful glee in *Lyrical Ballads*. The poetic spirit is once more defined in relation to its opposite.

The mother's compensatory defence against the injustice of betrayal (we are free of all knowledge relating to its circumstances) is to make of her baby and her own maternal feelings an icon all-powerful to protect her against the violence of her fears, guilt, and anger. 'She has a baby on her arm, / Or else she were alone.' In what Mary Jacobus calls this 'precarious allegiance to a fantasy world created to protect her against the reality of desertion',[18] she tries by song to win 'sad and doleful' experience into enrichment of her love; but her own violence is too strong for that which remains good in her. The holiness of her icon is possessed of a devilish counter-spirit, which makes her see herself as a witch, a familiar imp at each of her three nipples, draining her dry in a dull and fiery pain. Subjective passions bedevil the work of her eye in terrifying ways:

> 'My little babe! thy lips are still,
> And thou hast almost suck'd thy fill.
> – Where art thou gone my own dear child?
> What wicked looks are those I see?
> Alas! alas! that look so wild,
> It never, never came from me:'

Is she afraid her baby is abusing her need, lapsing into hostile male independence as soon as he has taken his fill? is she afraid of what she may be giving him? is she afraid of her own hatred of him? The exchange at the heart of love is suddenly a terror to her, full of a nightmarish ambivalence that also infects her attitude to nature – for the greenwood where this strangely foreign woman feels strangely at home is full of lurking poisons, the nature which protects her is also powerful to prompt suicidal fantasy and all the dangerous excitements of risk.

The Thorn similarly explores the disorder that an unmanageable ambivalence may bring to the gleefulness of the poetic spirit, but here the ambivalence operates in the most ordinary way – in gossip, which, in its infectious fascination for and revulsion from its subject, parodies the love and grief that draw minds truly together. Lawrence in *Lady Chatterley's Lover* distinguished the 'spirit of fine, discriminative sympathy' which is a respectful creative interest in others from the 'spurious sympathies and recoils' of gossip.[19] Both novelist and poet define themselves in relation to their opposite; and the gossip of Wordsworth's narrator, obsessing the play-area of his mind, reveals him as a kind of counter-poet. It is important, therefore, in discussing the poem, to avoid the common mistake of concentrating upon either Martha's suffering or the narrator's character. Wordsworth's interest is in the relationship between them, in the fact that certain unassimilable human tragedies like Martha's may produce only unhealthy curiosity in minds as superstitious as those of his narrator and the villagers.

The narrator's fixation with Martha stems from a remarkable meeting when, a newcomer to the area, he was caught out in a storm on the mountain tops and found that the crag to which he ran for shelter was in fact the seated figure of a woman, alone, exposed and quite oblivious of him. 'I did not speak – I saw her face, / Her face it was enough for me': he turned tail and fled. There are perhaps three reasons for his subsequent fascination with her. First, the circumstances of their encounter were exciting; the low cloud of the storm, and its restriction of vision to details separated from their customary patterns, helps both to cause and to image his fascination. Second, the nature of Martha's exposure is a terror to him; she seems exposed not only to the storm but (like Lear) to the full destructiveness of unmediated passion – her behaviour is so different from his, as he scurries for shelter. Third, his flight from a woman remains to reproach him with an unforgettable failure in love and manliness. The whole of his narration seems an attempt to nail down the shadows cast by this failure of sympathy at a crucially incomplete meeting. He is in the grip of an unappeasable fascination. All his measuring of the world (it can bring no new information to light) cannot bring it to the proportion he wants, for he also needs the excitement of uncertainty. The villagers more crudely share these contradictory responses. On the one hand, it is said, they take their spades to dig up the mound: they wish to scale events to a pharisaical justice, to unravel Martha's experience in terms of cause and effect, extending not their love but their power. On the other hand, it is further said, when they approach the mound, the earth around it shakes: suspicion about the intimacies of a disturbed mind seems now more exciting than the possibility of discovering the truth.

The emblem of Martha is ambivalent to all whose curiosity is not a mode of love but merely (in the pedlar's words) 'vain dalliance' (478) with the experience of others for the sake of self.

Through the confusion of sympathies and judgements that characterise the narrator's mind, Wordsworth creates the true mystery of Martha's life – a mystery in which we are freed from what Danby called 'the police court interest in what happened exactly, and how'[20] in order that we might reverence her misery. Wordsworth tells us sufficiently little of Martha's history to inhibit our responding with easy attitudes like blame; such attitudes are rendered impotent by their embodiment in the evidently inadequate character of the narrator. Indeed the poem's whole purpose is to open up that vexed area where notions of justice, responsibility, punishment and mercy cross. We are not told whether Martha's suffering is caused by infanticide or by some other intolerable sense of failure. All we know is that she was betrayed in the heart of her expectations of love and that all the blithe outgoing energies of her mind were turned back upon themselves in violence. This is her tragedy; weathers and seasons are all alike to her, neither external nor internal stimuli have power to break the habits of her mind. She will talk to no-one save herself, and her only words cry out her sense of eternal separation: 'Oh woe is me! oh misery!' Part of the cause of the narrator's ignominious flight, as of his furtive fascination, lies here in the remorseless self-punishment of her guilt, the self-violence of her despair. Alienated herself, and longing for justice, she has the power to infect others and to alienate them from the only stable justice, whose heart is mercy.

Perhaps the most remarkable writing in *The Thorn* is in the first five stanzas, where we see how Martha's exclusive obsession with that spot where she sits in all weathers has alienated the narrator in his own relationship with nature. He sees strangely significant beauty in the thorn, the pond and the mound, beauty whose significances cannot be disciplined to the plain narrative of fact or the inductions of detective work. The spot has become taboo, and yet he has dared to measure it from side to side . . . and so these stanzas play superstitiously and quasi-symbolically with meaning, taunt with the occult powers of suggestion and animism. The thorn is old and grey, yet stands no higher than a two-year-old; it is alive, yet like a stone; it bears a crop that yet would embrace it to death; the mound is like an infant's grave yet

too beautiful. . . . Such writing lacks the precision and liberty of a
healthy symbolism because it is so marvellously true to the
confusions and contradictions of the narrator's superstition, as he
uses nature for his own purposes. *The Thorn* is perhaps the most
impressive of these five poems in *Lyrical Ballads* that seek to carry
relationship and love into extreme alienated states of mind, trying
to counteract their infectiousness by doing them the justice they
deserve and reclaiming their meaning for the human community
to which they belong. The last remaining ballad poem of the
collection undertakes this challenge with regard to a still more
difficult and still more frequently disowned state: that of idiocy.

(d) *THE IDIOT BOY*

'I never wrote anything with so much glee': the exultant comedy
of *The Idiot Boy* is Wordsworth's most daring adventure in *Lyrical
Ballads*. The strength and originality of the poem disperse at once
the archly affectionate tones that have always tended to gather
round pastoral comedy about village life. There is nothing
superior in the many voices of Wordsworth's narration; educated
poet and uneducated villagers, despite their real differences, are
all enabled to speak for themselves, and they show themselves
united in what the *Preface* calls 'the essential passions of the
heart'.[21] The poem is, in Danby's phrase, a 'comedy of the
passions';[22] and like all great comedy, it looks into the possibilities
of the pain to which our human passions expose us. It looks into
the vanities and the kaleidoscopic inconsistencies and
contradictions to which the maternal passion exposes Betty Foy
and survives, as we shall see, to celebrate the glory of our common
folly. The poem's parody of Bürger's *Lenore*, described so well by
Mary Jacobus,[23] exerts the same democratic discipline upon us. A
knight, girded up for heroic enterprise by his lady, gallops off on
his steed through all the dangers of darkness to rescue another
lady in distress; or Johnny is sent by his mother to fetch the doctor
for Susan Gale – true romance is rescued from the spurious, and
literature is reclaimed for the common business of life.

Johnny's quest, of course, is a failure, and he is discovered lost
in delight by the waterfall. It is the story of a lucky escape, such as
any family might tell; and Wordsworth's glee is an appropriate
idiom for the folly of the enterprise, the exhilaration of its danger
and the final gladness at its happy ending. But it is also his idiom

for Johnny's particular joy, for (in Danby's words once more) 'the invulnerability of the joy that goes with him'.[24] Wordsworth has challenged himself in *Lyrical Ballads* with childhood, old age, strange states of alienation and insanity, and now with Johnny's idiocy, in the confidence of his sympathetic faith that he might live in all the people that surround him. But what is it to be Johnny? *The Idiot Boy*, like many of the *Lyrical Ballads*, is focused by a strongly visual image, to which meditation has given the force of an archetype:

> His heart it was so full of glee,
> That till full fifty yards were gone,
> He quite forgot his holly whip,
> And all his skill in horsemanship,
> Oh! happy, happy, happy John.
>
> (92–6)

The image of horse and rider which Wordsworth subverts is an ancient emblem of man in control of his passions; but Johnny is gently led off by his loving pony into a night of owls and moonshine. Wordsworth's celebration of the wisdom of folly has behind it a long tradition of literature both religious and secular: 'God hath chosen the foolish things of the world to confound the wise.' To remember St Paul (and Cervantes too) is to appreciate the humility of Wordsworth's response to the sublimity of Johnny's joy, as he sits in idle self-surrender. What is it to be Johnny? The glee of the poem – its ecstatic exclamations, its imitative sounds, its pleasurable jingling of rhythm and rhyme, its delight in repetition – takes us as far as possible into the pleasures in life and language that Johnny might feel; but finally the question remains unanswered. Wordsworth can no more measure Johnny's thoughts than he could measure the thoughts of the birds that hopped and played about him in *Lines written in early spring*. As he wrote in 1802, 'I have often applied to Idiots, in my own mind, that sublime expression of scripture that, *"their life is hidden with God"*' (*EL* 357): and the strange nocturnal air of Shakespearean romance that encloses the poem, dissipating with the adventure's end at dawn, is his best response to the extraordinary hidden poetry of Johnny's life.

Wordsworth's glee in Johnny, that is, is no airy subjectivity; it is hard-won in the discipline of a tender attentiveness to what he

cannot fully understand. For Johnny is capable of anything and
poet and villager alike fall into panic at their thoughts of what he
might do. Betty's fears are of gipsies, ghosts and goblins (232–41)
and – in the ecstasy of her panic – anger, despair and self-pity chase
such fears across her mind. The poet's imagination too is baffled
by Johnny's absence and falls into melodramatic fantasies of
'strange adventures' (351); and the mock-heroic satire of these
lines (322–51) should not blind us to Wordsworth's feelings that
his muse has deserted him. He finds in himself some of the
superstitious activity of mind that characterised his narrator in
The Thorn, and for the same reason: inhibition of the sympathetic
imagination at a critical moment. However, the anxiety of both
mother and poet relaxes into the trust which is at the heart of their
love when Johnny reappears: ' "Oh! Johnny, never mind the
Doctor; / You've done your best, and that is all" ' (407–8). The
poet too, reporting Johnny's account of his travels, is finally
content to trust himself to the boy's own words:

> 'The cocks did crow to-whoo, to-whoo,
> And the sun did shine so cold.'
>
> (460–1)

A prose interpretation of these lines (Johnny meant he saw the
moon and heard the owls) wholly misses the point of the strange
inscrutable glee of Johnny's mind and of the strange wealth
brought to the poet's mind by a love that works where knowledge
fails. For *The Idiot Boy* achieves something of what Foucault
attributed to Freud: it opens up 'the possibility for reason and
unreason to communicate in the danger of a common language'[25]
– and this achievement is characteristic of *Lyrical Ballads* as a
whole. If it is true, as Masud Khan says, that 'the *need* of the mad is
not so much to know as to *be* and *speak*',[26] *Lyrical Ballads* recognises
the same need in glee and ecstasy of all kinds. To be in silence and
to speak in freedom from interruption . . . the superstitious and
the healthy illusions of subjectivity are honoured in *Lyrical Ballads*
by a poet who remains alert to 'similitude in dissimilitude, and
dissimilitude in similitude' but who wishes to assert that glee and
ecstasy, whether healthy or sick, are also ways of knowing the
world. Wordsworth in these poems, it seems to me, succeeds in
meeting a challenge to 'live / In all things' that surround him –
and in so doing he enriches both our sense of the human

community and our sense of the life of the mind. It is natural now that in *Peter Bell* he should return to grapple with the challenge of a mind predatory upon the community and (in Winnicott's words) 'out of touch with the subjective world and with the creative approach to fact'.[27]

9 *Peter Bell: A Tale* (1798)

Peter Bell explores the deadness of subjectivity in a mind dominated by the lovelessness of pride; its concern is the disease of feeling not too much but too little.

> A primrose by a river's brim
> A yellow primrose was to him,
> And it was nothing more.
>
> (248–50)

The poem is Wordsworth's most considerable study in hubris since *The Borderers*. It shows a mind which in its inability to love can only seize the world and its inhabitants for use, a mind habituated to disguise its own deadness in the noise of self-glorification. Quite characteristically Peter was 'wont to whistle loud / Whether alone or in a crowd' (623–4); he must fill time and space with his own personality, lest silence confront him with his emptiness. *Peter Bell* is crucial in a consideration of Wordsworth's work because Peter's pride, like that of Rivers, leads him actively to evil; he presents a far more serious challenge than anything in *Lyrical Ballads* to the spirit of love in which Wordsworth would know the world.

The poem, however, begins not with Peter's temptation to hubris but the poet's. The long prologue shows us, through the rise and fall of its arc of enterprise, a poet who would at first fill time and space with his powers but who then becomes content to tell the tale of Peter Bell to a small company of local people in his own back garden. It is a prologue perfectly fitted to the poem it precedes; for it shows Wordsworth's awareness of the psychological dangers latent in his playful glee, his awareness of kinship with Peter in his pride. At first the poet's impudence is boundless: urged by strong access of power and exhilarated by danger, he desires – desires, and at once enjoys – an excursion far amongst the heavenly bodies. None of the traditional materials of poetry, learning or cosmology is sacred to him in his small

140

crescent moon of a boat. All things fall under the rule of his poetic muse. His caprice is his rudder and, could he but escape the touch of pity at his friends' fears for him, he would laugh at them until his ribs ached. But the pity he feels is part of the strong gravitational pull that draws him back to earth. He feels the emptiness of a space self-filled and subject only to the law of his taste. 'I've left my heart at home' (55): epic presumption and self-delight yield to the discipline of common humanity.

Yet it is not an act of will to return – a fact of great importance to the whole poem. The arc of its enterprise returns to earth out of the glories of its inner-space fiction because the poet's habits of mind leave him dissatisfied anywhere else. The sureness with which Wordsworth separates one state of mind from its parodic imitation, true glee from panic exhilaration, is won by attentiveness to the quality of his own experience. The poetry of his return, homing in affectionately upon the earth and the country of his birth, has a warmth not found in the outward journey: here, he says, 'I feel I am a man' (70). Who dares do more, is none . . . the mind that seeks to expand through self-regarding fantasy finds only the sterility of a world mirroring itself. Nevertheless, the two directions of the poet's flight have shown a tension in his mind, and in the long dialogue between boat and poet that follows, Wordsworth scrupulously examines that tension in order to understand the direction in which he finds himself going. It is a self-examination confirming the habits of his mind, an analysis of temptation in the process of relaxing its hold upon him.

The boat's temptation is to a mistaken poetic; and its *invitation au voyage* is reminiscent of many earlier seductions in literature. Like Mephistophilis it promises all things, urging apparently unconditional offers upon its chosen pilot with a haste and bewildering variety that bedevils the space between them. Like Lady Macbeth it taunts with accusations of faint-hearted effeminacy and goes on to offer its services with all the insinuations of sexual seduction: 'I am a pretty little Barge / Then come I pray you come with me . . .' (86–7, app. crit.). Like Satan it perverts language from its true meaning and codes the world in an arbitrary structure of its own: so it would have heart mean courage, for instance. When Wordsworth finds himself resisting the seductive powers of his boat, he is resisting the blandishments of all poetry in which he feels that the author's self-delight

distances him from man and nature. This, of course, is at the heart
of his critique of *The Rime of the Ancient Mariner*, which *Peter Bell*
burlesques episode for episode; for when he objected in 1800 that
the hero of Coleridge's poem had 'no distinct character',[1] he was
objecting to a poetic manner which drew the mind away from the
discipline of its daily dramatic meetings with external reality.

> 'Sure in the breast of full-grown poet
> So faint a heart was ne'er before,
> Come to the poet's wild delights,
> I have ten thousand lovely sights,
> Ten thousand sights in store.'
>
> (81–5 app. crit.)

But *Peter Bell* will have nothing to do with the esoteric spirits from
fairy lands forlorn that tempted Coleridge in his ballad poetry.
Wordsworth will be neither magus nor overlord in his poetic
empire – and hence the motto he prefixed to the poem in 1820:
'Brutus will start a Spirit as soon as Caesar!' Hazlitt had written
only three years earlier that 'the principle of poetry is a very
anti-levelling principle' and that the imagination is an
'aristocratical' faculty;[2] but *Peter Bell* proves him wrong as its
prologue rejects a mistaken poetic which is also a mistaken politic.

That Wordsworth's absent-mindedness in his prologue was no
charade but a real trouble to him is evident from the wry comedy
of the return to his friends awaiting him in his garden. The boat
had deserted him disdainfully,

> And I, as well as I was able,
> On two poor legs, toward my stone-table
> Limped on with sore vexation.
>
> (173–5)

Wordsworth begins his tale badly; arriving late, to cover his
confusion he draws upon his stock of poetical know-how and
begins eventfully, *in media re*. His head is still full of epic schemes,
but his audience cuts him down at once to size: he must begin at
the beginning – and his compliance is surely not only an
expression of attention and common courtesy but also of gratitude
to the people who recall him from his fantasy. Nothing could be
further from the ancient mariner's imposition of his story on an

unwilling audience. Furthermore, Wordsworth's mariner will not spread the isolating knowledge of a loveless act that cannot wholly be won back into the sympathies of the living; he will spread the humanising knowledge of a loveless act that can. Wordsworth's neighbourliness goes much deeper than good manners; it is a respect for the healthy potential of his listeners' minds. The prologue that began in flights of self-delighting fantasy ends disciplined by love to purposes of love in an English cottage garden.

Under the correction of his audience, Wordsworth abandons epic presumption for the more important work of characterisation; the first twenty stanzas of the poem picture the selfish habits that constitute Peter's life – habits that only the excitement generated in the pain and terror of personal suffering will have power to overthrow. It is a tale that George Eliot too was to tell in *Silas Marner* and *Adam Bede*, and then more subtly in *Middlemarch*, a tale searching the causes in nature that make these hard hearts, and then searching the cures in nature too.

Peter at the story's start is an emotional bankrupt who, for all he has to give, might as well have been imprisoned 'in the Fleet' (236). He neither gives nor receives; he takes, both in business and all the other relations of his life. The poet came down to earth in his prologue aware of the *debt* he owed to others (the word was introduced in Ms. 5), but Peter is unaware of all the wealth that lies in exchange. He is hard, cunning and energetic, elated not with glee but with the exhilarated sense of his own power and glory. His mind cannot relax in play for it is anxiously wrought up to the endless scheming of 'his *"whens"* and *"hows"* ' (313). His delight, as his dozen wedded wives suggest, is in his own aggressive masculinity and the lawlessness of his own desires and whims; and his narrowly masculine aggressiveness hardens him against the gentle approaches of the natural world. Burke, as we saw, traced the origins of our sense of beauty to 'the passions which belong to SOCIETY',[3] including the sexual passion; and this connection became conventional in the late eighteenth century. Wordsworth too always showed himself delicately aware of the sexuality of the human response to natural beauty – a sexuality that might mature into the holy love of *Tintern Abbey* or degenerate, as here, into the coarse promiscuity of Peter Bell:

> Though Nature could not touch his heart
> By lovely forms, and silent weather,
> And tender sounds, yet you might see
> At once that Peter Bell and she
> Had often been together.
>
> (286–90)

His forehead is wrinkled with frowning against the sun (311), his face is hard through being fixed 'against the wind and open sky' (320). Everything around him is his antagonist, to be subdued to his male good pleasure; the sense of otherness upon which the cooperations of perception and love depend serves in Peter only his feelings of antagonism.

What we see is a function of what we are: Peter sees the world with neither love nor pleasure, it exists to him 'in disconnection dead & spiritless' (*The Ruined Cottage*, Ms.B 49^r). Object exists in separation from object, locked in antagonistic separation from subject; and yet this sense of antagonism is crucial to Wordsworth's characterisation of Peter – for such egotism is, to quote the pedlar again, 'an impious warfare with the very life / Of our own souls' (Ms.B50^r). His hubris, like that of Macbeth or Edmund, is perpetual self-violation, perpetual warfare against that goodness which remains alive in him and which will eventually effect his reclamation; and Wordsworth will show how the passionately damned are closer to salvation than the hollow men with no life in them.

The twenty stanzas which describe Peter weave around him a rich web of poetry, through which he passes with comic ignorance. Like *The Ruined Cottage*, *Peter Bell* contrasts diseased with healthy excursiveness of mind. The poet, disciplined in the presumption of his earlier wandering, returns to earth with an affection for its places and place-names beyond what Peter could sustain:

> At Doncaster, at York, and Leeds,
> And merry Carlisle had he been;
> And all along the Lowlands fair,
> And through the bonny shire of Ayr;
> And far as Aberdeen.
>
> (216–20)

The writing recalls the feeling for place that we find in ballad literature, a feeling deeply rooted in the affections of popular culture; and this sense of richness and society isolates the buoyant Peter in a poverty of which he is quite oblivious. He will not give himself away in feeling, any more than he will gaze himself away before a landscape (266–70); for a man so exuberantly at war has neither time nor place for the returns of trust and fellowship. The harmony of Wordsworth's own cooperation with man and nature, however, exposes the 'medley air / Of cunning and of impudence' (304–5) with which Peter exploits them. The poet, disciplined during a prologue in which he found his kinship with men like Peter, can now trust himself to his own creative sensibility as the touchstone by which Peter must be judged.

Why does Peter beat the ass? The poem's mock-epic beginning opens upon an emblem of exhilarated violence which recalls the violation of the bower in *Nutting*: we see a face-to-face act of cruelty, an excited attack upon trusting meekness, aroused to its bitterest pitch precisely by that meekness. So the father beat his son in *Adventures on Salisbury Plain*. Such violence, we must remember, is in its inner reaches self-violence too; the sado-masochistic alternations between activity and passivity are crucial to the developing rhythms of *Peter Bell* and to an understanding of its hero's final reintegration. The attack, however, as it happens, seems in its relish to strike destructively at the worth of Wordsworth's faith in the natural expansiveness of love: how can such things be?

The circumstances in which Peter meets the ass are part of the answer – circumstances we understand differently from Peter. The tale tells us that Peter lost himself one evening in taking a short cut and that he stumbled across the ass by accident. But we know more than this. We know from the poet's conspicuous story-telling mantle that this is but the start of things; we know from his glee that there is mystery afoot; and we know from the echoes of the style that the unravelling of the mystery will be patterned after the religious literature of conversion. We recognise at once, as the parson and his wife would have recognised, the short cut that leads a smooth way over the fields: we have gone that way before in *The Pilgrim's Progress*. The wood too we know as 'the wandring wood' of *The Faerie Queene*,[4] the wood near Athens, the wood of *Comus*, the wood of countless fairy-tales in which men lose their bearings. The poem in the very manner of its telling invites the reader at once into a common culture from which Peter has exiled himself: a culture of shared religious, literary and folk imagination, whose heart is the human affection with which the poet speaks. The poet's glee plays the part in *Peter Bell* that divine grace plays in the literature of regeneration, or that the deep urgency towards a happy ending plays in fairy-tale: it moves us towards reintegration, both as individuals and as members of a society. Hence of course the preparatory importance of the prologue, with its reassuring rediscovery that his glee is grounded not in whim but in the discipline of reality; Wordsworth is seeking the psychological truth to which so much literature of miraculous transformation bears witness.

For Peter too the circumstances of the meeting are strangely meaningful, as though to put him signally to the test. It is an opportunity too good to miss: the ass is a prize to be seized piratically. Peter's first impulse is to appropriate, and when the ass gently resists him he becomes alternately violent and suspicious, as the active or passive side of his nature is uppermost. Each is as extreme as the other, the suspicion being a confidence that the powers of witchcraft are ranged against him, the violence a blind will to force his purposes upon the world. All things are for or against him. The panic exhilaration of the blows that Peter gives the ass for refusing to move from its station (a marvellously chosen word) shows the trap in which he is caught: in conceiving of the world as his antagonist, he dare not conceive of it as independent. All the cunning and violence of his life is an attempt to resolve this contradiction, where failure is unendurable and success impossible. He beats the ass in these challenging circumstances partly because he must deny, in the ass and himself, that principle of gentleness in which the independence of others is acknowledged. Hence his preoccupation with his own desires and fears, filling the world with the sound of his own voice; it takes him over sixty lines to notice the ass's wretched emaciation. The strangeness of their meeting in this secret bower; the curious obduracy of the ass; its pregnant movements of ear and eye – these hints create in the reader a sense that the ass might have a story of its own, but in Peter they merely arouse the violence of possessiveness and fear. He does not feel the sense of mystery that can lead him in respect to another being – only the superstitious fear that 'there is some plot against me laid' (407).

The richest comedy of the poem has its source in Peter's paranoia – comedy which sets a trap for the reader too, as Wordsworth will playfully tempt us to see the connected events of a village evening through the disconnecting superstitiousness of Peter's mind. A family tragedy, a mining detonation, a methodist meeting, a village pub. . . . These circumstances will seem to Peter, who can only refer all happenings to himself, the signs of a divine plot laid against him; and to the unsympathetic reader perhaps they seem the signs of an excessively coincidental plot that the poet has laid against him. Yet the ass does not make this mistake as it journeys home through the familiar goings-on of life. It is not the marvellous and miraculous that interest Wordsworth but the wonderful face that the familiar may be brought to wear – as happens, for instance, in paranoia.

Peter in his need to master the world wraps his arms around the ass and tries to lift it bodily, calling it a 'sturdy thief' (406–42 app. crit.); and when the ass brays – a terrifying noise which he cannot master – he draws closer to it as though he would creep into its skin (491–500 app. crit.). The executioner is also victim, for the world will not be subdued to his will. He depends for his sense of himself on the excitement that betrays him; it is an impossible situation. Then, as he stoops forward to seize the ass around the neck, his imagination reels in panic at what he sees in the water and he faints, perhaps twice. What he sees, of course, possibly through his own reflected image, is the drowned body of the ass's master – death. Such a *memento mori*, recalling the common end to the pride of human power, is frequently met in the religious tradition that *Peter Bell* imitates, but Peter here meets death not in the formulations of meditative self-examination but as a direct assault upon his sensibility in all its rage of omnipotent fantasy. His fear, guilt and paranoia are only slight exaggerations of a common human reaction to the unexpected discovery of death, and it is upon the excitement of these passions that Wordsworth concentrates in his experiment with Peter's reintegration: only passion has power to overthrow habit.

What Peter does not feel is the grief necessary to integrate the knowledge of death into creative living – the ass feels this. Its love is stronger than its fear, so that it is able to lick Peter's hands (the same hands that had been beating it) when they begin to busy themselves about its dead master. It is a love and a grief so strong that it constitutes a theodicy for Wordsworth, written in the necessities of that animal's nature. The effect upon Peter of his twin discoveries of the drowned man and the ass's reaction to that discovery is quite remarkable. For the first time he forgets his *whens* and *hows*. He understands that despite his terror he must raise the body from the stream; he understands that the dead man must have been the ass's owner; and when the ass kneels, he understands that he will let himself be taken to the dead man' house. Each of these new understandings originates in the traditional pieties and stories of a village community, and shows how little even the proudest mind is its own place; each works to connect Peter more closely with the world to which formerly he was so antagonistic. At the sublime terror of the dead man's body upright emergence from the water, Peter feels pain pass 'like a weaver's shuttle' (583–5 app. crit.) through his body Wordsworth's reference is to Job vii:6: 'My days are swifter than a weaver's shuttle, and are spent without hope.' It is death, the antagonist before whom Peter must fail, that drives him in shock and despair towards his fellow men; and the rest of the poem stands in measured hope against Job's dread of oblivion, as the dead man is brought home to the grief of those who will mourn him.

The ass kneels in the trust of entreaty; Peter mounts in a reciprocal trust and thereafter during the course of the poem sits passively still, awaiting what will happen. As Mary Jacobus wittily puts it, he becomes 'a comic inversion of the picaresque adventurer, taken for a ride by the ass he tries to steal'.[5] His passivity, self-punishing as it often seems, is the dialectical opposite of his earlier restless wandering and scheming; and it is the means by which he develops 'a heart / That watches and receives'. Throughout the long central section of the poem, as events increasingly press upon Peter and his mind veers fantastically from mood to mood, adrift amidst ideas which he cannot master or use, we see once more the horse in charge of its rider. Like some picture out of fairy-tale, it is an emblem of the 'silent and regularly progressive'[6] power of love over the wild passions by which Peter formerly had lived. It is a spiritual guide – not a messenger bringing doctrine and not (like Coleridge's south-pole spirit) an allegorical invention, but a living symbol partaking of the realities of love which it renders intelligible.

The ass carries Peter past a ruined chapel like the one in which he had married his sixth wife; and no longer hard with antagonism, he gives himself up to its suggestive power over him, recalling that sixteen-year-old Scottish girl whom he had betrayed into marriage. For the first time in the poem Peter's mind works in harmony with the poet's, as together they picture the girl she was, the hopes she had and the despair that ended them. For the first time Peter's imagination is seized, in guilt, by the independent existence of another person – and significantly it is of a woman. His sympathetic re-creation of a woman's experience is Peter's first creative contact with the female side of his own nature too (which, indeed, previously he could only contact by abusing it) – the side which here symbolises that capacity for relaxed being, as opposing to doing, which according to Winnicott 'forms the only basis for self-discovery and a sense of existing',[7] and also the only basis for the sympathetic discovery of others. 'The truth is', said Coleridge once, 'a great mind must be androgynous.'[8] What Coleridge asserted of men of genius, Wordsworth with equally typical emphasis explored in relation to all human creativity: the need for harmonious interchange between male and female in the same mind. It is an insight originating in the polarisation of sexual role and nature so common in eighteenth-century thought, and one which Wordsworth explored in many places – in the first of the *Poems on the Naming of Places*, for instance, in *Michael* and the sonnet to Bonaparte *1801*. Also, it always underlay his perception of his relationship with his sister, from *An Evening Walk* onwards; and here it serves to elucidate the first stage of Peter's reintegration with his own creativity.

Despair and self-punishment, however, accompany Peter's newly-awakened sympathetic memories at first: his wife's death and her dying appeal to her mother affirmed a love which excluded him then and excludes him now. There seems no escape from the purgatory of past deeds. It is the Methodist sermon (appealing to the will in a way the poem as a whole distrusts) that, touching him in his fear of death, assures him too of the possibility of a fresh start. His iron frame relaxes and he melts into tears, able at last to grieve. His tears have the sacramental quality of infant baptism, when grace is received but nothing taken; they relax his male aggressiveness and reestablish communion not only with his female sympathies but also with the helplessness of infancy, in which is the beginning of trust and creative cooperation.

The poem now comes home to its final scene, as silently the ass bears Peter to the dead man's family; and here the pattern repeats itself. Once more Peter finds himself excluded from the circle of human love, just as he hoped to enter it. He is not the man the family wanted to see. Yet when the widowed woman collapses, she breaks the spell in which he has sat on the ass; he dismounts and raises her head against his knee – perhaps the first time in his life that he has held a woman for her sake and not for his.

> And now is Peter taught to feel
> That man's heart is a holy thing;
> And Nature, through a world of death,
> Breathes into him a second breath,
> More searching than the breath of spring.
>
> (1071–5)

Perhaps in time the woman, helped by her faith, her love and neighbourly kindness, may come to mourn her loss; but now her suffering is inconsolable and Peter, his heart full of love, is made to feel just how little he can do – he must submit his love to the discipline of the real. Yet in his exclusion he once more rediscovers his past. For, as the woman rushes away to be alone with her pain, Peter sits apart, entranced, 'as if his mind were sinking deep / Through years that have been long asleep!' (1093–4). It is this act of meditation that finally sets him right with time, retrieving the past and thereby establishing creative living in the present and hope for the future; it restores his inner goodness to him and returns him back upon the present with a voice no longer needing to fill it.

> 'When shall I be as good as thou?
> Oh! would, poor beast, that I had now
> A heart but half as good as thine!'
>
> (1098–100)

After ten months' melancholy, we are told, he became a good and honest man. The presumptuous bully who in his boasted manhood had retained something of the infant's delusive sense of omnipotence has been reborn through that delicate disillusion which is the gateway to the real world and the beginning of the capacity to love.

The *Eclectic Review* said of *Peter Bell*: 'A more extraordinary conversion never excited the scorn of the sceptic, in the annals of what is termed Methodism.'[9] Yet the poem is not a conversion narrative but a history of reintegration, of the recovery of lost goodness, grounded in Wordsworth's faith that (in the words of *The Old Cumberland Beggar*) there is 'a spirit and pulse of good' inseparably linked to 'every mode of being'. It is just such a history as he was shortly to begin about himself in *The Prelude*. But although so deeply characteristic of its author, *Peter Bell* has never been much liked. John Beer calls it 'one of Wordsworth's strangest productions',[10] whilst Mary Jacobus says it is 'Wordsworth's most doctrinaire celebration of the human heart';[11] and these are sympathetic critics. I think what is commonly misunderstood is the nature of Wordsworth's glee. It is no naive optimism – the invocation to part third is under no illusion about the *likelihood* of the events the poem describes – but the glee of a man 'bold to look / On painful things'. The poem is perhaps best approached as a fairy-tale; and certainly it should be *told* as a fairy-tale is told, to bring out all its tones and teasings, all its terrors contained by the reassuring presence of its narrator. Like a fairy-tale the poem images, with a certain mock solemnity, the worst that may be known, but then moves towards its happy ending with an inevitability which is a condition of its being. The happy ending of such a tale, Bettelheim says, is 'the ultimate in emotional security of existence and permanence of relation available to man; and this alone can dissipate the fear of death.'[12] Here in *Peter Bell* the poet's glee serves the purpose of theodicy, justifying the worth of society and life in the face of predatoriness and death. His presence is pedagogic, as he makes for his happy ending after the discipline of the prologue, but it is certainly not doctrinaire.

> I've played, I've danced with my narration;
> A happy and a thoughtless man
>
> (791–2 app. crit.)

Peter Bell seems to me the culmination of the lyrical ballad poetry of 1798 – a poetry which above all else, even in grief, is playful, freeing us to enter that play-area of the mind where, as in a young child's play, the real world is imaginatively invented only because it already exists in reality. In play the little cottage girl of *We are seven* made good her anxiety and loss; and here too in play Wordsworth makes good the evil and the suffering he depicts in Peter Bell.

Part VI
The Autobiographical Poetry
of 1798–9:
The Poet and the Child

10 *Tintern Abbey, Nutting* and 'There was a Boy' (1798)

The secret of the enjoyment of solitude lies in the sense of the continuing presence of things absent – of internalised good relationships, missing in the experience of loneliness. It was this same experience of what Wordsworth called 'peopled solitude' (*PW* v:341:viii) that Winnicott indicated when he wrote: 'the basis of the capacity to be alone is a paradox; it is the experience of being alone while someone else is present'.[1] The development of such trust in good relationship is what enables destructive emotions both to be admitted and to be given their due (we shall see that this is one way of describing the meaning of *Nutting*); and it also enables that relaxation in which the self begins to find itself through play. It frees the mind from the anxiety of restless striving like that of Peter Bell, who had contrived 'a false life built on reactions to external stimuli'[2] – a false life which at the end of the poem yields to his long-abused inner goodness.

The precariousness of Wordsworth's hold upon internalised good relationship was responsible for the nostalgia in his first published poem, *An Evening Walk*, and surely also in part for the sheer amount of mental work undertaken in that poem in order to secure a hold upon the presences of the visible world – and hence the gulf between its despondency and hope. Now once more, in *Tintern Abbey* and the two-part *Prelude*, he faces that same precariousness; once more the goodness of his own past life seems lost. Both poems are impassioned dramatic meditations beginning under the pressure of that fear; and because Wordsworth is so scrupulously cautious about the dangers of cheering himself up with false comfort, they are poems that secure their final hope only through the adventure of their meditative unfolding, as anxiety relaxes again into play and rediscovers those relationships in time and place that were feared lost. The poems, that is, are triumphs of trust rather than of the will – and for this reason they are more confident in their hold upon inner goodness, and less strenuous in their hold upon external reality, than *An Evening Walk*. It is a relaxed confidence which leads as they unfold to a deepening understanding of the distinctions between solitude and loneliness, society and exile, love and betrayal, true self and false self, in which we shall find Wordsworth's maturest challenge to the political society of his day.

(a) *LINES WRITTEN A FEW MILES ABOVE TINTERN ABBEY*

Tintern Abbey, like *The Ruined Cottage*, explores two modes of meditation, one creative and one (shadowing the other) sterile; and it is with the latter that I wish to begin, with Wordsworth's gradual identification during the poem of those habits of mind that he found sterile in himself. The poem opens with a cry like that of a man awaking distressed from a bad dream:

> Five years have passed; five summers, with the length
> Of five long winters!

The anxiety of that exclamation is unassuaged by its relief. The sense of loss – of time lost, of the self and its continuities lost, of the worth of life itself lost amongst unseasonable and unnatural rhythms – is a sharp pang of disillusion which disrupts the habits of Wordsworth's sensibility. Where has his life been? Where is it now? Suddenly he feels, in the words of the two-part *Prelude* which I use in this and the following chapter, a sense of 'blank desertion' (1:124) in which the relationship between inner and outer, past and present, has broken down, leaving him with neither the language nor the understanding to do more than cry out at this sudden awakening consciousness of pain.

The cry, however, in the same grammatical sentence, yields responsively to the disciplinary power of nature ('and again I hear / Those waters'), and it is this simple reaction of attentiveness to the world outside that will gradually bring about, through renewal of relationship, a full understanding of that sense of desertion. By the time in the second paragraph that Wordsworth comes to write of 'the heavy and the weary weight / Of all this unintelligible world', he has already traced its origins to the suddenness of his awakening out of a city life where the mysteries of pain and evil had been reduced to mere confusion. Already he sees the alienation of that life in terms of his own loneliness and the noisy unintelligibility of the city, two interrelated aspects of the same failure in relationship; and I think he means literally *unintelligible* – he could not read between the lines of his experience there, his creativity and capacity to play were inhibited, subject and object remained in a spiritless disconnection.

The short third paragraph recreates that sickening sterility even more intensely and with deeper understanding. Towns and cities are built in the unreal world of Plato's cave: they are full not of forms but of joyless shapes, phantom meanings, frenzied activity, unprofitable profiteering. The allusion here to Hamlet's 'weary, stale, flat and unprofitable' world seems to me to suggest precisely that sense of anxious sterile meditation which Coleridge had identified in Hamlet when the '*equilibrium* between the real and the imaginary worlds' had broken down and his mind had withdrawn into seeing external things 'as hieroglyphics'.[3] The city life that Wordsworth conjures up is one in which relationship of all kinds has withered into shadowy and superstitious soliloquy.

The last paragraph of the poem, in a tone at last free of the nauseous weariness that had lingered through its first three paragraphs, reaches a precise understanding of the abuses of language that had bedevilled relationship in towns and cities – and not just in towns and cities, for the poem increasingly frees itself too of the naïve opposition between town and country. With Lutheran confidence, Wordsworth comes to declare his faith that

> neither evil tongues,
> Rash judgments, nor the sneers of selfish men,
> Nor greetings where no kindness is, nor all
> The dreary intercourse of daily life,
> Shall e'er prevail against us

Here is the heart of the poem's concern: to find a reliable language through which relationship can flourish. But language is only one mode of human communication, and words are only one mode of human experience: Wordsworth in *Tintern Abbey*, as more generally in the poetry of this period, uses 'language' as a metaphor to express all those relationships of passion and feeling

which infuse the verbal language we use and which constitute our
health and sickness. If a healthy language partakes of the reality
which it renders intelligible, the language of urban culture for
Wordsworth partakes of an unreality which it leaves confused.
For such culture, he thought, tended particularly to inhibit
relationship, deaden feeling, swamp the sensibility and promote
selfishness. The tenor of these complaints is commonplace in the
literature of the period; we have already seen Mrs Radcliffe's
lament in *The Mysteries of Udolpho*: 'How then are we to look for
love in great cities, where selfishness, dissipation, and insincerity
supply the place of tenderness, simplicity and truth?' (1:5). *Tintern
Abbey* is the first and in some ways the simplest of Wordsworth's
many attempts to do justice to city life; and the power and interest
of the poem, as opposed to the naïvety of Mrs Radcliffe's
judgement, lies in the urgency of his struggle to clarify *in himself*
the difference between his purer and impurer mind, between
creative and sterile meditation, between the feelings he associated
with the city and those he associated with the country. I want now
to illustrate the picture of creative meditation that we find
exemplified in the poem before returning to the question of the
value of these contrasts.

The meditation of *Tintern Abbey* is in fact a species of dialogue, a
self-dialogue made possible through the agency of natural forms;
and as Wordsworth trusts himself to the discipline of the
landscape during that long first paragraph, we can perhaps
distinguish three tones in his voice. First, we feel at once the great
relief in the poet's return to substantial things, and second, we
sense that this relief is obscurely crossed by 'somewhat of a sad
perplexity'. We hear, amidst relieved recognition of familiar
objects, an anxiety: he tells the objects of the landscape as though
they were beads in a rosary, superstitiously hoping they will yield
the pleasure he obscurely misses, listing them because none can
focus his attention. Relief which cannot subdue anxiety, present
pleasure disturbingly incomplete – in this compound reaction of
direct and reflective response lies the mixture of satisfaction and
dissatisfaction, of trust and doubt, in which the poem finds both
its drive and direction.

Third, we sense behind the onward movement of the poem the
guiding rhythms of the Wye itself; it is as though the sweet inland

murmur of that 'wanderer through the woods' exerts a discipline upon the current of the poet's thoughts. Geoffrey Hartman noticed this when he wrote beautifully of the poem's *'wave effect* of rhythm whose characteristic is that while there is internal acceleration, the feeling of climax is avoided'.[4] Wordsworth's suggested image, of life beginning to flow once more from a spring that had been stopped, has the archetypal quality of so much of his poetry; and it indicates what the sentence lengths too indicate, the gradual relaxation of anxiety during the first paragraph. We have so far only seen the indefiniteness that belongs to unintelligibility; but there is also an indefiniteness that belongs to play, and the opening paragraph in its attentive response to the landscape gradually relaxes into play. There is a continual flow towards and ebb from the precise frontiers of definition. The plots of cottage ground, or rather orchard tufts, lose themselves amongst the woods and copses, they do not disturb the landscape; the hedgerows seem hardly hedgerows but little lines of sportive wood run wild; the farms are green to the very door. . . . This relaxation into playful affectionate creativity under the discipline of the landscape is the key to the first paragraph. Gradually Wordsworth's mind is freed to play fancifully with what he sees, until at the last he guesses from the spiralling smoke at 'vagrant dwellers in the houseless woods' or at a hermit by the fire of his cave – fancies learned perhaps in the pages of a Gilpin but nevertheless expressive of creative surmise. The culminating fancy of the hermit, indeed, focusing in one point the poet's playfulness with the deepening meditative earnestness that underlies it, has the same power as a bridge passage in music, mediating between the present and the future; it provides Wordsworth with the space and the peaceful intensity in which he can begin to face his anxiety. From the orchard to the hermit, the frontiers between the wild and the civilised have dissolved until the two can interpenetrate – as they do in play. In play, we remember, the wildly clad little cottage girl of *We are seven* had peopled her mind; and so too has Wordsworth here.

More confident now, Wordsworth is able silently to confront his anxiety before breaking out into speech again: no, during these five years the powers of the landscape have not been dead, blank, as though they had never been. Gradually the poem composes its anxiety and makes it intelligible; we glimpse the discontinuity that had frightened Wordsworth through his gathering

confidence to look into it, as he begins to relate not only to the self
that he had been five years before but also (more importantly) to
the less worthy self that he has been in the intervening time.
Characteristically, looking into himself, Wordsworth discovers
debt. He is not the separated individual he had feared to be: bonds
abide, relationships abide. The first debt Wordsworth names,
incurred during those five blank-seeming years, is that of sweet
sensations 'felt in the blood, and felt along the heart'. Nor does the
poetry merely name, as Paul Sheats claims;[5] it enacts the poet's
wonder at the gifts he relives. De Quincey's descriptions cannot be
bettered here: 'the motion of the feeling is *by* and *through* the ideas
. . . the sentiment creeps and kindles underneath the very tissues
of the thinking'.[6] The very care of the writing seems an act of
responsive gratitude, testifying that these experiences are still
current in Wordsworth, the life-blood of his mind; and it is their
recollection that enables him to begin to reclaim those past five
years, even as he distinguishes what has been pure in them from
what has been impure.

The further debts that Wordsworth names, as his anxiety
relaxes more, are debts that must be taken on trust, since their
origin cannot be traced with any certainty to the Wye Valley. The
second, indeed, is by definition a matter of trust since it is beyond
recall: those feelings of unremembered pleasure that Wordsworth
believes build up the best habits of the mind. The third –
described by Wordsworth in traditional Protestant language
softened to the new eighteenth-century appreciation of the
importance of mood in perception – is to that mood in which, by
the agency of the affections, the mind is gently liberated from the
body until it comes to perceive that the life of things is grounded in
joy and harmony. In each of these cases, as Wordsworth finds
continuity where he had feared to find separation, what is
significant is that the mind is passive and relaxed. It is sustained
not by what it does but by what it is, by feelings, pleasures and
intimations that *are* relationship across the widest fields of time
and place; and though in the short third paragraph Wordsworth
recoils upon himself in a doubt that defines the experimental
quality of his belief, he nevertheless recoils to the reality of his
responsiveness to the rhythms of nature: 'how often has my spirit
turned to thee!'

The long fourth paragraph, returning to the cautious
exploration of the second under the influence of the vivid emotion

of the third, has now the confidence to face directly that 'sad perplexity' which, unnamed and unmanageable at the start of the poem, had threatened to overwhelm him. 'Though changed, no doubt, from what I was' – this ungrudging, almost casual concession in the course of his self-dialogue is Wordsworth's fullest indication so far of what underlay his initial anxiety. He was anxious (the articulation will gradually become complete) because he saw the landscape with the disappointment, the disillusion, that accompanies betrayal or faithlessness. The words unite the sexual and religious language of the poem – a language not merely illustrative but insistent that Wordsworth's feelings for nature are consubstantial with his feelings for God and man. Each symbolises the others, each constitutes his general sense of the worth of life; and hence, of course, the threatening significance of that blank desertion in which the poem began.

Something has been lost; but disillusion is not only malign, it may also be enrichment when experienced in the context of a sustaining environment: and here we have already seen the Wye Valley sustain Wordsworth through the long relaxing development of the first paragraph. What he has gained is a new substantial language through which he can place what has been lost: an intensity of feeling which he can now perceive as adolescent turbulence, first love, an anxiety of search that was more than half flight. There is something of iconic status about the objects he sought so passionately, 'the tall rock, / The mountain, and the deep and gloomy wood', each was a talisman to the superstitious eye of his love. His absolutism, his exclusive concern for the senses, his certainty that nearest was best, his lack of interest in the remoteness of thought – all testify to the lost contradictory longings of youth for self-confirmation and self-oblivion.

At all this the adult can only wonder gratefully; it is part of his adult sense of debt to the bounty of life, alongside the specifically new debts of maturity that he now goes on to name: that he sees nature hearing the still, sad music of humanity, and that he feels the sublime disturbance of elevated religious thought. Both gifts have brought creative disturbance, both have opened out excursively into wider worlds of political and religious experience; and we should notice once more that the poem does not merely name these gifts, it has embodied them in the very movements of its own meditation – and in so doing it has once again achieved the purposes of theodicy. The sufferings as well as the moments of relief in those apparently lost five years have been integrated into a new trust in the worth of man and the benignity of the universe – a universe where, in a striking phrase of Benjamin Whichcote, 'Man's Understanding is every-where transcended'.[7] 'Therefore', Wordsworth concludes, first love has matured into adult relationship. This is not a logical conclusion but an achieved self-discovery; he does not take a new decisive vow of faith but rather discovers that all the while, even in the midst of apparent faithlessness, faith has been kept.

Wordsworth has now achieved a full confidence in the creative relationship between 'nature and the language of the sense' which the waters of the Wye had initiated in the first paragraph; and in the final paragraph he is released to turn from self-examination to his sister. There he sees what is often neglected by readers of the poem: namely, that human love may equally have given him what he has just received from the landscape – the ability to recapture those past energies without which the present seems unreal and blank. For the adult in whom the child is dead experiences sterility; and Wordsworth, if he is to avoid the false life that he had invented so powerfully for Peter Bell, knows that he must feel in himself that same loving wildness that he sees in his sister. He must be confirmed in his enjoyment of that blend of culture and wildness which he had playfully perceived in the landscape of the opening paragraph; for in that sense of boundaries transcended lies the essence of the mind's creative excursiveness. Love itself depends upon it; and the scheme of things (Nature) is so ordained that love, if it be perfect, cannot be betrayed. All shall be well, and all manner of thing shall be well. . . . The poem concludes with exultant faith in the power of the love of man and the love of nature, beautifully interfused in the poetry, over all forces that threaten the '*equilibrium* between the real and the imaginary worlds': over triviality, callousness and vice, solitude, fear, pain and grief, absence and the final separation of death. Almost unnoticeably, Wordsworth's exhortations pass into prophecy, so confident is he in his trust; and the poem's final sentence harmonising steep woods and lofty cliffs with pastoral landscape, natural love with human, presence with absence, future with past, celebrates that marriage between the objective and the subjective which is at the root of play and which has been at the root of his creative meditation during the course of the poem.

It is quite clear that in *Tintern Abbey* Wordsworth was trying to understand and to integrate two seemingly opposite kinds of experience which had suddenly and bafflingly become juxtaposed in his mind; one which he relates to his purer mind and which was associated with his sense of personal creativity and his capacity for relationship and love, and the other which he relates to his impurer mind and which was associated with fretfulness, striving and sterility. But the poem is not simply subjective self-analysis, of course, for experience is relationship and the experiences that Wordsworth describes are learned in the imagery of country and city, of a 'natural' and a man-made environment. Raymond Williams has written justly that 'what is often being argued . . . in the idea of nature is the idea of man; and this not only generally, or in ultimate ways, but the idea of man in society, indeed the ideas of kinds of societies'.[8] I certainly think this is what is being argued, quite consciously, in *Tintern Abbey*; and I think it is generally what Wordsworth argues, often with an excessively essentialist appeal to human nature and often with an appeal to religion, but almost always – as *Hart-Leap Well* shows wonderfully well – with a historical awareness of the new perspective he holds upon what man has made of man and what ideally man yet might make of man.

In *Tintern Abbey* the idea of nature is inseparably bound up with Wordsworth's idea of man and his societies; it is not only that the presence of Dorothy reminds us that Wordsworth's feelings for landscape were consubstantial with his feelings for man, but that the landscape itself is clearly seen in terms of its relation to human labour and agricultural community. The alienating size and pace and the 'unprofitable' busyness of the city seem suddenly to Wordsworth to reduce men to a mere shadow of what they might become, and this recognition comes to him at the sight of country life – itself no single thing, of course, as the variousness of *Lyrical Ballads* made plain, but perceived here at an emotional moment in time and place, a distance where the most valued feelings of the self were free to flow again. In *Peter Bell* Wordsworth had depicted a man whose feelings for nature and human society were dictated by his antagonising desire to exploit and to dominate; but now in the great autobiographical poetry of 1798–9 he is concerned to discover and celebrate those feelings for man and nature alike which might transform such estrangement into a genuine sensibility to the otherness of the created world – feelings of love, respect and relaxed affection, feelings which might subsume the business sense of utility into a richer, more equally shared sense of pleasure.

(b) *NUTTING* AND 'THERE WAS A BOY'

Nutting takes the whole question one stage further, for it is Wordsworth's finest exploration of the problem that had excited him in *Adventures on Salisbury Plain* and *The Borderers*: the problem of the ambivalence at the heart of those feelings of love and trust which he had celebrated in *Tintern Abbey*. Its central image of the defaced bower, the despoiled garden, locates the origins of human evil and the beginnings of human morality precisely in this primary ambivalence. Wordsworth is well aware of the attractiveness of violence, of the powerful temptation to 'touch / The ark in rashness'[9], of the perverse pleasure that lies in the violation of the sense of inner goodness – as he had shown in *Peter Bell*. He is aware too of the dangers besetting the mind unable to integrate its own destructiveness; and yet in *Nutting* he has found himself able to celebrate in his own life the power of destructiveness to strengthen love. The day that was heavenly to the child, we might say, in its Edenic infinity of wealth, remains heavenly to the adult in the beauty of the theodicy it continues to teach: that violence may be safely and enrichingly experienced by the child in a good-enough environment.

Geoffrey Hartman has noted how the poem is true to patterns both of romance and psychology.[10] The boy (Sir Fool, in the adult's tenderly indulgent retrospect) sallies forth disguised in motley accoutrement, as though a knight upon a secret quest: he forces his way against the dangerous hostility of nature until, mysteriously, he gains the unblemished bower which guards the unanticipated profusion of the treasure he sought. Or: a small boy dressed in an assortment of old clothes for protection stumbles across a remote dell full of hazel-trees. The romance echoes do not only serve the adult's need for a poetry true to the felt sense of moral experience; they are true to the quality of the child's play. For the romance of his excursion lay in his sense of adventure and his self-dramatisation, so obvious in the ritual disguise he wears with such pride – a disguise sufficient to overcome the natural guardians of the place he seeks. It is in this combination of security and fear, familiarity and strangeness, that the creativity of his play develops.

What makes this day's play so memorable is that the quest is more than met in the bounty of nature. The boy's expectations are transcended in the beauty and the profusion of what he sees; it is a 'sudden happiness beyond all hope' before which he can only exclaim in wonder. With the instinct of a voluptuary, he dallies with what he knows is to come, preparing himself in a kind of foreplay of anticipation and suppressed excitement. The rhythms of the poetry change as the boy's play changes; secure in the secrecy of his joy (and the sense of secrecy, like disguise, releases power from its habitual restraints), he is free to indulge emotion and fancy. 'Perhaps it was a bower . . .' – the wandering rhythms of this long sentence, with its invocation of fairyland and its fanciful comparison of mossy stones to sheep, embody the pleasurable excesses of the boy's subjectivity. It is a disequilibrium through which finally he finds himself ready to rise to his challenge; and in what has come to be an extraordinary action, he stands up and pulls down branch and bough mercilessly, self-assertively, in a pleasurable orgy of destruction. It is an action reminiscent of a child's attack upon its mother; and the consequence of all his expense of spirit is familiar enough, if Wordsworth's memory does not play him false: a sense of pain in seeing what he has done. Winnicott has written: 'In the play-analyses of young children we can see that the destructive tendencies, which endanger the people that the child loves in external reality and in his inner world, lead to fear, guilt and sorrow.'[11] Nor is this true only of people: the boy here, confronting 'the silent trees and intruding sky', feels painfully how much he has failed to measure up to the beauty and wealth he had earlier perceived in the landscape.

The languages of sexuality and imperialism in the poem serve this crucial sense of anticlimax, in which the discipline of pain and guilt was learned (and relearned). The language of sexuality, blended with the terms in which an infant might see its mother, is clear to see: the milk-white clusters were too tempting to resist, the virgin scene was ravished until, sullied and deformed, it patiently gave up its quiet beauty. In romance terms the rose in the garden has been torn down and, in terms of *Paradise Lost*, 'Earth felt the wound' (IX:782) – a bond of trust and love has been assaulted. This language, of course, in which the poet recognises the perverse in himself, is adult; yet it is true too to the rhythms and sexuality of a familiar pattern of childhood play, a pattern of which Winnicott wrote: 'if when a child is playing the physical excitement of instinctual involvement becomes evident, then the playing stops, or is at any rate spoiled'.[12] This throws interesting light on Hartman's description of the wavelike rhythms of *Tintern Abbey* in which 'the feeling of climax is avoided'. Here, however, the boy's play epitomises 'the wantonness in which we play / With things we love',[13] and we watch him pass through a variety of moods and pleasures into the instability of passionate climax and final disappointment. He has imposed a male aggression upon a Nature felt to be female (the delicacy of Wordsworth's animism suggests the classical world of dryad and hamadryad); and yet for all his doing it is the passive mutilated survival of nature after the full onslaught of his ravages that educates him in the consequence of his actions. For it is the survival of the bower that enables him to confront his own destructiveness, to create a value for passivity, gentleness and silence, and to teach the worth of a play and creativity grounded not in antagonism but in harmony, both with the world and with himself.

The language of imperialism too serves this final discipline of anticlimax. The plundering boy discovers a virgin territory that excites him to a merciless ravage of devastation; but when he turns away 'exulting, rich beyond the wealth of kings', he feels acutely the poverty of such wealth. *Nutting* explores the Tamburlaine hunger in man to incorporate all things into himself, especially all living beautiful things, in order to make them declare his glory; and it shows how the small boy who had eyed the banquet before him so eagerly was put in the way of learning that 'though eating may satisfy the desire to have the good thing in one's own possession, it certainly does not preserve that thing's essential identity and nature'.[14] Wordsworth suggests too, I think, that the agrarian capitalism of his day is possessed by something of this hunger. Certainly the poem makes a fascinating contrast with Thomson's celebration of nutting in *Autumn* (610–24). In Thomson we find that the whole hierarchy of natural creation is fulfilled in serving man, as the lower classes of the social hierarchy are fulfilled in serving the higher. But Wordsworth's aim was quite different, as a rejected opening to the poem makes plain:

> I was early taught
> To look with feelings of fraternal love
> Upon those unassuming things which hold
> A silent station in this beauteous world.
>
> (*PW* II:505)

The poem is describing one moment in the education of those republican feelings that had set Wordsworth against not only the lingering feudalism of the time but also against its agrarian capitalism and nascent utilitarianism, whose effects he was now beginning to identify and attack.

Nutting is an account of one of Wordsworth's 'primary consciousnesses' (*PW* II:440 n.). The silent beauty and the plenty of Nature aroused strongly ambivalent feelings in the boy (wonder and the wish to possess, love and the wish to destroy) and, through the temptation to violent action, furthered the long process of integrating them. Male and female, self and other, mind and nature – in one sense the point of the poem lies in its final moment of disillusion, which enabled the boy to begin to recognise and integrate these opposites. But in another sense the meaning of the poem remains incomplete; for everything it relates has gone into the making of the poet's sensibility and remains an active, unbounded power within it. What is important to grasp is Wordsworth's *gratitude* for his boyish destructiveness; for as Winnicott says, by virtue of the survival of the reality attacked, 'destruction plays its part in making the reality, placing the object outside the self'.[15] It saves the self, that is, from what Wordsworth called the 'abyss of idealism', the excess of subjectivity in which he was 'unable to think of external things as having external existence' (*PW* IV:463); and equally importantly it gives not only the world but also the self its sense of reality, enabling it to confront those aggressive impulses whose disavowal leads to feelings of futility and unreality. Perhaps the loveliest quality of the poem, the radiant affection of its mock-heroics, expresses this gratitude of the creative adult looking back to the playful child still unpredictably alive within him, its aggressive energies still surviving but disciplined now to a tender respect for the otherness of the world.

'There was a Boy' makes an interesting companion piece to

Nutting; it too explores, in a milder key, the growth of healthy creativity under the discipline of a nature which first provokes the boy to play and then transcends him. The play is enjoyed, under the eye of those first moving stars of evening, in a peopled solitude. Standing with fingers interwoven, palm to palm, hands raised to mouth, the boy, 'blew mimic hootings to the silent owls / That they might answer him'. The gratification of his sense of mastery and skill – part of the end of all play – is not the orgiastic pleasure that it was in *Nutting*, and the climax of satisfaction is correspondingly less troubled.

> And they would shout
> Across the wat'ry vale and shout again
> Responsive to his call, with quivering peals,
> And long halloos, and screams, and echoes loud
> Redoubled and redoubled, a wild scene
> Of mirth and jocund din.

The expectations of the waiting boy are transcended in the variety and wildness of the glee he both causes and shares; in such mimicry, such response and counter-response, the mind develops the relationships in which it lives.

There are times, of course, when the owls remain silent, apparently 'mocking' his skill. These are times of particularly 'feverish and restless anxiety' (*PW* II:440 n.) when the boy feels the possibility of blank desertion; and yet, as a parent weans a child from over-excited expectations of play with gentleness, so too the landscape gently weans the boy away from his anxiety. It is the complementary discipline to that of *Nutting*. With 'a gentle shock of mild surprise', the boy's mind passes from the activity of play to passive perception of the abiding independent beauty of nature. The wish to make the world answer him is succeeded in an instant by the answer of his own heart to the world. In Lindenberger's words, 'the outer scene assumes the active role which had earlier belonged to the boy'.[16] The fear of separation is dissipated in the transcendence of the self by a world that may be trusted, and the possibilities of reciprocal relationship are once again reborn. From the poem's opening line, with its confident assertion that the cliffs and islands of Windermere knew the boy, to its closing description of the uncertain heaven received into the bosom of the steady lake, it creates beautifully those extraordinary interfusions and interchanges characteristic of the reciprocities of sympathy. The scene passes into the boy's mind and becomes the geography of his imagination; its height, depth, movement, stillness, contrasts, moods and harmonies are the capacities of his soul.

The boy now is dead; in the 1800 version of the poem he died at the age of ten. Wordsworth seems to have wavered between making the poem autobiography or elegy, but his chosen form of elegy focuses our attention upon the possibilities of blank desertion that death may bring. The second paragraph repeats with adult sobriety the boy's experience in the first, its rhythms insistent upon the muteness of the poet's station by the boy's grave: 'A full half-hour together I have stood, / Mute . . .'. The poet's evening silence here after the excitements of the day parallels the boy's anxiety at the unresponsiveness of nature. Such moments of disillusion recur – and of comfort? If the poet's muteness is anxiety, it is also the genesis of elegy: the boy's mimic hootings have their precise equivalent in the mimesis of adult creativity, where the world also is recreated in play because it has already existed in reality. The difference between adult and boy, however, communicated in the much balder verse of the second paragraph, lies in the adult's consciousness of the finality of death – a consciousness in which his love of man and nature alike seems threatened, their excursiveness immobilised in his vigil by the grave. The poem has the open unassertive irony characteristic of so much Wordsworth. Like the Lucy and the Matthew poems, it is delicately aware of the possibility that disillusion may damage the mind irrecoverably; and delicately it tests that fragile equilibrium of the adult mind which in *Tintern Abbey* and *Nutting* had seemed so strong. Is it in this case sufficient to say that the playful boy is still alive in the creative adult? Will his 'feelings of fraternal love' for man and nature hold? These questions were to be worried again in the composition of the two-part *Prelude*.

11   The Two-part *Prelude* (1798–9)

> Was it for this
> That one, the fairest of all rivers, loved
> To blend his murmurs with my Nurse's song . . . ?

The questioning out of which the two-part *Prelude* grows shares something of the sad perplexity that prompted *Tintern Abbey*. It is inarticulate and confused, certainly 'self-reproachful' as Jonathan Wordsworth has said[1] in its contemplation of vast poetic tasks as yet unstarted, but – more importantly – it is anxious with fear of a much more fundamental failure, of which that poetic dilatoriness might only be an expression. The questions that Wordsworth puts to himself suggest the literary form of funeral lament for one who has died young, in a death which threatens the value of life for those who survive. Only relationship with the boy he used to be, alive within him, provided Wordsworth with the springs of coherent power and purpose; and suddenly he fears that this relationship has failed him. Is there relationship at all? and if so, is it creative or merely nostalgic? This last question points to the particular spiritual dilemma of the elegist, which Wordsworth had embodied in that problematical figure of the poet stationary by the grave in 'There was a Boy'; and it is a dilemma which he indicates again here by means of his allusion to *Frost at Midnight* in line 8. For Coleridge's hold upon the goodness of his own past life was always precarious, and in poem after poem, with the polarising logic of depression, he tends to define his present self in opposition to the blessed and happy. *Frost at Midnight* begins as a vexed meditation with the poet unable to escape the nausea of his own mirror image in the world around him; and though the gentle rhythms of his baby's breathing later recall him to the reality of relationship and stimulate his imagination to work in love, he can nevertheless only imagine vicarious enjoyment for himself in the future blessedness of his child. Similarly Wordsworth, in writing the two-part *Prelude*, is afraid he may only be able to find vicarious pleasure in contemplation of a distant childhood estranged from his present self; he is afraid that the adult and the child within may be at cross purposes.

As in *Tintern Abbey*, it is only gradually that the poet's perplexity yields to his understanding; for the poem begins with a blind turning back to childhood out of what Wordsworth later calls 'the weakness of a human love for days / Disowned by memory' (I:444–5). By the conclusion to the first part and the introduction to the second part of the poem, he has become able to articulate something of his fear of these seductive dangers of nostalgia, and also of his hope that he might harness the powers of his past to present enterprise. But he offers many different explanations of what he is about; and the tranquillity that has composed his spirit seems to express a dormant rather than an integrated anxiety. Still he is not sure of his relationship to his own past:

> so wide appears
> The vacancy between me and those days
> Which yet have such self-presence in my heart
> That sometimes when I think of them I seem
> Two consciousnesses, conscious of myself
> And of some other being.
>
> (II:26–31)

It is at best a fragile equilibrium; and yet by the end of the second part he is able with marvellous confidence to express a recovered faith in the creative powers of his own mind which is also a faith in the mind of man – 'a more than Roman confidence, a faith / That fails not' (II:489–90), he writes, and he writes it as he wrote in 1793, with 'a republican spirit'. As E. P. Thompson justly remarked, 'one must look far in European Literature to find any affirmation as proud'.[2] The two-part *Prelude*, therefore, resembles *Tintern Abbey* in this respect too, that it is only when we reach the end of the poem, where anxiety has relaxed and become intelligible, that we understand fully the sense of failure, of betrayal and loss out of which it began – a failure not simply of personal application but of European political liberation, in which the poet had momentarily lost his faith, his theme and his hope of an audience. I want now to trace the meditative process by which Wordsworth recovered that faith through recovery of the child within him.

If it is true that 'the mind of man is fashioned and built up / Even as a strain of music' (i:67–8), then the spots of time in the two-part *Prelude* are the great themes of Wordsworth's mind upon which his subsequent experience played its variations. Their re-creation in poetry is in itself reopening communication with the deepest powers of his life. However, there is a difficulty for the reader here: for we are dealing not simply with memories but with powers constitutive of the mind, not merely with meanings but with the makers of meaning, with experiences that transcend self-consciousness and create both the self and the world as they are lived. Despite the temptation to link the poem with Christian confessional writing like *Grace Abounding*, or with derivative forms like Rousseau's *Confessions*, the difference is crucial. For Wordsworth's spots of time, though attracting moral or religious ideas to them, surpass those ideas; and in consequence (this is the difficulty for the reader) they are communicated in verse of exceptional openness – an openness which emphasises both their primariness in establishing and sustaining consciousness and also their mysteriousness of origin and operation. The writing, unglossed as it is, is as difficult to interpret as a musical score. It denies us the familiar moral and sentimental landmarks by which we commonly know the world; for the morality which interests Wordsworth is not to be authenticated by appeal to an objective code or tradition but by appeal to the subjective quality of the relationships between the self and the world. In this way, it is not only difficult but subversive poetry: it is dedicated to the re-creation of powers that will transform present perception and open upon the future in quite unpredictable ways. That unpredictability, in fact, is its hope, its means of keeping faith with the future, its sense that the future is worth living at all.

'The Reader cannot be too often reminded that Poetry is passion' (*PW* ii:513): Wordsworth is offering a wholly new account of the nature and development of thought and the moral consciousness. It is an account grounded in a recognition of the primary importance of passion and of the fact that passion is relationship, which the mind experiences by means of imagery. 'Man thought and still thinks in images', wrote Lawrence;[3] 'no mind is more valuable than the images it contains', wrote Yeats.[4] Wordsworth too, over a century earlier, thought of the mind in terms of its formative images; and he too saw this as subversive of the utilitarian, rationalist civilisation of his time. To Wordsworth in 1798–9, the poet's business seems to have been to fulfil the democratic prose revolution of the seventeenth century in a poetic regeneration of man; and the two-part *Prelude* is his attempt to re-create in all their unpredictable strength and variety those passionate images upon whose regenerative powers his own mind depended.

They are images intertwined 'not with the mean and vulgar works of man,/But with high objects, with eternal things' (i:135–6) – and this, of course, is the heart of the counter-culture that we find throughout all versions of *The Prelude*. In DC MS.16 (Ms.18A), there are several blank verse fragments dating from this period that trace a variety of ways in which the official cultures of the day famished the mind by feeding it with mean and vulgar images. All kinds of pressure are brought to bear that inhibit the mind's capacity to symbolise: educational pressure (see the discarded preface to 'There was a Boy', *PW* v:345–6); economic pressure (see the story of the factory boy, in de Selincourt's apparatus and notes to *Excursion* viii:283–332); and, most striking of all, the ethical pressure to conform exerted by a pharisaical society (see the apparatus and notes to *Excursion* ix:1–152). This last passage is a wonderful attack upon the 'negative morality' whereby the false self is confirmed in its civilised compliance, and a celebration of the liberty brought by creativity:

> 'tis expressed in colours of the sun
> That we were never made to be content
> With simple abstinence from ill, for chains,
> For shackles and for bonds, but to be bound
> By laws in which there is a generating soul
> Allied to our own nature,
>
> (*PW* v:287 app. crit.)

Wordsworth's great argument is that our passions and feelings, alienated from us unequally as they are by everything that man has made of man, are nevertheless the 'birth-right of our being' (ii:316); and that the discipline of the relationships in which these passions and feelings find their images is crucial to the development of the sensibility. The two-part *Prelude* traces the symbolising process whereby Wordsworth himself came to feel at home in the world, first through relationship with his mother, then with nature and lastly with man; and it shows how each of these relationships, developing in its due order, comes finally to symbolise the others, so that it may make sense to speak of a mind peopled with natural forms or of kinship with the otherness of the created world. The poem, it seems to me, is a journey of self-discovery that proves to be, as all such journeys are, an act of faith – of faith in a benign religious universe and faith in a radical politic, certainly, but above all of faith in those feelings (that is, in those relationships) in the child that make such adult beliefs possible. They are feelings which Wordsworth reads in the colours of the sun; and the poetry sets out to re-create them in the trust that they will prove to be 'an active principle' spreading unpredictably far 'beyond themselves' (*PW* v:286 app. crit.).

Wordsworth distinguishes two ways in which the favoured being is disciplined by its guardian spirits:

>   I believe
> That there are spirits, which, when they would form
> A favored being, from his very dawn
> Of infancy do open out the clouds
> As at the touch of lightning, seeking him
> With gentle visitation; quiet Powers!
> Retired and seldom recognized, yet kind,
> And to the very meanest not unknown;
> With me, though rarely, [in my early days]
> They communed: others too there are who use,
> Yet haply aiming at the self-same end,
> Severer interventions, ministry
> More palpable, and of their school was I.

>   (1:68–80)

It was through the way of gentleness that the River Derwent wooed him in his infant days, its ceaseless music 'with its steady cadence' (10) tempering human waywardness and promising a future calm against which to measure the fretfulness of human life: so the poem's long second sentence encompasses human agitation and composes it to peace. His nurse's song and his dreams were blended with the moving river, his conscious and unconscious mind alike attuned to harmony in the play-area of their earliest relationships; and this archetypal power of Wordsworth's mind was over twenty years later to shape the course of *Tintern Abbey*.

The gentle discipline of beauty, however, although crucial to the balance of all the blank verse of 1798–9, is not the chief mode of his education. This is the one way, and the other is the same – the sublime discipline of 'severer interventions' working through more violent transcendence of the self, through fear or an exhilarated delight of the same family as fear. The episodes that follow (16–258) are all in illustration of the severer ministry of nature upon him: the boy's energetic games at Cockermouth, the trap robbing, the nesting, the boat stealing, the skating, the card playing and finally the description of the other childish sports of nutting, fishing and flying kites. The principle of intervention is in each case similar; the child absorbed in the rhythms of his own play is suddenly made conscious of other rhythms, of other modes of perception that transcend and claim him. The fantasies of omnipotence which he has ritualised in play suddenly yield to a sense of terror, of wonder or more simply of relaxed passivity in which he is made aware of his own smallness amidst a vast world. Nor is it simply that the world is vast, it is *transformed* to the boy's perception; and Wordsworth deliberately uses the playful language of nature spirits here to be true to his sense of metamorphosing powers that are subjective but that are imaged in the appearances of the objective world and are active in response to them. Unto every one that hath shall be given, and he shall have abundance. . . . It is only the child who can give himself to the excursiveness of play, impressing 'the characters / Of danger or desire' (I:194–5) upon the face of the world and subordinating it to his own subjectivity, who can find himself countered and transcended by such transformation.

The trap robbing may serve as our paradigm. In the uncanny nocturnal beauty of autumn Wordsworth delighted

> To wander half the night among the cliffs
> And the smooth hollows, where the woodcocks ran
> Along the moonlight turf. In thought and wish,
> That time, my shoulder all with springes hung,
> I was a fell destroyer.   (I:31–5)

The young boy was, archetypally, the Hunter, intent with passionate eagerness upon the chase, and the adult in his affectionately punning description of that little fell destroyer captures perfectly the child's self-absorption and self-dramatisation. Yet even in the anxious hurrying of his sport, he felt the weight of other modes of being on him; there were moments of delight not only in his hunting prowess but also in the beauty of the running woodcocks, in the exhilaration of late nights amidst wild moonlit landscape. That is, the wish to hunt down beauty (the wish later to drive Sir Walter in *Hart-Leap Well*) was but one of the responses available to the boy; and the excitement of the hunt that narrowed his response until he was aware only with dim unease of the eyes of the crags upon him was obscurely felt to be a denial of those other possibilities.

Occasionally Wordsworth's excitement led him to steal a bird from someone else's trap – a temptation to usurp the rights of others which the mature man sees as the archetype of his understanding of *Macbeth*, and which informed his own play *The Borderers*:

> and when the deed was done
> I heard among the solitary hills
> Low breathings coming after me,
>
> (I:45–7)

The allusion to *Macbeth* captures perfectly his appreciation of the child's dramatic sense of wickedness and instant retribution. The mysterious intervention of those low breathings among the solitary hills, of those strange sounds of undistinguishable motion, induced in him a sublime and guilty terror, a terror in which the limits of his anxiously relished mastery could not but be felt. As in *Nutting*, he could not rest in the unmediated exercise of cruel desire and the subjection of the world to his own uses. Through the counter-rhythms of terror, rooted deep in his earlier moral education and imaged in both the real and the hallucinated features of a loved landscape, he was given the opportunity later to confront his own ambivalence, to perceive his cruelty and rapacity as aspects of his love.

Clearly the meanings of such a passage cannot be encapsulated in an exhortation not to trap birds or not to covet the birds of others. Such negative morality denies the delight and energy in which the worth of the moment and its poetry lies. Eager to suppress naughtiness, it would suppress vitality too, and disavow the nodal complexity and rhythmic sequence of an experience in which ambivalence was learned amidst imagery that dignified it. Most importantly perhaps, terror was given its worth; for here it proved a sublime and liberating experience. It taught guilt, but not demeaningly, and it put the child in the way of learning the power of mind to transform the material world. Upon these powers the adult's mind has been raised, and for their energy of mischief and their discipline alike he feels gratitude.

The spots of time that make up the first 258 lines of the two-part *Prelude* arise from sports and play associated with the various seasons of the year's 'delightful round' (i:201) – a natural balance of discipline, it seems, that we can see in miniature in the description of autumnal kite flying:

> The kite, in sultry calms from some high hill
> Sent up, ascending thence till it was lost
> Among the fleecy clouds, in gusty days
> Launched from the lower grounds, and suddenly
> Dash'd headlong – and rejected by the storm.
>
> (i:242–6)

The ascent of the kite is the infinite wonder and exhilaration of the mind, its crashing down is turbulence and disappointment. The balanced difference in rhythm and syllable between those light aspiring lines and the veering plunge of the lines that follow expresses the adult's debt of gratitude to the harmony which the kite's behaviour has imaged between the various movements of the mind, one countering the other, each saved from dominance by the other. Such balance is especially important in the case of difficult emotions such as disappointment; the variety of the real world, even in its seasonal changes, saves the boy from its becoming the habit of his mind. So he felt together 'the growth of mental power / And love of Nature's works' (i:257–8).

Both the ascent of the kite into the clouds and its rebuff by the wind epitomise one feature common to all these spots of time in their pattern of transcended play: the sense that the world may not be mastered by the individual mind. Our feelings and passions look out everywhere through their relationships upon infinity of possibility. For instance, the experience of the boy as he daringly clung to the cliff-face, the ingloriousness of his pursuit utterly transcended in the generosity of the powers about him, can only prompt the adult now to awestruck exclamation at the transformation of the world he saw:

> With what strange utterance did the loud dry wind
> Blow through my ears! the sky seemed not a sky
> Of earth, and with what motion moved the clouds!
>
> (1:64–6)

The mind is not able to settle into cosy unchallenged familiarity with the world, to master it in a complacency of naming, even to transform it according to its own wishes. As significant to Wordsworth as the speaking face of nature that made him feel at home in the world is this indecipherable language of unfamiliarity; in the tensions of this balance is the stimulus to further growth and deepening relationship.

Even more striking is the experience of 'blank desertion' (1:124) which beset Wordsworth after he stole the shepherd's boat. The same boy who had rowed out across a scene of faery beauty in all the romance of adventure and pride of achievement rows back in guilty terror. The archetypal power of the adventure developed an insight into the nature of moral causality that Wordsworth later explored in *Peter Bell* – an insight not bounded by the naïve vocabulary of offence and retribution (though perhaps the child thought this way) but rather exploring the necessity by which pride, having first created the world in the image of its own glory, then experiences it in the image of its own terror. The sense of that seemingly final separation never left Wordsworth; such blank desertion was always for him the true measure of the worth of the connections of love. In the skating scene, the glory of skilful skating is succeeded by the exhilaration of a self-induced vertigo, common amongst children, in which the boy experiments with his power over the landscape. The potency of these experiments is in turn succeeded by 'a passive attitude towards his vertigo' in which he allows himself 'to enjoy it'[5] – a transition like that of Peter Bell from omnipotent fantasy to relaxed passivity, enabling communion with a world 'tranquil as a summer sea' (1:185) and releasing the mind from the dominion of will and senses alike. In

the card-playing scene, the splitting of the ice brings uncanny
fears and bookish thoughts of wolves in Scandinavia – fancies
which suddenly bring pleasurable outward-looking liberation to
the mind preoccupied with the pleasurable downward-looking
intensity of those fanciful card games. In each case nature frees the
mind from the narrowness of its play and the literalness of its
perceptions. Its discipline encourages the transformative power of
the passions and opens out on all sides upon a liberty where (in the
playful words of *Tintern Abbey*) the boundaries between inner and
outer 'lose themselves'. For the spots of time are, to quote Marion
Milner, 'moments in which one does not have to decide which is
one self and which is the other – moments of illusion, but illusions
that are perhaps the essential root of high morale and vital
enthusiasm for living'.[6] For the favoured being, secure in his trust
of a benign world, there is nothing to fear: even the experience of
separation enriches him.

The second half of the first part of the poem (258–412) invokes
spots of time – the drowned man, the visionary scene above the
gibbet and the homecoming before his father's death – that are not
regularly classifiable. They belong neither to the annual cycle of
Lake District life nor to the average expectation of Lake District
childhood; they owe their origin to accident and are particular to
Wordsworth. The raising of the drowned man from Esthwaite
Water is sublime in its lack of commentary. The strangeness of the
man's clothes at night, the darkening shadows on the calm water,
the occasional disturbance of a leaping fish all create a sense of
expectation, of unrealised potential, none the less to be
transcended next day when the corpse emerges bolt upright
amidst 'that beauteous scene / Of trees, and hills, and water'
(1:277–8). The terror of the moment impresses the natural beauty
of the landscape on the boy, but speaks too of human tragedy, of
disharmony between man and nature, of the insufficiency of a
human love that comes too late. This stark contrast is fertile for
the future of Wordsworth's poetry; and once again it maintains its
fertility for the poet because of his own basic trust in the
relationship between man and nature. It is a relationship that,
saving the mind from despair and yet always vulnerable, gives
tragedy its worth.

The visionary scene above the gibbet is even more remarkably
suggestive. The adventure aimed ambitiously high; the fearful
solitude; the subdued terror of the gibbet; the 'visionary

dreariness' (I:322) felt before the bare pool, the beacon and the girl
with the tossing clothes struggling into the wind – all the stages of
this history foreshadow later poetry of Wordsworth, and their
sequence too perhaps shaped poems like *Adventures on Salisbury
Plain* and *Peter Bell*. But it is in particular the desolation of the
journeying mind which has lost its guide, and the bearings that
link it in kinship to the world, which is the recurrent nightmare of
Wordsworth's poetry. It is in this moment that he must have
found his understanding of *King Lear*; for that rough and strong
moor, where human beings pursue their lives under hostile
conditions, is the landscape of his most characteristic studies of
human desolation.

What Wordsworth calls a kindred excitement was aroused by
his anxiety to return home for the Christmas holidays when his
father died. The child, finding himself in the naïve egoism of
childhood centre stage in the moral theatre of life, found in the
feverish impatience of his initial desire and the general sorrow of
subsequent bereavement a source of personal guilt that deserved
to be punished; and so he humbled himself before God. The adult
now, smiling at his earlier naïvety, nevertheless venerates 'the
deepest passion' (I:359) which drove the child to this submission –
a submission in which indeed the child's desires were corrected.
And yet the imagery the adult retains is at least as much of storm
as of submission, of passion as of discipline. The boy's 'anxiety of
hope' (I:357) survives, mediated by the recognition of the need for
discipline, in the adult's enjoyment of the wildness of storm and
rain – an excitement learned not in the school of negative morality
but in the play of childish turbulence. The first part of the
two-part *Prelude* celebrates this power of the passions; their
energy, character and interplay constitute the nature of the
individual mind, their imagery sustains it both in growing
familiarity with the world and growing independence from it, and
their balance secures its health. The unmoralised openness of
Wordsworth's writing is true to their primary power and abiding
creativity; for their nature is perpetually to challenge those
meanings that they constitute.

The second part of the poem deals with the growth of pleasure in
nature from a secondary to a primary power in Wordsworth's life;
it is concerned rather for the beautiful than the sublime, for the

blended feelings of the growing boy than the passions of the child. Its first half (46–236) deals no longer with those moments when the mind is surprised or shocked out of itself by the severer interventions of nature; instead, in mellower and more affectionate poetry, it dwells upon moments remembered with pleasure because nature reciprocated his love with abundance. Their epic sports, for instance, rowing on Windermere 'with rival oars' (II:56), foster a state of mind not found amongst the 'conquered and conqueror' (II:67) of old literatures. Selfishness and the pride in mastery are interfused with chosen objects that gradually subdue them, nurturing not a competitive or militaristic manhood but 'a quiet independence of the heart' (II:72). So the growing boy was matured out of those passions which most civilisations perpetuate into those feelings of fellowship and independence which will eventually sustain the republican hopes articulated in the poem's final paragraph; and an agent in this process was the various and the bountiful beauty of nature, sought out by the boy, and epitomised here in those three lake islands of Windermere towards which they used to race.

The excursions which follow, to Furness Abbey (twice), to Coniston and to the eastern shore of Windermere, are similarly moments where his pleasures in nature were transcended in the bounty he met:

> Thus day by day my sympathies increased
> And thus the common range of visible things
> Grew dear to me:
>
> (II:215–17)

Wordsworth is not only thinking of the increasing range of natural objects to which he feels affinity and for which he feels affection (the affectionate detail of the writing is important); he is thinking too of the increasing range and character of his own subjective life. The landscapes of nature were becoming the syntax of his sensibility; their imagery extended the powers and the *dramatis personae* of his mind. For example, during the excursions to and from the 'holy scene' (II:111) of Furness Abbey, peace gained upon the boy whilst he was galloping thunderously along the beach, whilst he was breathing his horse along the sides of steep hills and whilst dismounted amidst the abbey ruins – a characteristically balancing variety of natural abundance, both of landscape and of feeling, which can still move the adult with animistic gratitude to the spirits of nature. These excursions to that 'spot of holy ground' surely helped to form the nodal point of growth in Wordsworth's mind that later directed the search of *Descriptive Sketches*. Furthermore, the wren that he once heard singing sweetly to itself (an emblem recurring at the start of *The Ruined Cottage*) made him long, even when about to gallop home, to make that holy spot his permanent dwelling-place – an impulse that haunted Wordsworth always (and variously as in *The Danish Boy* and *Home at Grasmere*) in his wish for a home where he might write a poetry that would work in alliance with natural power.

Again, in the cloistral calm of Coniston, the dying sun (personified once more by the animistic imagination) prompted the boy to prophesy that his last thought would shine upon that scene – a 'memorial gleam' (II:171) in which we feel the awakening activity of a mind learning its own integrity in time and place, and in which we also recognise the elegist and writer on epitaphs that Wordsworth was to become. On Windermere, an evening's experiment in picturesque sensibility was transcended in the binding power of sky and lake upon the boy, holding him as though in a dream – that state where, in the relationship between self and other, subjective illusion is masterful and the conscious mind is passive. Increasingly at home in the world, the boy is made increasingly aware of the growing range and independence of his powers.

The retrospective movement in which Wordsworth meditates upon the beginnings of creativity in the relationship between mother and baby (II:267–309) is no casual interpolation but a crucial moment of the poem's development. It is here that, with gathering confidence, he first trusts himself to pass beyond the particularities of the spots of time to that more sustained, passionately philosophical verse which is characteristic of his maturity and which will finally support the 'more than Roman confidence' of his conclusion. He trusts himself to adventure more boldly upon the past and to surmise his beginnings in the mute dialogues which he held by touch with his mother's heart. The mother's arms, the mother's breast, the mother's eye – the baby learns to struggle, through the energy that love releases, to unify the promises of the vocabulary of the senses into the fulfilment of the syntax of mastered perception; and at the same time he learns a sense of the infinite and inexhaustible worth of what he perceives. His 'apprehensive habitude' (II:286) – a marvellous phrase, suggesting not only the physical movements in which the baby's mind grasps the world but also something of the necessary anxiety which is subsumed in happy play – works by the agency of his mother's love to create the world in its true bounty. I must declare myself at least one exception to Jonathan Wordsworth's assessment of this passage as 'nobody's favourite sequence of *The Prelude*';[7] for it is one of mine. Nor is this simply a matter of the truths that Wordsworth for the first time sees (and there is a sense in which one might describe the whole twentieth-century school of object-relations psychology as a systematisation of such insights as we find in this paragraph). It is also a matter of the way in which those truths are felt. Jonathan Wordsworth finds that 'the tones and rhythms are expository' and that the diction is 'sometimes very pompous'.[8] But to me the tones seem full of tenderness, gratitude and wonder at the ordinary miracles achieved by adequate maternal love ('*Bless'd* the infant Babe . . . !'); and the diction is extraordinarily careful in order to embrace the momentous psychological significance of the baby's rudimentary physical gestures. The passage is characteristic of Wordsworth's very best writing; it is a meditation for what *Hart-Leap Well* calls 'thinking hearts', written by a poet whose eyes are steadily fixed upon the particularity of his subject. Furthermore, and characteristically, although the two-part *Prelude* remains an intimate address to a friend tracing the author's development as a favoured being, this passage marks the moment when it begins to be transformed into a political credo; for Wordsworth sees in the infant sensibility the 'great birth-right of our being' (II:316).

His mother's love was the necessary precondition of Wordsworth's love of nature, and this later love (disturbing though it felt at the time) in turn sustained him when his parents died and left him orphaned (317–26). Love created the world and saved the baby from finding himself an outcast, and then the world extended that love and saved him again. The process of symbolisation that Wordsworth is describing is a virtually universal one as the horizons of our senses of home and excursion reach beyond the cot and out into the world where we all come to live; and the remainder of the poem describes the completion of that process. It is ground we have already covered with the pedlar: the boy matures through adolescence into adulthood, developing the complementary powers of 'this most watchful power of love' (II:340) and 'the visionary power' (II:360), so that nowhere is the world exhausted and the boy is led at last into the man's religious trust.

The climax of the poem subsumes the poet's love for family, nature and God in a passionate recovery of the political idealism whose loss we suddenly see to have underlain his initial confusion and betrayal. Now at last Wordsworth finds in himself the articulate strength to face the malice and mean-spiritedness of post-revolutionary Britain and to speak out on behalf of the common potential in man against

> all that silent language which so oft
> In conversation betwixt man and man
> Blots from the human countenance all trace
> Of beauty and of love.
>
> (II:502–5)

Now is a time of indifference, apathy and the exultation of bad men over good; of fear and the lack of moral courage; of the breaking of the bonds of trust and duty, when good men betray their beliefs for the pretended sake of quiet, peace and domestic love. Wordsworth walks like Christian through the wilderness of this world; even amidst such a 'melancholy waste of hopes o'erthrown' (II:479), he is preserved in a confidence cheerful and spontaneous beyond the willed restraint of stoicism. For he has taken firm hold on what inside himself he feels to be good. The powers of the spots of time have gradually restored him from self-doubt, from the fear of betrayal and the seductions of nostalgia into a renewed faith in his relationship with the world. This rediscovery of his own creativity is for Wordsworth a rediscovery of the potential of man in general; and it is the 'visionary' (II:486) quality of his republicanism that he emphasises most strongly, for it is here that the spirit of his childhood is most active in him. Grounded in the love and pleasure of his own familiar debts, the adult in his political faith can, like the child in his play, adventure upon the future with an energetic confidence in the worth of the world that love will introduce him to. Even in a time and place of disillusion, there is no need to despair of those aspirations whose beginnings he sees in the baby's struggle to bring his world into clear focus.

In the play of the child, the illusions of subjectivity are central; and the same is true of the play of the adult in affection, love, art, faith and value of all kinds. Equally central, however, is the discipline of objectivity; and what is interesting about Wordsworth is his concern to identify objectivity as potentially an ally to the development of subjectivity rather than as necessarily its enemy, the cause of its inhibition and frustration. He subsumes the oppositional cast of most radical politics into a vision of human possibility – based upon what seemed good in past experience – which he images most accurately in the marriage between mind and nature celebrated in *Tintern Abbey* and the *Prospectus* to *The Recluse.*

But all relationship is vulnerable. A full account of Wordsworth's poetry of 1798–9 would give weight to the Lucy and Matthew poems, short ballad utterances too sharp and ambivalent to integrate into meditative harmony, delicate witnesses to the dangers of idealisation and the possibilities of loss and disillusion beyond the reparative powers of elegy. They suggest the openness and tentativeness of Wordsworth's mind at this period; and so too does *Ruth*, a kind of miniature counter-*Prelude*. It is one of Wordsworth's most unsettling poems, not least because of the apparent conventionality of its narrator; and, point for point a parodic imitation of the two-part *Prelude*, it tells of two favoured beings whose liberty is licence. The wilfulness of Ruth's childhood play, for instance, is an escape from the slight of her father's remarriage; and it is the unresolved aggression aroused by this that leads to her future undoing. Her tragedy will be that she meets an illusionist, a young man who is seduced by the scintillating play of his own imagination and whom she, with nothing sufficiently good in her own past to steady her, idealises excessively. Before he deserts her, they live out one of those little sentimental idylls of love between two children of nature that had proved so attractive to eighteenth-century readers; and through this Wordsworth reinforces the purpose of his poem: to show the seductive power that nature may exert on minds insufficiently educated in 'the discipline of love' (*Prelude* II:281). The objective world has failed to do them justice, and they in turn fail to do justice to the objective world: as in *Peter Bell*, nature once more proves to be what men make of it.

But how shall we judge nature from nature? country from city? the mean and vulgar works of man from the worthy? the impurer from the purer mind? The poetry of 1798–9 seems to me, in its great variety of consciousness and its reluctance to trust itself to assertion abstracted out of experience, to refer these questions to the values and beliefs that we each of us evolve out of our early formative relationships. Wordsworth is aware of how much we make the world in the image of our own experience (we need only contrast the different religious consciousnesses in the Lucy poems, the two-part *Prelude* and *Ruth* to see that); and so here in the two-part *Prelude* he does what he knows he can do, he celebrates and argues passionately for the imagery of those relationships which he believes to be best in his own experience. He recognises, of course, that Coleridge had arrived at 'the self-same bourne' from quite different starting-places 'in the great city' (ii:496–9); and we today would arrive, if at all, there or thereby, by quite different roads again. But the questions that the poem raises still remain: how do we reconcile the contradictions between nature and man – that is, the contradictions within man himself – that are perpetuated by the societies and the natures that we have made? How most may we do justice to the objective world to make it most fully our ally? The contribution that the two-part *Prelude* makes to these questions lies in the challenge of the relationships that it champions, in the value of those 'feelings of fraternal love' that Wordsworth feels for man and nature alike. Power disciplined to tenderness: Wordsworth's love is preserved for him by the free play of the child still alive within him, composing the play of his adult verse into a hope for a future where all men might at last come home into the great birthright of their sensibility – as Wordsworth himself was now about to come home to Grasmere.

Part VII
The Grasmere Poetry of
1799–1800:
The Poet at Home

12   *Home at Grasmere* (1800)

The *Odyssey* is the epic account of Odysseus' return after many years of wandering to his home; the *Aeneid* is the epic account of Aeneas' military occupation of the territories which had been the homeland of his ancestors and which the gods had chosen now for the future centre of Roman civilisation. *Home at Grasmere* is Wordsworth's epic of homecoming. From its opening aerial survey of 'in narrow room nature's whole wealth'[1] to its final invocation of Urania, the poem demands to be read with reference to Western epic tradition. It uses the language of invasion, occupation and possession to refine it of its militarism; and it uses the language of the promised land and paradise to refine it of religious superstition. The poem is, as Hartman says, 'a personal myth-making';[2] but it looks far beyond 'the transitory Being' (1038) of the poet himself towards the creation of a history and a civilisation in which the radical regeneration of man would be at last complete. It is a millennial poem, looking for 'the milder day / Which is to come, the fairer world than this' (238–9); and its myth is thus a founding myth. To see the poem in this way is to begin to resist those charges of self-centring complacency which have been levelled against it.[3] To come home, as Aeneas found, was to struggle to establish empire. The poet too, in his higher aim to bind together 'the vast empire of human society, as it is spread over the whole earth, and over all time', is similarly committed to struggle. Simply, home is where one starts from, the necessary resting-place from which the mind makes its excursions.

Home is a matter of both time and space; and in *Hart-Leap Well*, a poem closely bound up with *Home at Grasmere*, Wordsworth sets out to explore the present in which he finds himself at home in relation to the past. The poem re-creates the vanished conditions of feudalism at its height when the glory of the local lord was the fulfilment of all inferior creation. Vassal, horse, hound, hart, woman, sculptor, minstrel, dancer, artists too, found their purpose in the service of their patron. Wordsworth (once a 'fell destroyer' himself, we remember) is imaginatively generous

189

towards the past and finds it in himself to understand the nature of Sir Walter's joy – his joy in mastery over man and nature alike. Yet the new poet that Wordsworth shows himself to be, as he journeys from Hawes to Richmond, is joyous in a new and gentler spirit of liberty. He is free to travel, observe, muse and converse as he will; he is free of the burden of patronage; and he is free to talk in genuine interchange to the shepherd who, for all their difference in class, seems to feel free too to talk, to fancy and indeed to tell the tale upon which the poem is based. It is this recognition of democratic advance already achieved, in which the poet has been freed and the vassal enfranchised, that constitutes Wordsworth's sense of being at home in the present; and of course to be at home in the present is to have hope for the future. Sir Walter's memorial to the quarry upon which he had proved his maistrye is succeeded by Wordsworth's own memorial poem, 'that what we are, and have been, may be known' (174); and by this memorial Wordsworth hopes to help advance 'the milder day' (175) when the transformation of the social order will be complete. He has come a long way from the desperate hope of *Descriptive Sketches*.

The place that Wordsworth chose for his home was Grasmere; and we shall see that the choice is as much a siting in time as in place. He was obeying the same impulse in his life that he had obeyed in his poetry, and it would shape the political content of his pastoral poems now as it had already shaped the content of his autobiographical verse – the impulse, that is, to face the future by securing to himself what he felt was best in the past. *Home at Grasmere* undertakes this with a fascinating mixture of confidence and trepidation, whilst the Grasmere pastorals undertake it as elegy; but elegy is an authentic mode of the radical imagination, and its end is the same – to lay hold of the good, even in the moment of its passing.

To understand fully what it was that Wordsworth found good in Grasmere, we should remember the extent to which the political economy of Adam Smith had entered the national consciousness. One correspondent in *The Monthly Magazine*, defending the 'consolidation' of small farms into one another, thought that *The Wealth of Nations* had persuaded everyone in Britain of the value of the free market economy, with the solitary exception of the man to whom he was replying:

The logic of Adam Smith has, at length, *almost* persuaded us to

think, that trade, and commerce, in general, will prosper most
when left to act alone, uninterrupted by any authority, but
reason; or any legislative restrictions upon the individual, but
such as are necessary to secure the more complete free agency of
the whole.[4]

This laissez-faire individualism and rationalism had been at the
heart of the radicalism of the early 1790s – for Paine, as E. P.
Thompson says, 'the *Rights of Man* and the *Wealth of Nations* should
supplement and nourish each other'[5] – and thus Wordsworth's
attempt to grapple in Grasmere with the principles of political
economy was also an attempt to resite radicalism itself, by
reference to a culture whose spirit was very different from that of
the capitalist enterprise which he now clearly identified all around
him.

The Wealth of Nations is a historical and scientific classic of a
historical and scientific age; and perhaps its most remarkable
feature is its assumption that economics is an independent
science, generally separable from moral considerations. Smith
was able to find it so in part because he had a supportive theology
that saw the mysterious workings of providence in the fact, visible
only to the adept, that the individual pursuit of self-interest
tended always towards the common good. 'It is not from the benevolence of the butcher, the brewer, or the baker that we expect our
dinner, but from their regard to their own interest'[6] – this famous
sentence encapsulates Smith's belief that it has been the desire
for self-betterment that has prompted the technological
achievements, and the increasingly complex division of labour, by
which man has transformed himself from hunter to shepherd, to
farmer and now to his highest stage of civilisation yet, to
merchant. *The Wealth of Nations* is a celebration of the capitalist
credit economy and its characteristic embodiment in the modern
city, where our political liberties have been won and where the
countryside itself has been freed from the stranglehold of feudal
power.

Smith's ideas were as widely accepted as they were convenient;
but of course there was resistance where there was hardship, and
E. P. Thompson has shown how in particular 'the final years of the
eighteenth century saw a last desperate effort by the people to
reimpose the older moral economy as against the economy of the
free market'[7] – an effort in which they were supported by a

scattering of old-fashioned paternalists. This is the background against which we must understand Wordsworth's choice of home – a *place* where he saw small independent statesmen working hereditary land with no real space for 'consolidation', and a *time* when he saw men still living at an earlier stage of civilisation with simpler technology and less developed division of labour. There are two aspects to this older economy that Wordsworth found in Grasmere which I wish to emphasise here. First, the aspect of community. It seems to me that what Wordsworth found in Grasmere was precisely equivalent to the total societies that twentieth-century anthropologists have found in primitive tribes:

> in these 'early' societies, social phenomena are not discrete; each phenomenon contains all the threads of which the social fabric is composed. In these *total* social phenomena, as we propose to call them, all kinds of institutions find simultaneous expression: religious, legal, moral and economic.[8]

Grasmere was just such a society for Wordsworth, enabling the individual to develop his capacity for symbolisation intelligibly, to begin to apprehend the whole in the part, and finally to fulfil himself in the community as it was spread over time and space; and the metaphoric richness of his moral language in the Grasmere pastorals is, as we shall see, his attempt to do justice to the interwoven fabric of that life. Second, and complementing this aspect of community, the aspect of independence. It seems to me that in Grasmere Wordsworth found an image of property as the guarantor of that independence of emotional life and moral judgement without which a man cannot begin to look upon himself as good. It is the most serious weakness of *The Wealth of Nations* that, as it reduces community to a collection of atomistic individuals, it strips those individuals of their virtue by depicting them as slaves of their own self-interest. In the particular circumstances of Grasmere, however, Wordsworth found an image of property as responsibility, an image of what was owned as what was owed, of individual possession as communal enrichment. Property might be this too. . . . Threatened as Wordsworth saw Grasmere to be, from without by market forces as well as from within by its own instabilities, it was the potential of this precarious actuality that he wished to celebrate. It was this good of an earlier surviving time that he wished to secure, and bequeath as part of the knowledge upon which 'the fairer world' to come might be built.

The road to reality lies through the country of romance; from illusion to disillusion, benign or intolerable, it is the road we all travel. The first movement of the meditation of *Home at Grasmere* (1–170) traces the composition and then, it seems, the realisation of a dream: a dream come true. The dream originated in a young boy's sense of the impossible; he came to the brow of a hill that overlooked Grasmere and, gazing down into what seemed paradise, wished with 'one bright pleasing thought' (14) that he might live, perhaps might die, there. Grasmere had power to stop him in mid-track, to transcend him even in the preoccupations of adventurous play; and his response to that power showed the mixed feelings typical of childhood. On the one hand, it left him feeling impotent: the happy lot of others could never be his, it seemed his destiny to be excluded from such bliss. On the other hand, he felt an answering power within himself: he felt the unrestrained liberty of an angel, and suddenly the freedom of all his boyish pleasures in play, nature, tales and reading seemed epitomised by what he saw before him. The bower, the secret garden, paradise, the promised land, the fortunate fields – around that one bright pleasing thought of the boy to live in Grasmere gathered all the possibilities of idealism and disillusion amidst which we live and which are embodied in the imaginative creations of our fantasy, our literature and our religious faiths.

It is wholly characteristic of Wordsworth to begin the poem with the re-creation of a childhood spot of time. He must keep alive that sense of illusion which has made Grasmere such a special place to him; and we shall seriously misrepresent the poem if we miss the trepidation and the fear of disillusion which has always accompanied that illusion and which is so important now in prompting the course of Wordsworth's meditation. It is no light task to trust oneself to making a dream come true. Those readings of the poem that find it full of self-regarding complacence seem to me to mistake those temporary resting-places where Wordsworth's anxiety relaxes for affirmations of settled purpose. But *Home at Grasmere* is an extended meditation which, like *Tintern Abbey* and the two-part *Prelude*, only gradually comes to compose itself and reveal its inner tensions. Wordsworth's hope (it is the

hope of his mature poetic and politic alike) is to keep alive those
substantial relationships with the past which he sees depend upon
illusion, and at the same time to avoid the sterility of disconnected
fantasising. It is a delicate distinction to make, and yet essential if
his ideals are to be more than self-born mockers of his enterprise,
more than 'a gleam of light' (51) that fades. We sense at once,
however, that the brightness of the boy's response has survived,
not merely in the adult's memory but (like all the spots of time)
formatively in the ground of his sensibility. We can hear it in the
exultation of his pleasure: 'And now 'tis mine for life' (52), he
cries, or

> The unappropriated bliss hath found
> An owner, and that owner I am he.
>
> (85–6)

The boy's delighted omnipotence is still alive; and it is fascinating
all through this long prelude to the poem to watch the ebbs and
flows of Wordsworth's mind as he disciplines his sense of
'conquest' (67) to 'gratitude' (104), his sense of possession to debt.
Gradually, without extinguishing his delight, he begins to involve
his imagination in the realities of relationship – relationship with
the rich bounty of nature and the lowliness of his own home,
relationship with his sister and (most difficult of all) relationship
with the other human dwellers in the valley.

The reluctance of the poem to make its human acquaintance
is one of its most remarkable features, and it testifies to
Wordsworth's fear of the possibilities of betrayal at the very heart
of his faith. The celebration of the natural beauties of Grasmere
which reaches so far into the poem (until line 357) is not simply
the expression of spontaneous joy but also an apprehensive
self-preparation for what is to come, for what Wordsworth regards
as the greatest test of all: the nature of human life in Grasmere.
The extraordinarily beautiful passage in which he describes his
journey there with his sister (216–77) illustrates perfectly the need
that he felt to arm his imagination with the illusions of romance;
for the passage, in its mode of fairy-tale or Spenserian romance,
ritualises all the anxieties and hopes of their journey into an ordeal
which, by proving their faith, continues now to strengthen it. It
had seemed, in the intensity of their feelings, that nature had
indeed been testing them. The trees, the brooks, the shower and

sunbeam had worn the ambiguous faces of their own doubts and
desires; the guardian spirits of Grasmere, and the Lares of their
own house, had seemed uneasy at their presence; and finally, even
in the seeming moment of their success, there had been the long
last ordeal of two winter months of Lake District storm. In the
language of romance, it had been a test of faithfulness on the very
eve of marriage, a test of strength to be met if man's mind is ever to
be 'wedded to this outward frame of things / In love' (1000–1);
and Wordsworth needed to feel the reassurance of his past
success, the present comfort of the guardian spirits of Grasmere,
as it were, in order to feel truly at home there. The play of such
innocent superstition is, of course, the stuff of life; and it is
important in reading the poem not to lose sight of the ordinariness
of Wordsworth's feelings, even as we appreciate their
particularity to himself as a poet.

Wordsworth, then, the apprehensive newcomer, comes to the
indigenous population of Grasmere strengthened both by
confirmation of his original resolve to live there and by celebration
of the natural beauty already encountered (most notably in the
marvellous virtuoso flight of his imagination in his description of
the waterfowl). Yet still his approach is revealingly oblique. He
notices the absence of the pair of 'milk-white Swans' (323) in
which he and his sister had imaged themselves; and suddenly
their absence seems to adumbrate the most painful separations
that life may bring. His reaction is a violent flashing suspicion that
the dalesmen may have shot at the birds, killing perhaps one or
both of them. A murder in Eden: such suspicion is a natural refuge
for disappointment, especially in the unsettled mind of a
newcomer, and it shows something of Wordsworth's unease about
the people around him. But there is something in what he already
knows of Grasmere that recalls him in contrition and provokes an
extended fantasy of quite another kind – a fantasy that the
inhabitants of so holy a place must needs themselves be hallowed.
In such a home there must of necessity be peace, goodwill and
innocent love for all creation. Willingly Wordsworth trusts himself to the healing stream of a fantasy whispered to him by the
presiding genius of Grasmere; for 'by such forgetfulness the soul
becomes – / Words cannot say how beautiful' (386–7). It is his
confident belief, embodied in the various meditative movements
of his poem, that everything in the mind – passion, feeling,
thought, dream, imagination, even the most idle and superstitious

impulses of fantasy – may be trusted in so far as it is responsive to what he calls, in the language of the Eucharist, 'the visible Presence' (388) of Grasmere. Once more we see the importance of the benign illusions of fantasy and romance to Wordsworth. On the one hand, his hope that Grasmere is a latter-day Eden leads him finally, by that familiar dialectical impulse at the root of his desire for truth, to inquire into the actual merits and imperfections of the men and women around him. But on the other hand, it only initiates such an inquiry when he is fortified by faith and hope, guarded against the threat of cynicism and (since dreams are known to be dreams) guarded too against the sterility of romantic fantasising. In a fine phrase, which points to the blend of ordinariness and ardent idealism that characterises the seeing of his poem, Wordsworth says he has not 'wholly overlooked the truth' (399); and yet he knows that, in order to hope, it is necessary to look beyond it. It is not a perfect world that he hopes to find in Grasmere but a world in which his imagery of perfection may interplay with reality without catastrophic disillusion, a world in which the illusions of fantasy may be confirmed in the knowledge that they have a contribution to make. In short, it is a home he hopes to find.

The poem's expanding circle of relationship – the natural world, the animal creation, the people – embodies an actual process of making acquaintance in a new home; and now, smiling at the fantastic fears aroused in him by that 'awful voice' (407) of shepherd summoning his sheep, he is able at last soberly to assess the realities of the world he has chosen. What he sees in Grasmere is a subsistence economy free from extreme poverty and founded upon the independent ownership of hereditary smallholdings; and although men are much the same here as elsewhere, there are two great privileges that Wordsworth values – the fact that labour is a 'Freeman' (443) and that the charitable impulse is not overwhelmed by demands made upon it. Independence and community: men are in great measure in control of their own lives and also able to relate freely to others. Wordsworth's intention is quite clear. It is not to escape from the outside world (though of course he feels the wish to); it is not to turn the outside world into Grasmere (though he feels the wish to do that too); it is to bear witness to his own sense of the good, of what it might mean to be at home in time and space, in order to venture upon the unpredictability of the future.

At this stage in the poem, Wordsworth tells three histories to illustrate his growing acquaintance with the individual lives of Grasmere and his sense of the enrichment that its culture brings (469–645). It is an examination which is also a self-examination of his own hopes. The first tale, that of the so-called scholar, seems to me a stirring piece of work, a negative paradigm of everything that the poem understands by home. Wordsworth sees that the subsistence economy that may promote a modern heroism of austerity in some may mercilessly expose even the smallest faults in others. Here the scholar's small taint of generous carelessness and his wife's slight house-proud ostentation brought about a financial and then an emotional stress in which he seduced a young maid living under his roof. 'Wretched at home, he had no peace abroad' (517): the rhythms of relaxation and excursion are hopelessly disturbed.

> His temper urged him not to seek relief
> Amid the noise of revellers nor from draught
> Of lonely stupefaction; he himself
> A rational and suffering Man, himself
> Was his own world, without a resting-place.
>
> (512–16)

It is the nightmare that Wordsworth first explored in Rivers; and here the scholar is driven to the counter-creation of the world in the image of his own shame. The homeless twistings and turnings of his mind are a parodic opposite of the meditative tide of Wordsworth's own thoughts as seen in the poem; and yet the social conditions of Grasmere dignify his shame and give it a tragic intensity which Wordsworth works hard to recapture. The second tale, the tale of the widower's household, is a happy celebration of God's bounty in making returns far beyond what is taken away: a house which had lost its mistress found in its six growing daughters an abundance of gaiety, labour and fanciful invention, and a garden is created in the wilderness. If the first tale was pastoral tragedy, this is a pastoral of the golden age recovered; and the third tale, the widow's tale, is different again, tracing beautifully the height of Wordsworth's ambition in pastoral elegy. The variety of these histories shows that Wordsworth has already found in the people of Grasmere that sense of imaginative plenitude which he had found at once in

nature; and at the same time it shows his growing wish to bring
about an interplay between the various idealisms of past literary
convention and the present realities of life, humanising the former
as it dignifies the latter.

The confident security in which Wordsworth turns to his sister,
in the certainty that their choice is not a human solitude, prompts
a revaluation of everything that we have so far read; for once more,
characteristically, a fear that had been too deep to articulate has
been faced in the moment of its dispersal. It was a fear natural to
someone who would centre his whole understanding of man in
Grasmere: a fear of being misplaced, desolate, profligate of
feelings and fancies that were no more than subjective illusion and
would die with him.

> We do not tend a lamp
> Whose lustre we alone participate,
> Which is dependent upon us alone,
> Mortal though bright, a dying, dying flame.
>
> (665–8)

Wordsworth had been afraid of the kind of solipsistic
consciousness that he had portrayed so vividly in *The Danish Boy*,
whose central figure is a kind of homeless nature-spirit,
characterised (in Geoffrey Hartman's words) 'by no qualities
other than persistence, imaginative fixation, and the sadness of
incompletion'.[9] We can sense now that such a fear must have lain
behind the force of his earlier possessiveness as he approached
Grasmere; and what has saved him, of course, is what most he
feared he would lack – the excursiveness and reciprocity of human
fellowship.

More confident now in his participation in the human realities
of Grasmere, Wordsworth turns back from man to 'other
loves / Where no fear is' (720–1) – a return which is in part the
pleasure of recapitulation, in part the further extension of
sympathy, and in part the simple pleasure of classification,
placing his sympathies for birds and animals in just relation to his
sympathies for man. This new movement in his meditation
(720–874) rises with a gathering enthusiasm until finally he
completely overturns his original fear of isolation: isolation is not
here but everywhere else.

                    Society is here:
The true community, the noblest Frame
Of many into one incorporate;
That must be looked for here; paternal sway,
One Household under God for high and low,
One family and one mansion; to themselves
Appropriate and divided from the world
As if it were a cave, a multitude
Human and brute, possessors undisturbed
Of this recess, their legislative Hall,
Their Temple, and their glorious dwelling-place.
                                        (818–28)

This is an enthusiasm in which the idealisms of pastoral and classical republicanism blend, not to picture the truth of common day but to give voice to an aspiration delighted to find that, after all, it may breathe the air of common day. It is the buoyant relief characteristic of all new love that Wordsworth feels: that the airiest illusions of secret hope have taken on body, that life has kept faith with us. It is an experience in which (to quote the marvellous phrase from Ms.D) the line is invisible 'that parts the image from reality' (577); and Wordsworth is happy to enjoy the play of his mind whilst it lasts. Even if finally his enthusiasm passes, he concludes, nevertheless he and his sister, family and friends have joy enough to make themselves at home in Grasmere.

A new energy, sustaining the poem to its end (875–1048), springs from this resting-place. Suddenly the bounds of Grasmere feel restrictively narrow; his delight in home and nature, his restless energy and uneasy conscience, the imperative light of his own 'internal brightness' (886) all demand that he too, like the other inhabitants of the valley, should find a labour answering to his pleasures and his powers – and it will be a labour that will bring the seclusion of Grasmere into relationship with the larger world beyond. Yet it is typical of Wordsworth that, even here as he contemplates his own future, he should choose a language which suggests his sense of kinship with the dalesmen, his sense of similarity with them which humanises his sense of difference:

Possessions have I, wholly, solely mine,
Something within, which yet is shared by none –
Not even the nearest to me and most dear –

Something which power and effort may impart.
I would impart it;

(897–901)

His possession must be shared – and his sense of possession as responsibility, of property as inheritance to be laboured over and bequeathed, lies at the heart of Wordsworth's Grasmere poetry. It is perhaps most clearly seen in *Michael*, but it is evident in *Home at Grasmere* too, where the poet inherits the literary genius and idealisms of the past and works upon them according to the light of a historically new vision. Epic, romance, pastoral, tragedy, fairy-story, even the heroic adventures he had heard whilst a boy – for characteristically Wordsworth prepares himself for his labour by once more recalling his boyhood, in particular his unruly disobedience and his responsiveness to challenge. His most compelling memories are of the delight and exaltation that he found in the blind desire to dare all limits and pit himself against all dangers: 'deep pools, tall trees, black chasms, and dizzy crags' (918). Although subsequently Nature has helped to confirm in him the female principles of gentleness and calm, he sees that nothing has been wholly lost and that nothing needs to be denied. The boy's uncompliant independence and his wish to dominate reality, together with the adult's acquired gentleness of respect for reality, will cooperate to direct the enterprise upon which he is about to embark.

The 'great argument' (1014) of his work will be that of the new creation that might be wrought by the consummation of love between mind and nature. The heroic days have gone, as we saw in *Hart-Leap Well*, when the aspirations of men and nations were to be fulfilled through the glory of their leaders. Instead, Wordsworth looks forward, in a full expression of his republican hope and his faith in man's perfectibility, to a millennium 'of joy in widest commonalty spread' (968). The perfection which he anticipates will be grounded in a sense of the fittedness not only of mind to world (the scientist's emphasis upon the final irremovable facts of objectivity) but also of the world to mind (the poet's emphasis upon the final irrepressible facts of subjectivity). In the right relationship between these two emphases, of mind saved from exile by reality and in return made conscious of its own independence, Wordsworth finds the balance of his theme: man and nature, and what may be achieved in the play-area between the two of them, dependent upon the quality of passions and feelings at work.

Wordsworth speaks of himself as a prophet in these closing lines; and suddenly Grasmere is the promised land no longer. For the prophet is in the wilderness, preceded by the tents of beauty as the Israelites were led by Jehovah and his tented ark past 'the tribes / And fellowships of men' (1016–17). From this new perspective Grasmere is no more than one man's resting-place in the long homecoming of history. The poet cannot fully be saved from his alienation until the final regeneration of man is complete; and it is in this recognition that Wordsworth, with his own particular blend of the heroic and the tender, sets about his epic task of reestablishing those connections between Grasmere and the outside world which he had earlier seemed glad to break. For now more than ever before in epic man is seen to be at the centre of his own history, responsible for the world he sees and acts upon, and obliged by the best of what he inherits to work for the best in the future. Not only is this belief of Wordsworth's evidenced in his imitative method, reclaiming the literature of the past on behalf of 'the progressive powers' (1007) of the whole species. It is seen too in his conception of the moral life, where the favoured being of the poet must repay what he has received and make his life 'express the image of a better time' (1045); and also it shapes his political understanding, where the boy's vision of Grasmere has been made good in the adult's possession and bequeathed as a guide to accompany him on his adventure into the unimaginable future.

It was the subsistence economy, the patrimonial tradition, and the natural beauty of Grasmere that gave Wordsworth the confidence to trust himself to voice his prophetic hopes, both for himself and for man – hopes which are in themselves enrichment in so far as they seem to work in alliance with reality. Some of his hopes for himself were fulfilled and some not, as is the way; but his hopes for man were set in opposition to a social reality that was all the time confirming the capitalist connections between Grasmere and the outside world and threatening to destroy all the relations that Wordsworth valued. It was this process that he explored in his Grasmere pastorals.

13   The Grasmere Pastorals

Wordsworth apologised in a note to the *Lyrical Ballads* edition of *The Brothers* for the abruptness of the poem's start: 'This Poem was intended to be the concluding poem of a series of pastorals, the scene of which was laid among the mountains of Cumberland and Westmoreland' (*PW* ii:467). The second volume of *Lyrical Ballads* was a much more local collection than the first, largely devoted to Wordsworth's home-making in Grasmere; and many of its poems – short ballads and tales, short inscription pieces and the beautiful *Poems on the Naming of Places* – may have been destined for that projected volume of pastorals. The range of voice in the poetry is remarkable. At one extreme is the pastoral ballad, poems like *Andrew Jones* and *The Childless Father*, of which Stephen Parrish has written: 'by adapting the form to a homely and realistic purpose, carried out with jocular buoyancy, Wordsworth would have been accomplishing the sort of parody he had earlier managed by adapting the form of Bürger's ballads of terror to *The Idiot Boy*'.[1] The tone of these ballads is pastoral in a full sense of the word: they might be the affectionate words of a pastor possessed of great gaiety of spirit, participating in the interchanges of village society with tender indulgence, gentle reprimand or irresponsible idleness as circumstances prompt. They have a deep sanity of tenderness, expressed in many moods and quite unsubdued by the occasional meannesses they meet; their paternal feelings (strength and authority used with gentle respect) are quite free from paternalism. It is, however, upon a quite different form of pastoral that I wish to concentrate here – the long pastoral elegy of *The Brothers* and *Michael*, which saw Wordsworth's most powerfully felt adaptation of the pastoral genre and in which he was most free to bring into play the ideal value which he found in ordinary feelings. It is also the form through which he chose to engage with the economic and political debates of his day; and it is for this reason that I have postponed until now my discussion of *The Old Cumberland Beggar*, a poem written two years earlier than *The Brothers* and *Michael* but published with them and possibly intended too for that unfinished volume of Lake District pastorals.

(a) *THE OLD CUMBERLAND BEGGAR* (1797–8)

The Old Cumberland Beggar is a poem which often embarrasses the modern reader with the suspicion that it may, in the words of Mary Jacobus, 'equivocate with suffering'.[2] But such suspicion seems to me groundless; the purpose of the poem was to enable its readers to find in contemplation of the beggar their sense of 'kindred with a world / Where want and sorrow were' (107–8), and thus to intervene in that world only in ways sensitive to the obligations of such kinship. Wordsworth is well aware of the beggar's wretchedness and the abject poverty of some of the villagers from whom he begs. Yet he sees too that men and women, even in suffering and penury, may find values, derive benefits and enjoy connections whose casual destruction in the interests of social hygiene or enforced welfare may leave their last state worse than their first. The poem's respect for things as they are does not preclude hope of improvement; rather it guards against overhasty interference.

The subtitle to the poem in *Lyrical Ballads* is 'A Description'; and from its opening line ('I saw an aged Beggar in my walk') to its last ('So in the eye of Nature let him die'), *The Old Cumberland Beggar* embodies in its gathering complexity of relationship what it meant for Wordsworth truly to see. Its beginnings seem quite casual: subject perceives object in the familiar manner of scientific observation. At once, however, as the poetry moves on, we sense that the motive for Wordsworth's meditation lies in the insurmountable difficulty presented to his mind by his apparently simple observation of the beggar. He scans his scraps of food 'with a fix'd and serious look / Of idle computation' (11–12): what *can* he be thinking? Through Wordsworth's scrupulous and wondering attention to what he sees, we apprehend the width of the gulf between subject and object – a gulf not of space but of imagination. Certainly Wordsworth's careful description is a mode of respect for the beggar; but more than this, it is an attempt to cope with the bafflement he feels before a distance which his sympathies cannot cross – what can it be to be such a man? No wonder that Wordsworth concentrates upon the old man's doings, that his sentences sometimes veer away from the man and seek to know him in the things around him. Yet the beggar's presence recalls him, disciplines him again to almost prosaic, wondering attentiveness. The verse succeeds by its chastity, by its exclusion of those easy feelings (pity or compassion) which we might expect to bridge that gulf between them. Wordsworth is unmoved by the temptations of the picturesque, whose visual arrangements are also arrangements of our moral responses into the old familiar categories of paternalism: the Discharged Soldier, the Evicted Tenant, and so on. The literature and visual arts of the period are full of such pictures, aimed directly at arousing our pity; but Wordsworth's meditation is committed to an unknown future and to unprescribed feelings, as it follows the impulse of that initial disturbing wonder: 'I saw an aged Beggar . . .'.

The beggar seems wholly alienated from the natural and human stimuli of the world about him: 'one little span of earth / Is all his prospect' (50–1), says Wordsworth in a terse and troubling pun, and yet (because he looks) he sees that the beggar quite unknowingly exercises power upon that world. The toll-gate keeper leaves her work to open the gate for him; the post-boy amends his rattling pace without resentment; the sauntering horseman-traveller no longer tosses his alms upon the ground in the carelessness of opulence but places it carefully in the old man's hat and then turns back to look at him 'sidelong and half-reverted' (32) – in such small, even ambiguous impulses, for which Wordsworth scrupulously makes no large claims, the old man's presence is felt. He has the same effect upon others that Herbert and Matilda had; by the power of his helplessness he makes them adjust their pace and purposes to his own – adjustments of an almost automatic kind, yet without which there would not even be the possibility of the beginnings of sympathy. The poet too, halted in his walk, has adjusted the pace of his thoughts to the beggar's movement: 'on the ground / His eyes are turn'd, and, as he moves along, / *They* move along the ground' (45–7). The stumbling obstinate trudge of the rhythms in these two first paragraphs is the mode of Wordsworth's persistent scrutiny of the old man.

It is not only the helplessness of the beggar that disciplines the poet, however; it is also the power of the archetype that Wordsworth senses in him. Throughout the second paragraph it seems that the significances which gather around the old man are for Wordsworth, as he recollects all that he has seen and known of him, obscurely emblematic. The extreme old age that teases out of thought, the solitary traveller on the highway, the prospect of a little span of earth . . . these intimations, crystallising later into the perception of the beggar as 'a silent monitor' (115), enrich and

generalise the course of Wordsworth's meditation. The beggar
suggests what might have been, what might yet be, for all men: the
thing itself, unaccommodated man on his comfortless journey
from cradle to grave. He is an extraordinary figure; and the
extraordinary nakedness of his insentient solitude has power to
make men reflect afresh on their own lives, to appreciate anew the
value of the society they enjoy and to do so in a way sensitive to the
humanity that the beggar shares with them. The man who seemed
at first so alien is able to reconstitute, variously for various people,
their sense and understanding of society.

'Him even the slow-pac'd waggon leaves behind' (66) – at this
point Wordsworth too leaves the beggar behind him and turns
suddenly to challenge the politicians and political economists of
his day with the new insight that the beggar has afforded him into
his own understanding of society. He challenges the seeing of the
statesmen with his own: in their restless desire to reform the Poor
Laws (for parish relief was hopelessly unable to cope with new
urban densities of population), they are unable to adjust their
pace to the rural beggar that Wordsworth sees. In fact, says
Wordsworth, what they see is the reflected image of their own
'talents, power, and wisdom' (72). *Their* beggar is a nuisance, 'a
burthen of the earth' (73) – two legal terms emphasising the drain
upon the resources of others – and therefore, their argument will
run, he must be put to work in a workhouse to pay for the benefits
he receives. Adam Smith had grounded his sense of society in
man's innate (or rapidly acquired) 'propensity to truck, barter,
and exchange one thing for another';[3] and clearly each man must
have something material to contribute, since it is in vain to expect
from others' benevolence the help we can only secure from their
self-interest. Wordsworth's attack is directed here against a
utilitarianism which argued for the centrality of self-interest and
the final test of utility in human affairs, and whose assessment of
human contribution and exchange was always narrowly financial.
His evidence is what he sees in the total society of the Lake District
villages that he knows.

Wordsworth sets out to reconstitute the language of social and
political debate by appeal to an older religious language of natural
law – a natural law stating that good and evil were to be found
intermixed in all things earthly. 'Good and evil we know in the
field of this world grow up together almost inseparably', wrote
Milton in *Areopagitica*.[4] 'There is some soul of goodness in things

evil, / Would men observingly distil it out', Shakespeare has
Henry V say before Agincourt (iv:1:4–5). Characteristically it is
the good that Wordsworth sets out to find before demanding
change; for nothing – not even the beggar, he concedes ironically
to the statesmen – is wholly abandoned to evil. Gradually he
builds up the balance of his case. The beggar's visits sustain the
unlettered villagers in habits of charity and moods of kindness
which might otherwise wither into selfishness, and upon whose
survival the future possibility of their pleasure in conscious virtue
depends. Stronger minds find in the beggar's wretchedness the
first impulse of fraternal thought that binds them to a world of
want and sorrow. Other easy, well-to-do minds behold in the
beggar a silent monitor who makes them momentarily count their
blessings, even if (more grasshopper than ant) they take no
thought for the future. Others again delight to give and build their
hope in heaven. In each particular case – and Wordsworth once
again scrupulously makes no large claims – the old man prompts
feelings that are not merely self-interested. Sometimes they are
feelings which tend to 'refine the selfishness from which they
spring' (*Home at Grasmere*, 675) and sometimes feelings whose
benevolence seems to outweigh by far their self-interest; but
either way Wordsworth shows the political economists wrong in
vital ways. First, he shows that self-interest and benevolence in
the mind grow up together almost inseparably; and thus it is false
to construct a model of the world upon the former to the exclusion
of the latter. Second, it follows that men do not only think of
property in terms of the rights of possession but also in terms of the
duties of responsibility – in terms of what Wordsworth calls boon,
exemption, charter, words that reclaim old traditions of feudal
and Christian reciprocity for a modern republican consciousness.
For there is a kind of self-comparison with others that rises above
the meannesses of envy and vainglory, to ground our sense of
human difference in the fraternal recognition that 'we have all of
us one human heart' (146). Third, Wordsworth wants to honour
what is best in the mixed nature of men so that, enjoying being 'the
fathers and the dealers out / Of some small blessings' (143–4),
they may increasingly act their place in God's world, which is
itself upheld in the reciprocity of gift and debt.

   The final paragraph of the poem draws out the implications of
its religious language fully. It opens with the poet's gift of blessing,
his pastoral laying on of hands like a priest who feels and speaks in

accordance with the will of God; and it closes boldly in his faith that he has come like a prophet to see with the loving eye of God, sustaining in his poem the totality of the beggar's world as the eye of God in medieval painting sustains the totality of creation. 'Reverence misery': Herbert had tried to recall Mortimer from overhasty judgement and the hubristic belief that he could set the world to rights in the image of his own desires. Similarly Wordsworth's injunction to the statesmen that they should reverence the beggar's hope tries to recall their attempt to reconstruct the world in the workhouse image of a capitalist economy. Foucault has written of the 'restructuring of social space' that accompanied the internment of the various failures of bourgeois society who proved unable 'to participate in the production, circulation, or accumulation of wealth';[5] and of course it was a restructuring of inner space too. Against the cramped enforcements of the workhouse, Wordsworth pleads passionately for the *spaciousness* both of the beggar's liberties, harsh as they are, and also of the old rural economy upon whose charities he depended. 'Then let him pass, a blessing on his head!' – Wordsworth repeats the line as though to ensure the beggar's free passage across time and space alike. But the poem is an elegy for a class that Wordsworth believed would 'probably soon be extinct' (*PW* IV:445); and it is we who are the losers as much as the beggar. For the punishment of deviant behaviour of all kinds, like the institutionalisation of old age and charity in the arrangements of the welfare state, removes from our *presence* the monitors in whom we might see the need to reconstitute our society. The poem's purpose, authenticated in the clearsighted study of an older culture, is the regeneration of the new; and this is yet to be achieved.

(b) *THE BROTHERS* (1799–1800)

The Brothers is an elegy told by a poet conscious that his pastoral cure is both much wider than, and at the same time kindred to, the cure of the Anglican priest who is one of his central characters. Both the Ennerdale priest and the stranger returning home from slavery in North Africa are his parishioners; and in a dialogue where, despite increasing rapprochement, Leonard and the priest are unable to achieve full reciprocity of feeling, Wordsworth's success is the establishment of a language and poetic style able both to appreciate and to harmonise the differences between them. The poet perfects the work of the priest. He writes pastoral to bring under one discipline the rural community he describes and the larger world for whom he describes it; in a language and style whose heart is Ennerdale, he writes one of its remembered histories to claim its place in 'the great book of the world' (270).

Donald Davie found the verse of *The Brothers* 'undistinguished, and barely adequate';[6] but it is a verse consciously adapted to genre, a plain style dedicated to the ideal and inexhaustible wealth which it enables us to find in the most ordinary feelings. Even its narrative is the history of feeling:

> Towards the field
> In which the parish chapel stood alone,
> Girt round with a bare ring of mossy wall,
> While half an hour went by, the Priest had sent
> Many a long look of wonder, and at last,
> Risen from his seat, beside the snow-white ridge
> Of carded wool which the old Man had piled
> He laid his implements with gentle care,
> Each in the other lock'd; and, down the path
> Which from his cottage to the churchyard led,
> He took his way, impatient to accost
> The Stranger, whom he saw still lingering there.
>
> (25–36)

The rhythmic attentiveness of such writing is remarkable, a mark of Wordsworth's respect for the pace of the old priest and the emotions moving his mind – the pull of his curiosity, the story of that little ritual disposition of the implements he loves, the slow progress of his impatience down the path. Wordsworth's sympathy is rich with a variety of affectionate tones, none of which tends to diminish the priest; on the contrary, the plain and precisely weighted language venerates him in the habitual substantial relationships of his life. The writing is sacramental honouring the sublime truths that lie in everyday relationships; and in so doing it aspires towards the memorial power of that plain unornamental graveyard which it describes, opening out on all sides upon the infinite and eternal worth of life.

The priest's gossipy curiosity about the stranger is, in its freedom from malice, a mode of the wish to love. Knowledge is relationship; and characteristically Wordsworth celebrates in such simple everyday interest in the affairs of others that fundamental excursiveness of mind through which we each come to claim our kinship with the world. The priest on his way down the garden path is obedient to one of the most elementary motives of human nature. What is more, his presentiments that the stranger is a tourist, quite mistaken as they are, lead us straight to the heart of the poem; for Wordsworth's subject in *The Brothers* is the spiritual value and the spiritual danger of those 'hauntings from the infirmity of love' (236) which necessarily people our solitudes. The priest's curiosity and fantasies about Leonard adumbrate Leonard's own more passionate curiosity and fantasies about the fate of his brother; and still further into the poem Wordsworth depicts Leonard's calenture, creating land out of water, and James' somnambulism, creating land out of air. The priest in his gentle spirit of complacent mockery had expected Leonard to be a tourist; yet tourists too, living 'as if the earth were air' (3), are also haunted by the infirmity of love – and not only tourists but poets too, that other kind of scribbler and idler. They all in their own particular way search out relationship and love in their self-pleasing solitudes. Once again Wordsworth's subject is one in which he perceives human identity behind apparent difference; and it is a subject which finds its perfect setting in a country graveyard.

The dialogue that develops between the priest and Leonard in the graveyard explores both the creative and the destructive hauntings of love; it explores both fantasies that enrich and fantasies that embitter life. Quickly we sense how deeply the priest feels at home in Ennerdale. It is a society which, like that of Grasmere, we might also call a total society; for once more the fixity of social role is accompanied by a rich imaginative flexibility, so that each part of life seems to symbolise the whole and each man lives in the people and things around him. Everywhere we find the blurring of boundaries, the line invisible that parts the image from reality, and each man made of many beings. Walter Ewbank is one example of this in the poem, for in him youth and age, grandfather, mother and father meet; and the priest himself, of course, is another, made up of all the histories of all the valley lives he knows. He is no different from the other dalesmen in this. For the most strikingly blurred boundary-line in the poem is that between grave and surrounding turf: 'the dead

man's home / Is but a fellow to that pasture field' (174–5),
Leonard says, and is told at once that the Ennerdale dead need no
gravestones since they possess 'a kind of second life' (186) in the
living. Reciprocally, the living possess a kind of extended life in
the dead; and this is amongst the chief causes of the almost sublime
composure of the priest's heart.

> The thought of death sits easy on the man
> Who has been born and dies among the mountains.
>
> (183–4)

He is unafraid, in the appropriate winter season, to turn over (as
he puts it) the graves of the churchyard; the hauntings of past lives
hold no terrors for him, pain and death have their place at his
fireside. He enjoys an imaginative plenitude in Ennerdale; and if
this is responsible for an element of comic complacence in his
garrulous approch to Leonard, it inhibits neither his curiosity nor
his growing sympathy – his heart is still anxious to know.

Leonard, however, is more disturbingly haunted by the
presences of absent love. We first see him in the graveyard, raising
his eyes to the hills (the line echoes the Psalmist's hope of
salvation) and recreating the landscape in the image of his need.
He feels a sense of present incompleteness, learned in the past
plenitude of Ennerdale life; and it has led him into an excessively
romantic attachment to the object of his hope, the resumption of
his previous life with his brother. Stein's definition of such
romantic attachment in *Lord Jim* is strikingly relevant to *The
Brothers*: 'The way is to the destructive element submit yourself,
and with the exertions of your hands and feet make the deep, deep
sea keep you up.'[7] It is a sentence that hints at the dangerous
excess of what John Beer calls the 'buried yearning'[8] in the hearts
of both brothers; and it reminds us too of the complexity of
Wordsworth's seeing – that he is writing of love not only as the
source of all value but as *infirmity*. Leonard's venture to try his
fortune at sea was a romantic all-or-nothing gamble; and so too is
his return to find his brother. He shows the dread of disillusion
that lies at the root of the enterprise when he remarks that men
commonly die of a broken heart; and we sense it too, as does the
priest in his way, in his restless wish to direct the course and pace
of the conversation to his unadmitted end. When he learns the
truth, he lets everything go. The news of James' death is like the

lightning-stroke that split the crag in the hills, it is a violation perhaps embraced in the secrecy of dread but too elementally destructive from him to blend with the goings-on of life in Ennerdale. Despite the rapprochement between the priest and Leonard – the priest apologises to Leonard for the wrong he had earlier done him in his heart, and Leonard in return feels bound to apologise by letter for his secrecy – Leonard turns away. He rejects the hospitable invitation to supper, and exiled by the strength of his love, reckless in disappointment, he returns to sea.

The cause of his romantic hope and disillusion lies deep in the culture and the subsistence economy of Ennerdale. During the previous century and a half, the family smallholding had become increasingly unable to pay its way; and despite the Ewbank courage in bearing their burdens through torrents of disaster (the image is a shaping one in the poem), on the death of Walter Ewbank the land had been sold. What outside capital had taken away, only outside capital could recover: and so Leonard went to sea ('to the destructive element submit yourself'). It was a speculative testing of fortune, bearing himself the burden he did not think his weaker brother could bear, in order to win back the patrimony for them to share; and the tragic irony of his failure is precisely pointed by Wordsworth. It was Leonard's absence that led to James' sleep-walking, which led in turn to his death: it was the mountains to which Leonard had looked for hope that brought him disaster. It is love and Ennerdale that undo him.

The tragedy is universal in one sense, that the hunger to find ideal values in the ordinary facts and feelings of life may lead in all times and all places to catastrophic disillusion as well as to benign illusion (the pastoral poet is as aware here as he was in *Home at Grasmere* of the risks that *he* runs too). But in another sense it is a tragedy specifically related to time and place, a comment upon that characteristic history of eighteenth-century bourgeois fiction that brought success modestly and affectionately home from business enterprise to its birthplace. It is the tale of Richard Bateman that Isabel tells herself in *Michael*, the tale most extraordinarily told in Thomas Day's *The History of Little Jack*, where a baby brought up by an old man and a goat on a lonely heath becomes a partner in an iron-foundry and builds himself a modest country retreat in the middle of that heath. The ostensible intention of such tales was to rebuke and refine the nakedness of capitalist enterprise, but their effect was to mystify the real conflicts between landed and commercial interest – and this is the genre that *The Brothers* calls into question by its tragic shape. If Leonard is undone by love and Ennerdale, he is also undone by market forces operating upon Ennerdale – and if this is a challenge to understanding of which the Ennerdale priest was not aware, it is a challenge met by the pastoral poet in his consciousness of his wider cure. Wordsworth has no ideal picture, of course, of the relationship which he would like to see between Ennerdale and the larger world. But he has told the truth as he sees it, in an attempt to dispel mystification and to insist that the relationship matters. He has written a tragic elegy that calls their two cultures into play, and he has done it under the discipline of his republican conviction that 'we have all of us one human heart'.

(c) *MICHAEL* (1800)

The induction to *Michael* invites us to turn aside 'from the public way'. It invites us to adjust our pace in order to attend to the privileged knowledge which the poet (as though he were nature's priest) enjoys of the secret places of the earth. Yet the knowledge is not arcane; the tale which Wordsworth tells is a local history familiar to everyone in Grasmere, and the tones in which he invites us to hear it are the commonest tones of friendship. Yes, it may seem difficult and daunting, but courage! –

> The mountains have all open'd out themselves,
> And made a hidden valley of their own.
>
> (7–8)

Wordsworth's affectionately teasing tones of encouragement are an adult's version of the child's invitation to play. He urges us to turn aside in an activity where difficulty will be succeeded by ease, where the act of attention will be succeeded by that relaxed concentration which is, as Winnicott observes, in direct line with 'the *preoccupation* that characterises the play of a young child'.[9] That hidden valley, protected in the pastoral care of the mountains, will be our play-area. It will be the place apart where, like the graveyard in *We are seven*, the living and the dead, the present and the past are enabled to play together. For there is a loss to make good, a tragedy to mourn. Michael's request for Luke's collaboration, we remember, was made at this spot too.

'But we were playmates, Luke; among these hills,
As well thou know'st, in us the old and young
Have play'd together . . .'

(363–5)

The sheepfold in the hidden valley is the place where the past life
of Grasmere and the present life of the public way of the world
may intersect. It is Wordsworth's hope that the passer-by will
return armed with a new understanding of the transactions of
recent social history, and yet that this new understanding will be
grounded in nothing other than the commonest of human feelings,
justly honoured.

The history that Wordsworth tells is structured by this sense
that the present is not to be truly known without the past. Three
times he reaches back into Michael's earlier life to return with
increasingly rich understanding of those relationships that came
to comprise his life: relationships, in ascending historical order,
with his property and nature (40–79), with his home and wife
(80–146) and finally with his son (147–216). The individual is not
the atomistic unit invented by the political economists; nor is he to
be known without a sensitive historical curiosity, particularly to
what he finds best in his own life – hence the importance of the
structure and pace of the narrative that Wordsworth only
gradually begins to unfold. His purpose is the purpose that we
have already seen so often: to trace the excursiveness by which a
man's mind comes to live in all the things that surround it, in what
The Prelude calls a 'progress on the self-same path' (x:239), and
then to show the catastrophic effects of betrayal when that mind is
forced by grievous loss to take 'a stride at once / Into another
region' (x:241–2).

The first half of the poem is thus a celebration of all the
significant relationships of Michael's life – of the love he feels for
his property, for nature, for his home, his wife and his son. The
pleasure he takes in each is different, of course, but it is also
importantly the same: 'the pleasure which there is in life itself'
(79). That is why, as David Pirie says, 'the poetry is not
straightforwardly "symbolic" ' [10] – for each pleasure in such a life
is consubstantial with the others and serves to recall them. When
Wordsworth celebrates the family's 'cleanly supper-board'
(101), and 'their basket pil'd with oaten cakes, / And their plain
home-made cheese' (103–4), he sees what might have seemed the

prosaic realities of domestic routine as a ritual; and he describes it
with sacramental care because he sees that it embodies for them
the pride and pleasure that they take in all their activities. Each
aspect of their life symbolises the whole, it is all of a piece, with the
ritual interconnectedness of life in a total society; and the
plainness of Wordsworth's poetry is a conscious device to honour
the pervasiveness of their ritual feeling in all the daily events of
life.

But of course to Michael, with his patrimonial fields, it is his
property and his son that matter most; they bring the deepest
pleasures, and his pleasure in each increases his joy in the other.
Wordsworth in his most radical days had always valued the right
to private property; and although he had written much against its
abuse, it was only in the excitement of his new acquaintance with
the smallholdings of Grasmere that he found himself able to give
convincing poetic voice to his ideal vision. For ideally (we should
perhaps remember *Goody Blake, and Harry Gill* as counterpoise)
property was to him the truest interpreter of the mysteries of time
and mutability; it kept the past alive, gave meaning to the present
and hope for the future. It epitomised everything that since *An
Evening Walk* he had come to understand by home: it provided 'a
kind of permanent rallying-point' (*EL* 314–15) for the domestic
affections; it encouraged the growth of independence and
fellow-feeling alike in which a man might find his virtue; and it
provided scope for pride in the duty of labour. Hence the
peculiarly cruel irony of the choice that faces Michael, as he tries
to decide whether to sacrifice his property or his son, in whom that
property has its fullest meaning.

Michael's fear for the future cuts to the heart of the whole
interwoven tissue of his life; and the worst of it all is the fear of
betrayal of family by family. He struggles not to impute this sense
of betrayal to the conscious malice of his kinsman, and he
struggles to trust in Luke as he would trust in himself; he tries
hard, as with diminished heart he will continue to try hard after
Luke's desertion, to hold fast to what he has found best in his life.
But even so, like so many betrayed figures in Wordsworth's poetry
before, both he and his wife fall into strange extremes of mood,
flickering from bitterness to joy, from despair to hope and back
again; and occasionally the syntax of his mind breaks down
altogether into a darkly suggestive inarticulateness. His only
acceptable recourse, it seems, is the desperate remedy of hazard:

to commit his son to the same destructive element to which Leonard had committed himself in *The Brothers*. In what proves to be the climactic ritual of the poem, both parents then prepare their son against his departure, Isabel with needle and thread and Michael with the ceremonial request that he lay the cornerstone of the planned sheepfold; and in the farewell address that he gives him there, the past is once again retold in order to enrich the present.

It is important through all this to recognise the freedom from the language of blame in the poem ('Michael should have sold his land', and so on). It seems to me that Wordsworth allows us to entertain the possibility of blame and to discover its irrelevance; for blame implies that things might have been otherwise, whilst the poem traces the historical inevitability of the passing of an economy of life unable to adapt to new conditions. Also, of course, as in *The Ruined Cottage* and *The Brothers*, Wordsworth sees that infirmity is an inseparable part of the strength he celebrates, and to blame in these circumstances is simply trivial. When Michael tells Luke by the sheepfold that 'thou has been bound to me / Only by links of love' (411–12), he has a moment's insight into the tragic irony that structures the poem: the irony that the bonds of law serving capital are stronger than the bonds of love, that the covenant of law is stronger than the covenant of love redrafted at the sheep-fold, that economic debt is more powerful and more recoverable than the debt of love. The old moral economy, that saw property as debt and labour as responsibility and both as part of the whole duty of man, is yielding to the new market economy; a primitive total society is yielding to a new alienated society. Of course this distinction is not an absolute one but a question of degree, a transformation of the sensed quality of capitalism. Grasmere had never been separate from the world but a particular part of it; outside capital had always had its interest in Grasmere (Michael's lands had been mortgaged before) and Grasmere had always had its interest in outside capital (Isabel's hope is that Luke will repeat Richard Bateman's well-known success). But what Wordsworth has done in *Michael*, with that emblem of the coldly functional ploughshare passing through Michael's pasture, is to render the finality with which the aspirations of individual lives and families may be terminated, and through that to show that gradually a particular way of feeling and thinking and talking about the world is being lost.

Geoffrey Hartman is right: 'the poet is Michael's true heir'.[11] There is an attenuation involved, in that what was a matter of material practice (sheep-farming) has become a matter of cultural practice (writing poetry about sheep-farming). But there is also a broadening involved too, in that the poet's cure extends far beyond the shepherds it includes. For the poet will be Michael's 'second self' (39) not just in commemorating a way of life which is irrecoverably lost but in keeping alive his own vision of human potential which that way of life prophetically and incompletely embodied. Of course the poet is a very different person from Michael. For one thing, he has his own property to labour upon if he is to bequeath to 'a few natural hearts' (36), and more particularly to a few 'youthful poets' (38), the particular form of his vision. But what is impressive about *Michael* is what in general is so impressive about the poetry: Wordsworth's capacity to learn about himself through a disciplined attentiveness to the *otherness* of other people. The heart of his radical politic lies here, in his concern to find similitude in human dissimilitude. The poem is Wordsworth's sheep-fold, written to arm us against the future, and to celebrate our common potential for an unalienated life in an unalienated community – a community where property serves to bind men together rather than to drive them apart, and where the excursiveness of our better feelings may find a home in all the things that surround us. We shall disagree about what these things mean; but *Michael* brings them into play. For Wordsworth has written a poem where, under the discipline of his own radical sensibility, author and reader, past and present, ideal and real are free to play together – and where, moreover, it seems part of the pleasure which there is in life itself to do so.

Conclusion

Of all the attacks that have been made on Wordsworth's theory of language, the best still seems to me to have been the nearest in time – that of Jeffrey, made in the course of his review of Southey's *Thalaba* in the *Edinburgh Review* for October 1802; and it was so good because it sprang from the sure instinct of political hostility. Jeffrey wrote in defence of 'the establishments of language' against the new Lakeland school of '*dissenters* from the established systems in poetry and criticism' because he understood that their experiments with language were a political as well as a poetical dissent. What was at stake was the possibility of creating new alignments of feeling and understanding that would transform from within the hegemony of eighteenth-century paternalism; and Jeffrey's literary criticism was designed to put a stop to this, to secure culture for the buttressing of the establishments of church and state. The directness of his attack upon Wordsworth's ideas about language, however, is refreshing, compared with the political evasiveness of Coleridge's discussion in *Biographia Literaria* or with the further abstraction that has characterised much academic discussion since. For Jeffrey after all was right: Wordsworth's theory of language was inseparable from his general understanding of what was valuable in all modes of human communication and relationship; and a full discussion would involve us at once, as he says in the *Preface* to *Lyrical Ballads*, with 'the revolutions not of literature alone but likewise of society itself'.

Jeffrey directly contradicts the *Preface*: 'The poor and vulgar may interest us, in poetry, by their *situation*; but never, we apprehend, by any sentiments that are peculiar to their condition, and still less by any language that is characteristic of it'. That is the accent of the old paternalism; the poor are denied their voice and then, by that equation so common amongst intellectuals, their alleged impoverishment of vocabulary is equated with impoverishment of experience. 'The love or grief, or indignation of an enlightened and refined character, is not only expressed in a

217

different language, but is in itself a different emotion from the love, or grief, or anger of a clown, a tradesman or a market-wench. The things themselves are radically and obviously distinct . . .'. Yet Jeffrey is obliged to use the same word on two out of three occasions here; he is obliged to speak of the feelings of love and grief that the clown and gentleman share even as he asserts their discreteness. The *things* that he describes with such apparent objectivity are in fact *relationships* in which he participates; the very language he uses demands that he see similitude as well as dissimilitude. The relationships of his seeing, however, are patrician, and his language, though educated, is mean: 'poverty makes men ridiculous', he says. He is impervious to the lesson of *The Idiot Boy*, and the democratic potential involved in the perception of human similarity is snuffed out in his concentration upon cultural difference. This is the paternalism against which Wordsworth set himself in his constant emphasis that men who do not wear fine clothes or speak fine sentences can nevertheless feel deeply. He wished to draw people together in mutual recognition of their common humanity; and he valued an educated language only in so far as it tended to spread relationship and love.

Jeffrey writes of Wordsworth as a subversive, a man who had squandered the benefits of his education and betrayed the responsibilities of his class. It is an essential perspective upon the law-agent's son who, instead of turning out like Edmund Bertram as second sons should, had gone at the end of 1799 to live with his sister at Town End. We need to see the young Wordsworth in his hostility to the official culture to which he later assimilated himself and where he has been enshrined ever since. For he is indeed a subversive writer. Not, indeed, in the sense that he had a political programme to offer; for I suspect that he lost any such programme in 1793 and that in 1800 the world appeared a very intractable place to him. Yet none the less he is subversive. He is subversive in his opposition to negative morality and compliance. He is subversive in his desire to rescue nature, and thus man, from the spirit of capitalist exploitation. He is subversive in his desire to enrich our sense of human community in the recognition that we have all of us one human heart, enabling us to live in the worlds of infancy, childhood and extreme old age, of beggars and pedlars, of suffering, idiocy and madness. And he is subversive too in his energetic faith in the unlimited radical potential to be won in that area of the mind where self and other play together, where the ideal may entertain the real and yet preserve that delicate illusion which is the light of all our love, hope and faith.

Notes and References

1: *AN EVENING WALK*

1. Dr Samuel Johnson, *Lives of the English Poets* (Everyman, 1964) vol. II p. 292.
2. Geoffrey Hartman, *Wordsworth's Poetry 1787–1814* (Yale University Press, 1964) p. 357.
3. Jonathan Wordsworth, on the other hand, suspects Wordsworth at twenty did not feel 'very strongly' about either landscape or suffering. See *The Borders of Vision* (Oxford University Press, 1984) p. 310.
4. *As You Like It* (Signet edition) IV:1:15–17. All references to Shakespeare throughout are to the Arden edition, unless otherwise stated.
5. Edmund Burke, *A Philosophical Enquiry into the Origin of our Ideas of the Sublime and Beautiful* (2nd edition, 1759) I:v:55.
6. D. W. Winnicott, *Playing and Reality* (Penguin, 1974) p. 27.
7. Paul D. Sheats, *The Making of Wordsworth's Poetry, 1785–1798* (Harvard University Press) p. 35.
8. Burke, op. cit., introduction, pp. 35–6.
9. David Hume, *Essays* (World's Classics, 1903) p. 7.
10. Marilyn Butler, *Romantics, Rebels and Reactionaries* (Oxford University Press, 1981) p. 16. See also pp. 16–20.
11. Walter Benjamin, *Illuminations* (Fontana, 1982) p. 258.
12. Karl Marx, *Grundrisse* (Penguin, 1973) p. 162.
13. Burke, op. cit., introduction, p. 16.
14. Mary Warnock, *Imagination* (Faber & Faber, 1976) p. 34.
15. Samuel Taylor Coleridge, *Biographia Literaria* (Everyman, 1965) ch. 4, p. 48 n. 2.
16. Hume, *A Treatise of Human Nature* (Everyman, 1911) I:v:23.
17. Roger Sharrock, *The Figure in a Landscape: Wordsworth's Early Poetry*, The Warton Lecture on English Poetry 1972 (Oxford University Press, 1973) p. 15.
18. Burke, op. cit., pp. 63, 68.
19. Henry Brooke, *Universal Beauty* (1735) III:91.
20. E. P. Thompson, *The Making of the English Working Class* (Penguin, 1968) p. 60.
21. Marilyn Butler, op. cit., pp. 15, 23.
22. E. P. Thompson, 'Disenchantment or Default? A Lay Sermon', in C. C. O'Brien and W. D. Vanech (eds), *Power and Consciousness* (New York University Press, 1969) p. 152.
23. The couplet too draws on Ecclesiastes XII.
24. Sheats, op. cit., p. 57.
25. Hartman, op. cit., p. 94.
26. Ibid., p. 94.

2: *DESCRIPTIVE SKETCHES*

1. Carl Woodring, *Politics in English Romantic Poetry* (Harvard University Press, 1970) p. 85.
2. *Monthly Review*, vol. XXXII (January 1765) p. 50.
3. Geoffrey Hartman, *Wordsworth's Poetry 1787–1814* (Yale University Press, 1964) pp. 103, 104.
4. Donald Wesling, *Wordsworth and the Adequacy of Landscape* (Routledge & Kegan Paul, 1970) p. 14.
5. John Beer, *Wordsworth and the Human Heart* (Macmillan, 1978) p. 15.
6. Aldous Huxley, 'Wordsworth in the Tropics', in his collection of essays *Do What You Will* (Chatto & Windus, 1929).
7. Mary Moorman, *William Wordsworth: The Early Years 1770–1803* (Oxford University Press, 1968) pp. 134–7.
8. J. F. Turner, ' "Various Journey, Sad and Slow": Wordsworth's "Descriptive Sketches" (1791–2) and the Lure of Pastoral', *Durham University Journal*, vol. LXIX no. 1 (December 1976) pp. 38–51.
9. Paul D. Sheats, *The Making of Wordsworth's Poetry, 1785–1798* (Harvard University Press, 1973) p. 74.
10. Leslie F. Chard II, *Dissenting Republican: Wordsworth's Early Life and Thought in their Political Context* (The Hague: Mouton, 1972) p. 91.
11. Thomas Paine, *Rights of Man* (Penguin, 1969) p. 136.
12. See D. W. Winnicott, *Playing and Reality* (Penguin, 1974) ch. 7, 'The Location of Cultural Experience'. The second phrase comes from p. 127.

3: *A LETTER TO THE BISHOP OF LLANDAFF*

1. The text of Watson's piece is printed in full, excluding the first paragraph, in *The Gentleman's Magazine*, vol. LXIII (July 1793) pp. 633–6. These phrases are from p. 635, p. 633 and p. 633 respectively.
2. Edmund Burke, *Reflections on the Revolution in France* (Everyman, 1910) p. 58.
3. John Milton, *Areopagitica*, ed. K. M. Lea (Oxford University Press, 1973) p. 33.
4. Ibid., p. 39.
5. Thomas Paine, *Rights of Man* (Penguin, 1969) p. 117.
6. Ibid., p. 97.
7. Paine, *Common Sense; Addressed to the Inhabitants of America* (Penguin, 1976) p. 92.
8. William Wordsworth, *Prose Works*, vol. I, p. 103.
9. Preface to *The Borderers*, ed. Robert Osborn (Cornell University Press, 1982) p. 65.
10. M. H. Abrams, *The Mirror and the Lamp: Romantic Theory and the Critical Tradition* (New York: The Norton Library, 1958) p. 111.
11. Paine, *Common Sense*, p. 70.
12. Leslie Chard II, *Dissenting Republican: Wordsworth's Early Life and Thought in their Political Context* (The Hague: Mouton, 1972) pp. 163–4.
13. Karl Marx, *The Eighteenth Brumaire of Louis Bonaparte*, in *Surveys from Exile* (Pelican Marx Library, 1973) pp. 146, 149.
14. Burke, op. cit., p. 59.
15. Abrams, op. cit., p. 104, after A. O. Lovejoy.

4: *SALISBURY PLAIN*

1. *Paradise Lost,* III:20.
2. Joseph Conrad, *Heart of Darkness* (Penguin, 1976) p. 52.
3. Carl Woodring, *Wordsworth* (Harvard University Press, 1968) p. 9.
4. Michael H. Friedman, *The Making of a Tory Humanist: William Wordsworth and the Idea of Community* (Columbia University Press, 1979) p. 113.
5. Geoffrey Hartman, *Wordsworth's Poetry 1787–1814* (Yale University Press, 1964) p. 118. See also pp. 118–25.
6. Thomas Paine, *Rights of Man* (Penguin, 1969) pp. 91–2.
7. Enid Welsford, *Salisbury Plain: A Study in the Development of Wordsworth's Mind and Art* (Oxford University Press, 1966) pp. 17, 18.
8. See my forthcoming essay, an expanded version of this chapter, ' "A stride into another region": Wordsworth's "Salisbury Plain" Ms.I, 1793–4', to be published in the *Durham University Journal,* June 1987.
9. Compare *Descriptive Sketches* (1793) 571.
10. See Edmund Burke, *A Philosophical Enquiry into the Origin of our Idea of the Sublime and Beautiful* (2nd edition 1759) II:IX:133.
11. Paine, op. cit., p. 140.
12. William Wordsworth, *Prose Works,* vol. I, p. 103.

5: *ADVENTURES ON SALISBURY PLAIN*

1. William Godwin, *Enquiry concerning Political Justice* (Penguin, 1976) V:11:473.
2. Ibid, I:3, p. 90.
3. Paul D. Sheats, *The Making of Wordsworth's Poetry, 1785–1798,* (Harvard University Press, 1973) p. 115.
4. D. W. Winnicott, 'The Development of the Capacity for Concern', in his book *The Maturational Processes and the Facilitating Environment* (The Hogarth Press, 1965) p. 73.
5. E. P. Thompson, 'Disenchantment or Default? A Lay Sermon', in C. C. O'Brien and W. D. Vanech (eds) *Power and Consciousness* (New York University Press, 1969) p. 152.
6. Enid Welsford, *Salisbury Plain: A Study in the Development of Wordsworth's Mind and Art* (Oxford University Press, 1966) p. 28.
7. Ibid., p. 24.
8. Robert Osborn, in the introduction to *The Borderers* (Cornell University Press, 1982) p. 37.
9. D. W. Winnicott, *Playing and Reality* (Penguin, 1974) p. 128.

6: *THE BORDERERS*

1. *Collected Letters of Samuel Taylor Coleridge,* ed. E. L. Griggs (Oxford University Press, 1956) vol. I, p. 190, Letter to Joseph Cottle, 8 June 1797.
2. Enid Welsford, *Salisbury Plain: A Study in the Development of Wordsworth's Mind and Art* (Oxford University Press, 1966) p. 31.
3. Ibid., p. 47.
4. Ibid., p. 51.
5. Carl Woodring, *Wordsworth* (Harvard University Press, 1968) p. 19.

6. Marilyn Butler, *Romantics, Rebels and Reactionaries* (Oxford University Press, 1981) p. 65.
7. William Hazlitt, 'Lectures on the Dramatic Literature of the Age of Elizabeth', in *Works*, ed. P. P. Howe (London, 1930–4) vol. VI, p. 360.
8. Geoffrey Hartman, 'Wordsworth, "The Borderers", and "Intellectual Murder" ', in *Journal of English and Germanic Philology*, vol. LXII (1963) p. 765 n. 11.
9. Quoted in *Ghosts and Other Plays* (Penguin, 1964) p. 294 n. 24.
10. René Girard, *Violence and the Sacred*, trans. Patrick Gregory, (Johns Hopkins University Press, 1977) p. 31.
11. Ibid., p. 74.
12. Edmund Burke, 'A Letter from Mr. Burke to a Member of the National Assembly', in *Reflections on the Revolution in France* (Everyman, 1910) p. 263.
13. Ibid., p. 262.
14. Ibid., p. 267.
15. William Wordsworth, *Prose Works*, vol. I, p. 103.
16. Paul D. Sheats, *The Making of Wordsworth's Poetry, 1785–1798* (Harvard University Press, 1973) pp. 128, 129.
17. Friedrich Nietzsche, *Beyond Good and Evil* (Penguin, 1973) section 270, p. 190. The whole of this aphorism is strikingly close to Rivers' outlook.
18. See, for example, Erik H. Erikson, *Toys and Reasons: Stages in the Ritualization of Experience* (Marion Boyars, 1978) p. 50.
19. Girard, op. cit., p. 258.
20. Carl B. Cone, *The English Jacobins; reformers in late 18th century England*, (Charles Scribner's Sons, 1968) p. 110.
21. Girard, op. cit., p. 13.

7: *THE RUINED COTTAGE*

1. Sigmund Freud, 'Mourning and Melancholia', in The Pelican Freud Library (Penguin, 1984) vol. XI, p. 252.
2. Ibid., p. 254.
3. Ibid., pp. 260–1.
4. Jonathan Wordsworth, *The Music of Humanity* (Nelson, 1969) p. 168.
5. Ibid., p. 245.
6. Lionel Trilling, *Sincerity and Authenticity* (Oxford University Press, 1972) p. 82.
7. Samuel Taylor Coleridge, *The Statesman's Manual*, ed. R. J. White, in *The Collected Works of Samuel Coleridge Taylor* (Routledge & Kegan Paul, 1972) vol. VI, p. 30.
8. William Wordsworth, prefatory essay to *The Borderers*, ed. Robert Osborn (Cornell University Press, 1982) p. 65.
9. David Pirie, *William Wordsworth: The Poetry of Grandeur and of Tenderness* (Methuen, 1982) p. 63.
10. Erik H. Erikson, *Toys and Reasons: Stages in the Ritualization of Experience* (Marion Boyars, 1978) p. 49.
11. David Pirie, op. cit., p. 73.
12. Ibid., pp. 51–2.

13. *The Collected Writings of Thomas De Quincey*, ed. David Masson, (Edinburgh, 1890) vol. xi, p. 307.

14. David Perkins, *Wordsworth and the Poetry of Sincerity* (Harvard University Press, 1964) p. 116.

15. Paul D. Sheats, *The Making of Wordsworth's Poetry, 1785–1798* (Harvard University Press, 1973) p. 178.

16. Cleanth Brooks, 'Wordsworth and Human Suffering: Notes on Two Early Poems', in F. W. Hilles and H. Bloom (eds), *From Sensibility to Romanticism: Essays presented to Frederick A. Pottle* (Oxford University Press, 1965) pp. 373–87. See especially pp. 385–7.

17. David Aers, 'Wordsworth's Model of Man in *The Prelude*', in David Aers, Jonathan Cook and David Punter, *Romanticism and Ideology: Studies in English Writing 1765–1830* (Routledge & Kegan Paul, 1981) p. 80.

18. Francis, Lord Jeffrey, *Edinburgh Review*, vol. xxiv (November, 1814) p. 30.

19. William Hazlitt, 'Character of Mr. Wordsworth's New Poem, The Excursion', in *Works*, ed. P. P. Howe, (London, 1930–4) vol. xix, p. 20.

20. Jonathan Wordsworth, op. cit., p. 209.

21. Ibid., p. 249.

22. Edmund Burke, *Reflections on the Revolution in France* (Everyman, 1910) p. 33.

23. D. W. Winnicott, *Playing and Reality* (Penguin, 1974) p. 37.

24. Stephen Prickett, *Coleridge and Wordsworth: The Poetry of Growth* (Cambridge University Press, 1970) p. 44.

25. William Wordsworth, *Prose Works*, vol. i, p. 148.

8: *LYRICAL BALLADS*

1. Donald Davie, 'Dionysus in *Lyrical Ballads*', in A. W. Thomson (ed.), *Wordsworth's Mind and Art* (Oliver & Boyd, 1969) pp. 120, 138.

2. William Wordsworth, *Prose Works*, vol. i, p. 141.

3. Marion Milner, *On Not Being Able to Paint* (Heinemann, 1971) p. 89.

4. D. W. Winnicott, *Playing and Reality* (Penguin, 1974) p. 61.

5. *The Collected Writings of Thomas De Quincey*, ed. David Masson (Edinburgh, 1890) vol. xi, p. 294.

6. Geoffrey Hartman, *Wordsworth's Poetry 1787–1814* (Yale University Press, 1964) p. 12.

7. Ibid., p. 9.

8. *The Letters of John Keats 1814–1821*, ed. H. E. Rollins (Cambridge University Press, 1958) vol. i, p. 193, Letter of 27? December 1817.

9. Winnicott, op. cit., p. 76.

10. Hartman, op. cit., p. 145.

11. John Beer, *Wordsworth and the Human Heart* (Macmillan, 1978) p. 65.

12. Mary Jacobus, *Tradition and Experiment in Wordsworth's 'Lyrical Ballads' (1798)* (Oxford University Press, 1976) pp. 101–2.

13. John Danby, *The Simple Wordsworth* (Routledge & Kegan Paul, 1960) p. 46.

14. Dr Burney, *Monthly Review*, vol. xxix (June 1799) p. 207.

15. Hartman, op. cit., p. 144.

16. Wordsworth, *Prose Works*, vol. i, p. 126.

17. Stephen Parrish, *The Art of the 'Lyrical Ballads'* (Harvard University Press, 1973) p. 122.

18. Jacobus, op. cit., p. 197.
19. D. H. Lawrence, *Lady Chatterley's Lover* (Penguin, 1961) ch. 9, pp. 104–5.
20. Danby, op. cit., p. 71.
21. Wordsworth, *Prose Works*, vol. ɪ, p. 124.
22. Danby, op. cit., p. 54.
23. Jacobus, op. cit., pp. 250–3.
24. Danby, op. cit., p. 55.
25. Michel Foucault, *Mental Illness and Psychology*, trans. Alan Sheridan (Harper Colophon Books, 1976) p. 69.
26. M. Masud R. Khan, *Hidden Selves: Between Theory and Practice in Psychoanalysis* (The Hogarth Press, 1983) p. 85.
27. Winnicott, op. cit., p. 78.

9: *PETER BELL*

1. From Wordsworth's note to the 1800 edition of *The Rime of the Ancient Mariner*, quoted in *Lyrical Ballads*, pp. 270–1.
2. William Hazlitt, 'Characters of Shakespear's Plays' (Coriolanus), in *Works*, ed. P. P. Howe (London, 1930–4) vol. ɪᴠ, p. 214.
3. See Edmund Burke's *A Philosophical Enquiry into the Origin of our Ideas of the Sublime and Beautiful*, (2nd edition, 1759) ɪ:ᴠɪɪɪ. 60–2.
4. *The Faerie Queene*, bk ɪ, canto ɪ, stanza 13.
5. Mary Jacobus, *Tradition and Experiment in Wordsworth's 'Lyrical Ballads' (1798)* (Oxford University Press, 1976) p. 272.
6. William Wordsworth, prefatory essay to *The Borderers*, ed. Robert Osborn (Cornell University Press, 1982) p. 63.
7. D. W. Winnicott, *Playing and Reality* (Penguin, 1974) p. 97.
8. *Specimens of the Table Talk of the Late Samuel Taylor Coleridge*, ed. H. N. Coleridge (2nd edition, 1836), entry for 1 September 1832.
9. *Eclectic Review*, vol. xɪɪ (July 1819) p. 6.
10. John Beer, *Wordsworth and the Human Heart* (Macmillan, 1978) p. 128.
11. Jacobus, op. cit., p. 266.
12. Bruno Bettelheim, *The Uses of Enchantment* (Penguin, 1978) pp. 10–11.

10: *TINTERN ABBEY, NUTTING* AND 'THERE WAS A BOY'

1. D. W. Winnicott, 'The Capacity to be Alone', in his book *The Maturational Processes and the Facilitating Environment* (The Hogarth Press, 1965) p. 30.
2. Ibid., p. 34.
3. *The Literary Remains of Samuel Taylor Coleridge*, ed. H. N. Coleridge (London, 1836) vol. ɪɪ, pp. 205, 206.
4. Geoffrey Hartman, *Wordsworth's Poetry 1787–1814* (Yale University Press, 1964) p. 26.
5. Paul D. Sheats, *The Making of Wordsworth's Poetry, 1785–1798* (Harvard University Press, 1973) p. 234.
6. *The Collected Writings of Thomas De Quincey*, ed. David Masson (Edinburgh, 1890) vol. xɪ, p. 298.
7. Benjamin Whichcote, 'The Use of Reason in Matters of Religion', in *The Cambridge Platonists*, ed. C. A. Patrides (Arnold, 1969) p. 56.

8. Raymond Williams, *Problems in Materialism and Culture* (Verso, 1980) pp. 70–1.
9. This striking phrase comes from a fragment associated with *Nutting* and printed by de Selincourt on pp. 612–14 of his edition of *The Prelude*. See lines 80–1.
10. Hartman, op. cit., pp. 73–5.
11. D. W. Winnicott, *Through Paediatrics to Psycho-Analysis* (The Hogarth Press, 1975) p. 69.
12. D. W. Winnicott, *Playing and Reality* (Penguin, 1974) p. 45.
13. See *The Prelude*, ed. E. de Selincourt, p. 612, lines 3–4.
14. Marion Milner, *On Not Being Able to Paint* (Heinemann, 1971) p. 57.
15. D. W. Winnicott, *Playing and Reality* (Penguin, 1974) p. 107.
16. H. Lindenberger, *On Wordsworth's 'Prelude'* (Princeton University Press, 1963) p. 43.

11: THE TWO-PART *PRELUDE*

1. Jonathan Wordsworth, *The Borders of Vision* (Oxford University Press, 1982) p. 36.
2. E. P. Thompson, 'Disenchantment or Default? A Lay Sermon', in C. C. O'Brien and W. D. Vanech (eds), *Power and Consciousness* (New York University Press, 1969) p. 172.
3. D. H. Lawrence, *Apocalypse* (Penguin, 1974) ch. 8, p. 50.
4. W. B. Yeats, *Essays and Introductions* (Macmillan, 1969) p. 286.
5. See Charles Rycroft, 'Some Observations on a Case of Vertigo', in his book *Imagination and Reality* (The Hogarth Press, 1968) p. 16.
6. Marion Milner, *On Not Being Able to Paint* (Heinemann, 1971) p. 29.
7. Jonathan Wordsworth, op. cit., p. 73.
8. Ibid., p. 78.

12: *HOME AT GRASMERE*

1. *Paradise Lost* iv:207.
2. Geoffrey Hartman, *Wordsworth's Poetry 1787–1814* (Yale University Press, 1964) p. 171.
3. Hartman, for example, speaks of Wordsworth 'counting his possessions' in just such a spirit. Ibid., p. 173.
4. *Monthly Magazine* vol. i (June 1796) p. 361.
5. E. P. Thompson, *The Making of the English Working Class* (Penguin, 1968) p. 105.
6. Adam Smith, *The Wealth of Nations* (Penguin, 1974) p. 119.
7. E. P. Thompson, op. cit., p. 73.
8. Marcel Mauss, *The Gift: Forms and Functions of Exchange in Archaic Societies*, trans. Ian Cunnison (Cohen & West, 1966) p. 1.
9. Geoffrey Hartman, *The Fate of Reading and Other Essays* (University of Chicago Press, 1975) p. 185.

13: THE GRASMERE PASTORALS

1. Stephen Parrish, '*Michael* and the Pastoral Ballad', in Jonathan Wordsworth (ed.), *Bicentenary Wordsworth Studies in Memory of John Alban Finch*, (Cornell University Press, 1970), p. 68.
2. Mary Jacobus, *Tradition and Experiment in Wordsworth's 'Lyrical Ballads' (1798)*, (Oxford University Press, 1976) p. 183.
3. Adam Smith, *The Wealth of Nations* (Penguin, 1974) p. 117.
4. John Milton, *Areopagitica*, ed. K. M. Lea (Oxford University Press, 1973) p. 14.
5. Michel Foucault, *Mental Illness and Psychology*, trans. Alan Sheridan (Harper Colophon Books, 1976) p. 68.
6. Donald Davie, 'Dionysus in *Lyrical Ballads*', in A. W. Thomson (ed.), *Wordsworth's Mind and Art* (Oliver & Boyd, 1969) p. 131.
7. Joseph Conrad, *Lord Jim* (Penguin, 1957) ch. 20, p. 163.
8. John Beer, *Wordsworth and the Human Heart* (Macmillan, 1978) p. 101.
9. D. W. Winnicott, *Playing and Reality* (Penguin, 1974) p. 60.
10. David Pirie, *William Wordsworth: The Poetry of Grandeur and of Tenderness* (Methuen, 1982) p. 94.
11. Geoffrey Hartman, *Wordsworth's Poetry 1787–1814* (Yale University Press, 1964) p. 266.

Index

Entries in **bold** type indicate passages of detailed commentary. References to the notes indicate quotations unattributed in the text.